Systematic Instruction
for Students with
Moderate and Severe Disabilities

Systematic Instruction for Students with Moderate and Severe Disabilities

by

Belva C. Collins, Ed.D.
University of Kentucky
Lexington

·P A U L·H·
BROOKES
PUBLISHING CO. ®

Baltimore • London • Sydney

Paul H. Brookes Publishing Co.
Post Office Box 10624
Baltimore, Maryland 21285-0624

www.brookespublishing.com

Typeset by Integrated Publishing Solutions, Grand Rapids, Michigan.
Manufactured in the United States of America by
Sheridan Books, Inc., Chelsea, Michigan.

Library of Congress Cataloging-in-Publication Data

Collins, Belva C.
   Systematic instruction for students with moderate and severe disabilities / by Belva C. Collins.
       p.   cm.
   Includes bibliographical references and index.
   ISBN 13: 978-1-59857-193-6 (pbk.)—ISBN 10: 1-59857-193-1 (pbk.)
   1. Students with disabilities—Education—United States.   I. Title.
   LC4031.C647 2012
   371.9—dc23
                                                                    2011053440

British Library Cataloguing in Publication data are available from the British Library.

2021 2020 2019 2018

10   9   8   7   6   5

Contents

About the Author

Belva C. Collins, Ed.D., is Professor and Chair of the Department of Special Education and Rehabilitation Counseling at the University of Kentucky, where she serves on the program faculty in the Moderate and Severe Disabilities Program. Dr. Collins began her career as a teacher of students with intellectual disabilities in rural Southwestern Virginia before coming to the University of Kentucky to work as a research assistant on several federally funded grants to validate the use of response prompting strategies in special education. She has continued this line of research throughout her career in higher education and has been successful in guiding the applied research of her students in investigating variations of systematic instruction in classroom and community settings. This work provides the foundation for this text. In addition to disseminating her own scholarly writing, Dr. Collins serves as the executive editor of *Rural Special Education Quarterly*, the primary publication of the American Council on Rural Special Education.

Preface

When I was a beginning teacher in the mid-1970s and armed with a degree in special education to teach learners with low-incidence disabilities (in addition to a degree elementary education), I felt confident that I knew what to teach. My preparatory program stressed a developmental curriculum and required me to take courses in kindergarten methods. I also felt confident that I knew where to teach. I had completed my student teaching in a segregated school for students from kindergarten through age 21 who had been identified as having moderate to profound intellectual disabilities, and I took my first job in a rural elementary school that served students with low-incidence disabilities, ages 5–21 years, in a small two-room building not far from the school where general education students attended classes. I felt most confident in using the behavior management skills based on applied behavior analysis (ABA) that I had learned in my special education coursework, establishing clear rules and setting up a token economy to deliver reinforcement. All I knew about instruction, however, was how to write a good behavioral objective (with a condition, a behavior, and a criterion), how to construct a detailed task analysis, and how to shape desired behavior through reinforcing small approximations of the skill that was desired. After that, it was trial and error as I praised students for making correct responses and corrected errors as they occurred. I knew nothing about collecting data and making decisions based on what was and was not working.

It did not take me long to learn that my students needed to learn more useful skills than I had been led to believe, that they needed exposure to students without disabilities, and that they could benefit from being in the community. As special education began to evolve, so did my classroom. My team teacher and I began to teach functional skills that the students needed in their daily lives. We began to make trips to the nearby elementary school building, where they could participate in activities with students without disabilities (although not always at their age level), and we began to take trips into the community each week, where students could practice the basic skills (e.g., making purchases, crossing the street, making social greetings) that we were teaching. I still, however, struggled with how to teach. I continued to use a lot of trial and error and began using techniques that just seemed to make sense, like shadowing a student's movements and only giving assistance as needed. I realized that students needed the opportunity to respond independently when they could and to receive assistance only when they needed it, but I remained clueless as to how to teach them in a systematic way. I tried to apply the strategies I was learning in my master's degree program in elementary education, creating learning centers and exposing my students to a lot of hands-on opportunities for discovery learning. I did not, however, experience much success with these attempts.

When I entered my doctoral studies in the 1980s, I was blessed by the mentorship of three professors, Dr. David Gast, Dr. Mark Wolery, and Dr. John Schuster, as a whole new world opened to me. Under their guidance, I began working on classroom-based research projects and performing consultations with students with moderate and severe disabilities. In this way, I acquired the foundation for systematic instruction using response-prompting strategies and techniques for data-based decision making that would set my own research agenda in a multitude of classrooms during the following 20 years. I learned how to teach students with moderate and severe disabilities by applying instruction in a systematic fashion based on the principles of ABA. I learned how to collect instructional data on a daily basis, analyze the graphed data, and make modifications in instruction based on my analysis. In response, the students learned.

In time, I began to play with variations on the procedures I had learned through research studies I conducted with students and teachers in classroom settings that served learners with moderate and severe disabilities. As recommended practices in special education evolved to be more inclusive and age appropriate and core content gained importance following federal legislation, the way I used systematic instruction also evolved, but the basic principles remained the same.

The purpose of this book is to guide the reader in how to conduct systematic instruction with students with moderate and severe disabilities. It is not a book about where instruction should be conducted or what the curriculum should be. Whereas other authors (e.g., Browder, Brown, Kleinert, Snell, Spooner, Westling) have described the effectiveness of systematic instruction in their texts, no one has written a specific guide to systematic instruction using response prompting since Wolery, Ault, and Doyle (1992). Since that time, scores of new studies have evaluated numerous variables of systematic instructional procedures. Thus, this text will update their work.

It is my intention that readers will find this book to be user friendly. I have tried to limit the jargon involved but also have tried to clearly define basic terms because a working vocabulary of the terms associated with systematic instruction is needed for practitioners to be able to be consumers of the research in the field as well as to fluently converse with others on instructional practices. It also is my intention that this book will be useful to anyone who works with students with moderate and severe disabilities, including special education teachers, paraprofessionals, general education teachers, peer tutors, parents, and related services delivery personnel. Systematic instruction can be effective with individuals with moderate and severe disabilities, from preschool through adulthood, but it also can be effective with other learners, including those with mild intellectual disabilities or learning disabilities, as well as with students who do not have disabilities. (On a personal note, I found that systematic instruction was effective in teaching my own children tasks that required accuracy and fluency, such as multiplication facts, spelling of difficult words, and elements of the periodic table.) Systematic instruction is effective when used with simple discrete tasks, such as sight-word reading, as well as with complex chained tasks, such as those involved in working math problems, preparing a meal, or performing a personal management routine.

I have organized this book in a logical fashion. The first part of the book describes the components of systematic instruction, the collection and analysis of instructional data, and the basic response-prompting procedures that compose systematic instruction. Readers will find a list of key terms, step-by-step guidelines for implementing response-prompting procedures, sample lesson plans based on research conducted by classroom teachers, ideas for adapting the sample lesson plans, and sample data sheets to be used while conducting instruction. The second part of the book builds on the first by focusing on instructional variables that can be changed to increase the efficiency of instruction, continuing with guidelines and sample lesson plans that demonstrate those changes. Each chapter throughout the book ends with questions for reflection. At the end of the book, readers will find appendixes that contain reproducible flow charts for implementing response-prompting procedures, reproducible blank data sheets to be used during trials of baseline and instruction, a list of additional resources that contain more in-depth information about systematic instruction, and the glossary of key terms used in the chapters.

My purpose in writing this book will be accomplished if readers discover that systematic instruction is not limited to the direct discrete trial instruction in a one-to-one format that so often is associated with ABA. Systematic instruction should be a much more dynamic process in which instructional trials are not limited to one-on-one instruction at a desk or table but are inserted into the ongoing natural routines of students throughout the day. The key is having a plan for how to teach and implementing that plan in a way that makes sense for each individual learner.

Three items should be noted as this book is read. First, I have used the broad term *instructor* to designate the individual who conducts instruction because this term may include the special or general education teacher, paraprofessional, related services provider, peer tutor, or parent. In addition, I have used the broad term *learner* to designate the individual who is the recipient of instruction because this term may include preschoolers, elementary through high school students, and adults. Second, I have based the sample instructional programs on the research methods used in studies that my students or I have conducted; this is not to ignore the other fine examples of systematic research published in the professional special education literature, but to highlight work that I have seen actual teachers conduct in their classrooms. Finally, I have used the Core Content Standards from Kentucky (the state in which I work) as the sample objectives for the instructional programs that follow in the text. These are meant as examples in the context of this book and should not be construed as the only appropriate standards that can be used in similar instructional programs. In fact, at the time of this book's publication, there is a movement to adopt national standards (the Common Core State Standards) across the United States, and new standards are being adopted in Kentucky to replace those used in this book. Thus, readers should consult the latest standards in their respective states as they develop their own instructional programs.

REFERENCE

Wolery, M., Ault, M.J., & Doyle, P.M. (1992). *Teaching students with moderate to severe disabilities.* New York, NY: Longman.

Foreword

As few as 4 decades ago, relatively little was known about whether students with significant disabilities (e.g., those with autism, moderate to severe intellectual impairments—including those with concomitant sensory and physical disabilities) could be taught skills to allow them to care for themselves, communicate and socialize with family members and friends, function independently in their communities, and seek employment of various sorts. Until the mid-1970s, school-age students with significant disabilities were routinely denied access to public education, and younger children (infants, toddlers, and preschoolers) with significant disabilities were not granted access to education or early intervention services until the late 1980s and early 1990s. Furthermore, relatively little was known about how to teach them. Much has changed! Access to education, of course, occurred as a result of litigation, advocacy of parents and parent organizations, and brave legislators. The research field did relatively little to make the case that education was important, although in some instances it shaped the nature of services.

Access to education, however, would be of little value if the answers did not exist to questions such as, "What should we teach individuals with significant disabilities?" "How should they be taught?" and "How should we organize their instructional experiences?" For these questions, investigators played key roles in providing the field with viable answers, and Collins summarizes and describes this literature in this text. Several general findings emerged over the years. First, nearly all individuals with significant disabilities could learn skills (functional skills) that improved the quality of their lives. Second, the approaches used with students who did not have disabilities or who had mild forms of disabilities tended not to be effective with this population. Third, learning to do a skill, even a functional one, in one context with one instructor did not necessarily mean individuals with significant disabilities would apply that skill (i.e., maintain and generalize it) whenever and wherever it was needed or would be useful. In other words, they were similar to the rest of us; that is, often we acquire skills (e.g., certain instructional practices, progress monitoring, data-decision rules) in colleges and universities and then fail to apply them in public school classrooms. Fourth, many individuals with significant disabilities could be taught functional skills in the schools attended by their age-mates without disabilities—separate schools were not necessary. Fifth, instructional arrangements (e.g., small-group instruction) other than one instructor and one student were effective. Sixth, intentional and systematic instruction was often necessary. *Intentional* means specific skills were targeted and instruction occurred frequently and regularly with a purpose. *Systematic* means specific procedures with precise protocols were used, their effects monitored, and adjustments made based on the data.

As described in Chapter 1, the behavioral tradition, with emphasis on differential reinforcement and transfer of stimulus control, and social learning theory, with its emphasis on learning through observation and imitation, served as the conceptual foundations for the development and evaluation of the systematic procedures. The research approach used to evaluate those procedures was applied behavior analysis. From this tradition, emphasis was placed on careful description and implementation of procedures, use of time-series designs employing a replication logic for evidence generation, use of ongoing and continuous measurement of outcomes, and evaluation of the social importance of outcomes and acceptability of procedures.

A substantial cadre of investigators, including Belva Collins, who authored this text, conceptualized, developed, evaluated, refined, and replicated the systematic procedures and protocols. Those researchers generated a large body of studies documenting the effectiveness of a number of teaching procedures (e.g., response-prompting procedures—see Chapters 3 and 4). They found these procedures tended to be robust and flexible. The researchers went well beyond the simple question of whether a procedure was effective and did studies on instructional formats and arrangements to compare and increase the efficiency of instruction (see Chapter 5). Unlike most educational and special education research, the relative efficiency of the procedures recommended in this text is known, or at least known in part. In short, this body of research answers questions practitioners have (or should have): For whom, under what conditions, and for which skills are these procedures effective and efficient? Another unique aspect of this literature is the manner in which studies were conducted. First, the researchers often measured maintenance and generalization of skills across relevant contexts. Second, they measured the fidelity of the studies' procedures using direct counts; thus, the procedural fidelity of the studies is known. Third, they also tended to conduct their studies in actual schools, programs, and communities where individuals with significant developmental disabilities received their educational services. Fourth, they often involved the families or teachers of the participants in making decisions about what to teach in the studies. Finally, they also often involved the participants' caregivers and teachers as implementers in the studies. The result was a fairly large number of effective teaching practices for which procedural parameters are known and which are ecologically valid—their effectiveness and efficiency in real-world contexts are understood.

This text, however, is not simply about a handful of highly effective practices. The purpose of public schooling is to teach skills that endure and are useful to learners in situations other than where those skills were taught. Chapter 7 provides a practical summary of what we know about teaching skills in ways that cause learners to maintain them and to apply them in relevant situations when those skills are needed. In Chapter 8, a cogent discussion is presented about how to make core content functional to learners with significant disabilities. This straightforward discussion is a result of some very deep thinking concomitant with practical application. Although much of this text is devoted to how teachers should conduct instructional experiences for their students, Collins provides highly useful discussions in Chapters 9 and 10 for new teachers. She focuses on involving others in the schools (e.g., other professionals, students' peers, paraeducators). She also describes how to organize and structure the school day. Beginning teachers will find this information invaluable. The final chapter introduces the notion of using technology for instructional purposes.

Collins covers a great deal of ground in this text, which means many choices were made about how much detail to address in each chapter. In general, those decisions were made accurately. This is not a comprehensive treatment of each practice or issue with extensive citation of the existing research; it is not a reference source for advanced scholars. Rather, the key information is provided about the practices and issues that are central to providing evidence-based practices for students with significant disabilities. This information is provided in a highly accessible manner. Undergraduate students will find the text full of information with useful examples that are easily grasped. Instructors will find this to be a highly useful book and one from which courses can be easily organized. In this text, Collins includes many "pedagogical features." These pedagogical features actually work! Each chapter has clearly stated objectives, a list of terms used in the chapter, sample instructional programs, and questions for reflection. These features do not get in the way of acquiring the content—they supplement it and in some cases serve as advanced organizers for the chapters. In addition, the appendixes include flow charts of selected procedures, sample data collection sheets, and resources divided by content. An accurate glossary is included, and it will undoubtedly be consulted often.

As expected, Collins has presented a highly useful and potentially important text. She has taken a large body of literature, distilled it, found the critical elements, and described those elements clearly. This is a difficult task for accomplished researchers such as Collins. Most such individuals cannot write in such a straightforward or accessible manner. The field will thank her for her contributions; beginning teachers will be more skilled in their profession; students with significant disabilities taught by those teachers will learn more in less time; and their families will be pleased with the outcomes. This is no small accomplishment!

Mark Wolery
Professor and Chair
Department of Special Education
Peabody College
Vanderbilt University
Nashville, Tennessee

Acknowledgments

Even when a book or paper has a single author, writing is never a solitary endeavor. With awareness of this fact, I wish to thank those who helped to shape this text.

First, I want to express my gratitude to those who gave me knowledge of and experience with the content. As mentioned in the preface of this book, I remain eternally grateful to Drs. David Gast, Mark Wolery, and John Schuster for providing me with a sound foundation in the principles of applied behavior analysis, systematic instruction, and data-based decision making. Their feedback on my early research investigations helped shape my own research agenda. I also want to thank Dr. Melinda Ault and Pat Doyle for their wonderful text cowritten with Dr. Mark Wolery that preceded this book and has been cited repeatedly in my own work. I am grateful to the many colleagues who have continued to collaborate with me on systematic instruction research investigations over the years, especially Dr. Harold Kleinert, whose thoughtful comments helped to shape many of the research studies cited in this book. Finally, I must thank the top-notch teachers who have opened their classrooms to provide settings for research on systematic instruction. They are assets to the field of special education, and their students have benefited from their inquiring minds and competent instruction.

Next, I wish to express appreciation to the staff at Paul H. Brookes Publishing Co., who believed in my ability to write this book, who helped shape and improve my written work with their suggestions and questions, and who gave me reasonable timelines to keep me on track as I wrote.

Finally, I must acknowledge the great support I have received from my husband, Ted Collins, who unselfishly recognized that I needed large blocks of undisturbed time to write this book during weekends, holidays, and vacations. I know that he remains proud of my accomplishments, even when it means that he has to eat fast food alone so I can have the freedom to get away and devote myself to research and writing. No words can express how grateful I am for his support and partnership in our marriage.

In memory of Jeffrey Scott Boggs
(December 26, 1964, to November 22, 2010)

Using Effective Practices to Teach Students with Moderate and Severe Disabilities

CHAPTER OBJECTIVES

On completion of this chapter, the reader will be able to

- List and describe the components of an instructional trial
- Task analyze a chained task, and describe how it can be taught across three instructional formats: forward chaining, backward chaining, and total task presentation
- State principles for presenting a consequence following a correct response
- Provide examples of general and specific attentional cues and responses, and describe the rationale for delivering one over the other
- Provide examples of response prompts, and arrange them in a hierarchy that is appropriate for a given target skill and learner
- Distinguish between massed, spaced, and distributed trial presentation formats
- List the four phases of learning, and write a behavioral objective with observable and measurable behaviors to address each phase

TERMS USED IN THIS CHAPTER

applied behavior analysis (ABA)	task analysis	physical prompt
	forward chaining	controlling prompt
instructional programs	backward chaining	massed trial format
instructional sessions	total task presentation	spaced trial format
instructional trials	differential reinforcement	distributed trial format
antecedent	attentional cue	embedded instruction
behavior	attentional response	acquisition
consequence	prompts	fluency
stimulus	stimulus prompts	maintenance
response	response prompts	generalization
stimulus control	errorless learning	behavioral objective
observable behavior	prompt hierarchy	response cards
measurable behavior	verbal prompts	choral response
discrete behavior	gestural prompt	fixed ratio schedule of
chained task	model prompt	reinforcement

Before using procedures for conducting systematic instruction with students with moderate and severe disabilities, it is necessary to have a basic understanding of the principles of **applied behavior analysis** (**ABA**; Alberto & Troutman, 2009) and a working knowledge of the components of instruction. This chapter provides that foundation by defining, describing, and providing examples of instructional components and concludes with samples of lesson plans demonstrating those components.

BASIC COMPONENTS OF SYSTEMATIC INSTRUCTION

Instructional programs using direct instruction are composed of individual **instructional sessions,** and instructional sessions are composed of individual **instructional trials.** An instructional session may have as few as one instructional trial or as many as the instructor deems necessary for learners to have ample opportunities to perform a targeted behavior or skill. Instructional programs differ from lesson plans in that instruction continues across daily sessions until learners reach criterion on the performance of a behavior; lesson plans typically address a single day of instruction on a specific topic. Instruction on the behaviors targeted in instructional programs may be embedded across lesson plans. For example, an instructional program for a communication skill can be embedded across lessons in science, language arts, math, or social studies. In general, the more opportunities a learner has to perform a behavior, the more quickly learning will take place.

Instructional Trials

Every single trial of systematic instruction has three basic components. These include the **antecedent,** the **behavior,** and the **consequence.** It is easy to remember these components as the A-B-C of an instructional trial. The antecedent is the **stimulus** that precedes a behavior or a **response,** and the consequence follows the behavior. One way to do this is to envision systematic instruction through a simple formula (Collins, 2007, p. 119): A → B → C (A = antecedent, B = behavior, C = consequence) or S → R → C (S = stimulus, R = response, C = consequence). Throughout this book, the terms *antecedent* and *stimulus* are used interchangeably, as are the terms *behavior* and *response*.

If the correct response always follows an antecedent or stimulus, **stimulus control** has been established (Wolery & Gast, 1984). The goal of instruction is to establish stimulus control, especially under natural conditions.

Behavior

The target behavior is the one the instructor wants the learner to acquire and, therefore, is targeted for instruction. The behavior or response follows an antecedent or stimulus. When recording the responses of learners, it is important that behaviors be both **observable** and **measurable.** It is impossible to know what a learner feels, thinks, appreciates, or understands unless it is demonstrated in some tangible way that can be seen and measured by the instructor. For example, a learner who looks up and smiles in response to music may be demonstrating appreciation, and a learner who puts words together in a novel way to make a sentence may be demonstrating the understanding of the mechanics of writing a sentence. Appreciation cannot be measured, but the presence of a smile can; likewise, understanding cannot be measured, but the ability to put together nouns and verbs with punctuation to show meaning is measurable.

Discrete and Chained Behaviors

All behaviors that are taught to a learner can be classified as discrete or chained (Alberto & Troutman, 2009; Collins, 2007). A **discrete behavior** consists of a single step. When it is observed, it either occurs or does not occur. For example, a learner is performing a discrete behavior when reading a single word, writing a single letter, answering a question with a simple response, communicating "hello" in greeting someone, or raising a hand to gain the attention of the teacher.

A **chained task** consists of discrete behaviors that are linked together to perform a more complex behavior. When a chained task is observed, each step can be viewed individually to see whether it occurred or did not occur. For example, a learner is performing a chained task when linking several words together to read a sentence, writing a series of letters to form a word, answering a complex question by putting together a series of statements, communicating by emitting an utterance with several words to convey a thought, or performing a series of actions to prepare for class (e.g., open door, walk in room, sit at desk, get out book, open book to correct page).

A **task analysis** is a means of breaking down a chained task into small, discrete behaviors or steps (Alberto & Troutman, 2009). The number of steps depends on the ability of the learner. For example, writing a name could be considered a discrete task for a learner with a mild intellectual disability, it might be broken down into individual letters of the alphabet for a learner with a moderate intellectual disability, and it might be further broken down into the individual strokes necessary to form each letter of the alphabet for a learner with a severe intellectual disability. Although instructors may provide task directions to perform individual steps of a chained task during instruction, the goal is that, over time, the completion of one step of a chained task will serve as the natural stimulus for the learner to perform the next step of the chained task. For example, the natural stimulus for turning off the water tap is a full glass, not the instructor saying, "Turn off the water." In some chained tasks, it is necessary for learners to perform the steps in a specific order (e.g., crossing a street). In other chained tasks, it is acceptable if learners perform the steps out of sequence (i.e., in a functional order) as long as the desired outcome is produced (e.g., put either peanut butter or jelly on the bread first to make a sandwich).

There are three formats for teaching chained tasks: 1) **forward chaining,** 2) **backward chaining,** and 3) **total task presentation** (Alberto & Troutman, 2009). Forward chaining occurs when one step of a task analysis is taught at a time. As a step is mastered, the instructor begins instruction on the next step in the sequence until all steps are learned. Although this is time consuming, it can be an effective way to teach learners with significant disabilities who may require a great deal of time to learn single steps. An example would be teaching a learner to write the first letter of his or her name to mastery before teaching the next letter. Backward chaining occurs when the instructor performs all of the steps for the learner except the last step of the sequence and then teaches that step to the learner. When the learner masters the final step of the sequence, the instructor teaches the final two steps. Instruction proceeds in this backward fashion until the learner has mastered all of the steps. This format also is time consuming but has the advantage of allowing the learner to receive reinforcement for accomplishing a task. An example would be when an instructor performs all of the steps of tying a shoe except for the final step, in which the learner pulls the laces tight to secure the bow and is praised for tying the shoe. Again, this procedure may be appropriate for learners with significant disabilities. Total task presentation is the most natural way to present a task. During every single instructional trial, the learner has the opportunity to perform every single step of the chain. This allows the learner to perform the steps already known and to receive instruction on the steps yet to be mastered. Instructor judgment determines which format should be used when teaching different tasks to different learners. If the total task presentation format is too overwhelming for a learner, the instructor always can decide to teach in a forward or backward chaining format.

Antecedent

The antecedent is the stimulus preceding a behavior that the instructor wants a student to perform (Alberto & Troutman, 2009; Collins, 2007). The list of examples from our daily world is endless. The doorbell ringing is the stimulus to answer the door. Darkness approaching with nightfall is the stimulus to turn on the lights. The smell of burning food is the stimulus to check what was left cooking on the stove. The beep that accompanies an incoming message on a computer is the stimulus to check e-mail. The goal for learners is that they will, in time, perform the behaviors they have acquired in response to natural stimuli. While teaching, however, the instructor must ensure that learners have antecedents that will result in the desired behaviors. Most often, this is done by giving a task direction, such as, "Read the words on this page," or "Work these math problems." This tells learners what the instructor wants them to do, and it is paired with the natural antecedent—in these examples, the page of written words or the worksheet containing math problems. By pairing the task direction with the natural stimulus, it is likely that learners, over time, will begin to complete the task at hand in the absence of a task direction. For a more functional life skill, the natural stimulus for crossing a street is a white *Walk* sign. When first teaching this skill, however, the instructor would give the task direction "Cross the street" and then teach learners to wait for the white *Walk* sign as well as the absence of oncoming traffic instead of expecting them to respond correctly to an untrained stimulus.

Consequence

If correct responses are to increase, it is important that every behavior or response be followed by a consequence (Alberto & Troutman, 2009; Collins, 2007). The consequence consists of feedback to let a learner know if a response was correct or incorrect. A consequence, such as praise or a good grade, informs the learner that a response was correct; if this is reinforcing to the learner, it increases the likelihood that the learner will make the same response in the future. Error correction allows the learner to see where a response was incorrect and how it should have been performed. Asking the learner to correct the error allows the learner to practice a correct response, thus increasing the likelihood that the learner will recall how to perform the response in the future.

There are few rules that should be followed in delivering reinforcement following a correct response (Alberto & Troutman, 2009). First, it is important to provide consequences that are reinforcing to learners and not to assume that every learner is reinforced by the same consequence. For example, a learner who is tactilely defensive may not be reinforced by a pat on the shoulder. Second, it is important to vary reinforcers because they can lose their power when they are used repeatedly. For example, praise statements might include, "Good job," "Awesome," "Wonderful work," and "Great performance!" Third, it can be helpful to provide learners, at least initially, with descriptive praise statements because these provide feedback on what the learners did correctly. These can be statements such as, "I like the way you wrote your first and last names on the line with a space between," or, "You did a great job washing your hands; they are really clean!" Fourth, it is important to provide reinforcement during all instructional trials until learners reach criterion. Once criterion is reached, reinforcement can be faded, as described in Chapter 7. Fifth, reinforcement should be age appropriate. To illustrate, young children or learners with significant intellectual disabilities may not grasp the concept of earning points, whereas edibles or smiley face stickers may not be appropriate for older learners. Finally, artificial reinforcers, such as edibles, should be used sparingly and only when necessary. In every case, the artificial reinforcer should be paired with a natural reinforcer, such as social praise, so that it can be faded as the natural reinforcer becomes more valued.

A good principle to remember is that a consequence is not positive reinforcement unless the behavior increases. Sometimes instructors will find it necessary to change or strengthen reinforcers to motivate students to respond. Also, if a learner becomes dependent on teacher assistance, it can be helpful to use **differential reinforcement** (Alberto & Troutman, 2009), in which reinforcement is delivered for independent responses only and is withheld when students receive assistance.

Attentional Cues and Responses

Before every instructional trial, it is necessary to secure the attention of learners. Learners need to be attending to the stimulus and task direction to know how they are to respond and for learning to occur. There are two ways to secure a learner's attention: 1) general **attentional cue** and 2) specific attentional cue (Collins, 2007). Likewise, there also are two ways for learners to respond: 1) general **attentional response** and 2) specific attentional response. These responses let the instructor know that the student is attending and ready to learn. The addition of an attentional cue would change the previous formula to the following: AC → S → R → C (AC = attentional cue; Collins, 2007, p. 123).

Most learners will respond to a general attentional cue by giving a general response that indicates readiness to learn. There are many types of general attentional cues. The instructor may call out the learner's name; the instructor may say something to indicate that it is time for instruction to begin, such as, "Ready?" or "Look!" or "Eyes on me"; or, the instructor may perform an action that gains the learner's response, such as turning the lights on and off, raising or lowering voice volume, or touching the learner on the shoulder. In turn, the learner should respond to indicate attending in some way, such as giving the instructor eye contact, giving an affirmative verbal response (e.g., "Yes"), or sitting quietly and listening for further directions. Once attention is secured, the instructor is free to deliver the specific stimulus for the learner to respond. For example, the following exchange could begin an instructional trial:

General attentional cue: "Kaia, are you ready to work?"

General attentional response: "Yes."

Task direction: "Good, then answer this question. Who is the president of the United States?"

For some learners, a general attentional cue is not sufficient to secure attention. Some learners may be easily distracted or have sensory impairments that prevent them from picking up on natural general cues (e.g., cannot see or hear instructor). In these cases, the instructor will want to use a specific attentional cue in which the learner is required to perform a specific response to show attending. Specific attentional cues may require the learner to perform an action or to give a verbal response that may or may not be related to the task to be presented. A specific attentional cue that is not related to the task is illustrated in the following exchange:

Specific unrelated attentional cue: "Kaia, show me that you are ready to work by showing me your good sitting behavior."

Specific unrelated attentional response: Kaia stops talking, places her hands in her lap, and makes eye contact with the instructor.

Task direction: "Good, now answer this question. Who is the president of the United States?"

An example of an attentional cue that is related to the task is illustrated in the following interaction:

Specific related attentional cue: "Kaia, put your finger on the picture of the man in this picture."

Specific related attentional response: Kaia puts her finger on the picture of the president of the United States.

Task direction: "Good, now answer this question. Who is the president of the United States that is shown in this picture?"

There are a number of ways in which specific attentional cues can be presented to require the learner to attend to a relevant feature of the task to be completed. These can include naming the letters of a word before being asked to read it, tracing the letters of a word with a finger before being asked to write it, or naming the numerals in a math problem before being asked to work the problem.

Prompts

There are two categories of **prompts** that set up learners for success: 1) **stimulus prompts** and 2) **response prompts.** Using these types of prompts decreases the number of incorrect responses learners make during instruction, resulting in nearly **errorless learning** (Collins, 2007; Spooner, Browder, & Mims, 2011; Wolery, Ault, & Doyle, 1992; Wolery & Gast, 1984; Wolery & Schuster, 1997). Errorless learning typically is defined as an error rate of 20% or less in an instructional session. Errorless learning is advantageous because it decreases the opportunity for learners to make errors, decreases learner frustration when the correct response is unknown, and increases access to reinforcement for performing a correct response. The logic is that if a learner does not know how to perform a behavior, then the instructor should prompt the learner to perform it correctly rather than allow the learner to become frustrated, practice incorrect responses, or make guesses. Once the learner acquires the response by being prompted, prompts can be faded.

Stimulus Prompts

Stimulus prompts—prompts that are in place prior to instruction and that increase the likelihood that the learner will perform a correct response—can be conceptualized as follows: S/P → R → C (S = stimulus, P = prompt, R = response, and C = consequence; Collins, 2007, p. 124). As an example, instructional materials may be formatted to prompt learners to make a correct response to the targeted stimulus, as would be the case when the word *red* is printed in the color red. Over time, the red color can be faded as the learner begins to focus on the letters of the word as the relevant stimulus rather than the color of the letters. Commercial materials with stimulus prompts are available for purchase, or instructors who are skilled in technology use may develop their own on the computer.

Response Prompts

Response prompts and the systematic procedures for using them are the focus of the instruction described in this book. Response prompts are inserted in instructional trials to elicit the correct responses from learners, making the procedure nearly errorless, and can be conceptualized as follows: S(P) → R → C (S = stimulus, P = prompt, R = response, and C = consequence; Collins, 2007, p. 125).

There are several levels of assistance in a **prompt hierarchy**. Depending on the learner and the task, the prompts can be listed from least to most intrusive (Collins, 2007: Wolery et al., 1992) as follows: independence (no assistance or prompt needed), **verbal prompt, gestural prompt, model prompt,** and **physical prompt**. Verbal prompts can be further broken down into 1) direct verbal prompts (e.g., "The word is *dog*") or 2) indirect verbal prompts (e.g., "The word starts with a *duh* sound"; "The word is the name of an animal that barks"). Physical prompts can be further broken down into 1) full physical prompts (e.g., hand-over-hand guidance to write *dog*) or 2) partial physical prompts (e.g., a nudge to get the hand started to write *dog* or guidance from the wrist or forearm instead of the hand).

In most response-prompting procedures, the general rule is to use the least intrusive prompt possible that is still likely to result in a correct response. A prompt that facilitates a correct response is called a **controlling prompt** (Collins, 2007; Wolery et al., 1992). In some cases, it may be desirable to pair prompts. For example, an instructor might pair a verbal prompt with a physical prompt for a learner who needs physical guidance; the instructor can then fade the physical prompt when the learner begins to respond to verbal directions. Regardless of the type of prompt that is used, all prompts should be faded over time as learners acquire the ability to perform behaviors independently.

Trial Format

As previously noted, each instructional trial consists of an antecedent or stimulus, a behavior or response, and a consequence. An instructional session can consist of a single trial or a multitude of trials. For example, a learner may have one opportunity to hang up a coat when arriving at school, but he or she will have a vast number of opportunities to practice social greetings with peers throughout a school day. There are three basic trial formats in which instruction can take place: 1) **massed trial format,** 2) **spaced trial format,** and 3) **distributed trial format** (Collins, 2007; Wolery et al., 1992). Each of these formats has advantages and disadvantages. It is best to use all three when it makes sense to use them. For example, a learner who is acquiring a new skill may require one-to-one massed trial practice with the instructor during initial instruction on a skill, then may need to practice the skill again in a group setting while also receiving distributed trials as opportunities for using the skill arise naturally throughout the day.

Massed Trial Format

Massed trials occur when one instructional trial after another takes place in quick succession with no other activity in between. Massed trials can be conceptualized as follows: XXXXX, where X = instructional trial on a targeted skill (Collins, 2007, p. 122). The instructor may give a task direction repeatedly, one after the other, such as asking a learner to read a series of sight words; set out utensils, plates, and cups for the entire class before snack time; or fill a page with one trial after another of writing his or her name and address. Massed trials can be beneficial when learners are first learning a new behavior because such trials provide many opportunities to practice the targeted response.

Spaced Trial Format

Spaced trials occur when a learner has an opportunity to respond and then some time to contemplate the response or listen to others respond before receiving another trial on the same skill. The learner does not engage in any other activities between turns. Spaced trials can be conceptualized as follows: X X X X X, where X = instructional trial on a targeted skill (Collins, 2007, p. 122). Spaced trials occur naturally in group settings in which all learners are working on the same behavior. For example, learners may take turns being called on to answer questions in a science class, they may take turns reading sentences or paragraphs from a story, or they may take turns counting out money to each other as they simulate making purchases. Spaced trials can prepare learners for the real world by teaching them to take turns; such trials also can provide learners the opportunity to acquire skills from each other through observation between turns.

Distributed Trial Format

Distributed trials occur across activities at natural times throughout the day. The learner may participate in an instructional trial and then take part in another activity before having the opportunity to participate in another instructional trial. Distributed trials can be conceptualized as follows: XYXYXYXY, where X = the targeted task and Y = other tasks performed during the day (Collins, 2007, p. 122). Distributed trials have the advantage of facilitating generalization in that students learn to perform behaviors across natural settings with a variety of people or materials. Instead of having the learner repeatedly write a name on a single sheet, instructors would take the opportunity to conduct an instructional trial by having the learner write a name at the top of worksheets in academic classes, on attendance sheets at school activities, or on scorecards in physical education classes. Instead of having the learner read sight words on flashcards, the instructor would take the opportunity to conduct instructional trials when target words appear in books, on signage, or on web sites across settings.

It may take a learner longer to master a skill or acquire a behavior when using distributed trials for instruction because the learner has to respond during repeated trials over time across activities, materials, settings, and people. In the long run, however, the acquired response should be more useful because the learner can perform it when it is needed. Note that distributed trial instruction also may be described as **embedded instruction** because the trials can occur within the context of other activities (Grisham-Brown, Schuster, Hemmeter, & Collins, 2000).

Phases of Learning

The previous discussion noted that different trial formats may be appropriate for facilitating different phases of learning. There are four basic phases of learning: 1) **acquisition,** 2) **fluency,** 3) **maintenance,** and 4) **generalization** (Alberto & Troutman, 2009; Collins, 2007). Instruction should be designed to address the appropriate phase of learning for each individual learner and the specific task being taught. It is possible to address more than one phase of learning at a time if the instruction is designed to do so.

Acquisition

Acquisition is the initial learning of a new behavior or response. A behavior is targeted for instruction when assessment has shown that the learner does not have the behavior in his or her repertoire and the instructional team has determined that the behavior will be beneficial to the learner.

Fluency

Fluency is how well a learner can perform a specific behavior. This is usually considered in terms of how quickly a learner can respond. Some behaviors require fluency. For example, it is desirable to be able to count out money when making a purchase without holding up the other shoppers who are in line to pay. It is necessary to be able to enter a personal identification number into an automated teller machine before it logs out. It is necessary to be able to greet or respond to people before they walk away. Fluency also can refer to accuracy. Instructors often measure the number of words read correctly per minute to determine fluency in reading or the number of math problems worked correctly per minute to determine fluency in math. For the skill of playing a musical instrument, fluency would be measured by the percentage of correct notes as well as the timing.

Maintenance

Maintenance refers to the ability of a learner to perform a behavior over time. This is measured once a learner has met criterion and reinforcement has been faded. For example, a learner may have mastered the spelling of a group of words with 100% accuracy. It is important, however, to check whether the learner can still spell those words a week or a month later. Ways to facilitate maintenance are discussed in Chapter 7.

Generalization

Perhaps the most important phase of learning is generalization. *Generalization* is the ability to perform a behavior across different conditions, including people, settings, activities, materials, and times of day. For example, a learner who has been taught to read a list of words should be able to read them regardless of the font color or size and regardless of whether they appear on a worksheet, in a book, or on signage. If learners cannot generalize or apply behaviors that have been acquired, then learning has no purpose. There are a number of ways to facilitate generalization; they are discussed in Chapter 7 as well.

Objectives

Before beginning instruction, it is crucial that the instructor have a **behavioral objective** (Alberto & Troutman, 2009) for each and every behavior that will be taught. This gives focus to the lesson, allows the instructor to develop an appropriate data-collection system, and specifies how well a learner must perform a behavior before it is considered mastered. Each behavioral objective should specify 1) the learner(s) for whom the objective has been written, 2) the observable and measurable behavior that the learner(s) will perform, 3) the conditions under which the behavior will be performed, and 4) the specific criterion that must be met before a behavior can be considered mastered. An example of an objective that focuses on acquisition follows:

When seated at a computer and told to enter her personal information, Ripley will type her name, address, and telephone number with 100% accuracy for 3 consecutive days.

The above objective can be changed to address fluency as follows:

When seated at a computer and told to enter her personal information, Ripley will type her name, address, and telephone number within 1 minute with 100% accuracy for 3 consecutive days.

Although the objective specifies 3 days, the time can be lengthened to measure maintenance as follows:

When seated at a computer and told to enter her personal information, Ripley will type her name, address, and telephone number with 100% accuracy for 3 consecutive days and will maintain the skill until the end of the school year.

The objective also can be extended to facilitate generalization, as follows:

When seated at a computer and told to enter her personal information, Ripley will type her name, address, and telephone number with 100% accuracy for 3 consecutive days across the following activities:

When working on an assignment in the computer lab

When filling out an application on a laptop computer

When working on an assignment on the classroom computer

If desired, an objective can address all phases of learning, as follows:

When seated at a computer and told to enter her personal information, Ripley will type her name, address, and telephone number within 1 minute with 100% accuracy for 3 consecutive days and will maintain the skill until the end of the school year across the following activities:

When working on an assignment in the computer lab

When filling out an application on a laptop computer

When working on an assignment on the classroom computer

SAMPLE INSTRUCTIONAL PROGRAMS

The following instructional programs demonstrate the basic components of systematic instruction, although they do not use a response-prompting strategy. It is again important to note that, although similar in its components, an instructional program is not the same as a lesson plan. As previously stated, a lesson plan typically is designed for a single lesson that will be taught once. Instructional programs are ongoing units of instruction that are repeated until learners reach criterion. In some cases, instructional programs address behaviors that are embedded across lesson plans. For example, an instructional program for teaching letter identification can be embedded in lesson plans across science, social studies, language arts, and health classes as long as there are opportunities for learners to receive trials to identify targeted letters (e.g., name letters used to identify elements on the periodic table, name letters used in Roman numerals in a unit on ancient Roman culture).

Sample Instructional Program 1

Instructors can expect learning to take place more rapidly when a learner has more opportunities to respond per session or throughout the day. The following instructional program is an example of how an elementary teacher might structure a daily lesson to increase the number of trials per session per learner by using **response cards** (Skibo, Mims, & Spooner, 2011) to allow all learners in the instructional group to make a **choral response** each time a stimulus is presented. The procedures are based on a research study conducted by Berrong, Schuster, Morse, and Collins (2007).

Core Content Standards

Science • Students will describe patterns in weather and weather data to make simple predictions based on those patterns discovered.

• Students will make generalizations and/or predictions about weather changes from day to day and over seasons on the basis of weather data.

Math • Students will convert units within the same measurement system, including money, time (seconds, minutes, hours, days, weeks, months, years), weight (ounces, pounds), and length (inches, feet, yards).

Behavioral Objective

When presented with questions on the date, the weather, and holidays during daily calendar time, the learner will hold up a response card showing the correct answer to each question within 5 seconds with 100% accuracy for 5 days.

Instructional Context

Instruction will occur during daily calendar time in an elementary classroom at the start of each school day with the learners seated around tables with their materials in front of them. Classroom assistants will be seated behind those learners who will require support to complete the task.

Instructional Materials

Materials for each student will consist of 1) a laminated 8″ × 10″ blank calendar with a piece of Velcro glued to each section and 2) an assortment of small, laminated, Velcro-backed cards with black, computer-generated words for the days of the week and the months of the year; numerals for the days of the month and the year; and words with pictures for holidays, special events, and the weather. The instructor also will have a calendar and cards to use when modeling the correct response.

Instructional Procedure

Each instructional trial will proceed as follows.

Attentional Cue	• The instructor will give the general attentional cue, "It's time to work on our calendars. Is everyone ready? Okay! Look."
Task Direction	• The instructor will ask a calendar question (e.g., "Can you show me what month this is?").
Response Interval	• The instructor will wait 5 seconds for the learners to hold up the correct cards.
Consequence	• The instructor will praise correct responses (e.g., "Great job! This month is May. Now you can put the name of the month on the top of your calendar") while modeling the correct response for learners who did not hold up the correct cards.
Nontargeted Information	• The instructor will make statements about correct responses (e.g., "May is the fifth month of the year. Sometimes people write the number 5 to indicate the fifth month of the year. May is in the spring, when the weather is getting warmer") before proceeding to the next trial.

Data Collection

The instructor will scan the class during the response interval to see which learners make an incorrect response or fail to respond and will quickly record a minus sign beside the names of those learners. When the lesson is finished, the instructor can go back and record a plus sign beside the names of learners who made correct responses. A sample completed data sheet can be found in Figure 1.1.

Maintenance

Once all learners have met the criterion of 100% correct responses for 1 day, the instructor will thin her praise statements for correct responses to every fifth question (i.e., **fixed ratio** of 5, or FR5, **schedule of reinforcement**) until all learners have met criterion for 5 days. For the reminder of the semester, the instructor only will praise class performance at the end of the session (e.g., "Everyone did a great job showing me the correct answers during calendar today").

Generalization

The instructor will facilitate generalization by having learners apply the information from the calendar activity throughout the day (e.g., writing the date on assignments, discussing the weather before going outside for recess, doing art projects with holiday themes).

SMALL-GROUP DATA SHEET

Date: _February 4_   Instructor: _Ms. Ward_

Skill: _Calendar_

Questions	Barbara	Betty	Bobby	Dennis	Gary	Henry	Jackie	Keith	Larry	Rocky	Sandy	Thea
					Student names							
Month	+	−	+	+	−	+	−	+	+	−	+	−
Year	+	+	+	+	+	−	−	+	−	+	+	+
Day of week	+	−	−	−	+	+	+	+	+	−	−	−
Month of year	−	+	−	+	+	+	+	−	+	+	−	+
Holiday/event	−	+	+	+	−	+	−	+	−	−	+	+
Weather	+	−	+	−	+	+	−	−	+	+	+	−
Number correct	4/6	3/6	4/6	4/6	4/6	5/6	2/6	4/6	4/6	3/6	4/6	3/6
% correct	67%	50%	67%	67%	67%	83%	33%	67%	67%	50%	67%	50%

Key: Plus sign indicates correct response; minus sign indicates incorrect or no response.

Figure 1.1. Sample completed data sheet for Sample Instructional Program 1.

Behavior Management

The instructor will periodically praise learners for sitting in their seats, attending, and participating (e.g., "I like the way all of you are sitting up so straight and looking for the right answers!").

Lesson Variations and Extension

Although classroom time devoted to calendar activity is common for elementary learners, calendar skills should be inserted in more age-appropriate activities for secondary learners. For example, calendar skills can be discussed during homeroom by asking learners to find the correct day in their personal planners and to answer questions about the day's schedule and week's activities. During science class, learners can locate the daily high and low temperature and graph these as seasons change. During social studies class, learners can locate the date on the day's newspaper and answer questions about current events (e.g., candidates running for office on election day). Throughout the day, learners can write the date on the assignments that they submit, using their personal planners to locate the date.

Sample Instructional Program 2

In the second instructional program, an instructor also uses response cards, this time to increase the opportunities to respond during a lesson on telling time with middle school students with moderate and severe disabilities. The procedures are based on a research study conducted by Horn, Schuster, and Collins (2006).

Core Content Standards

Math	• Students will convert units within the same measurement system and use these units to solve real world problems.
Practical Living/ Vocational	• Students will identify individual work habits/ethics (e.g., respect, time management, problem solving) and explain their importance in the workplace.

Behavioral Objective

When presented with the time shown on a clock face, the learner will hold up a response card showing the correct answer within 5 seconds with 100% accuracy for 5 days.

Instructional Context

Instruction will occur during math class with the learners seated at their desks with their materials in front of them. Classroom assistants are seated beside learners who may require support to complete the task.

Instructional Materials

Materials for each learner will consist of a set of laminated, spiral-bound cards on which the times of day have been printed in black. The times for the hours and the minutes will be separated: The hour cards, numbered from 1 to 12 followed by a colon, will be on the left; the minute cards, numbered from 00 to 59, will be on the right. Learners will be able to flip the hour and minute cards separately to show a printed time. The instructor will hold a real clock with a clock face large enough to be seen by all learners.

Instructional Procedure

There will be 30 instructional trials per session. Each instructional trial will proceed as follows.

Attentional Cue	• The instructor will give the general attentional cue, "We're going to work on telling time. Show me you're ready by holding up your time cards."
Task Direction	• The instructor will set the clock to a specific time of day and give the verbal task direction (e.g., "Show me what time it is").
Response Interval	• The instructor will wait 5 seconds for the learners to flip their correct cards to the correct time.
Consequence	• The instructor will praise correct responses (e.g., "Nice work. It's 12:25. The hour hand is on 12, and the minute hand shows 25 minutes after

SMALL-GROUP DATA SHEET

Date: _September 4_   Instructor: _Mr. Brock_

Skill: _Telling time_

Time	Angie	Chad	Franklin	Lee	Jamie	Joey	Mark	Ricky	Scotty	Trina
					Student names					
11:01	+	–	–	+	+	+	–	+	–	+
3:22	+	+	–	–	–	+	+	–	+	+
12:40	–	+	+	+	–	–	–	–	–	–
4:45	–	+	–	+	–	+	+	–	+	–
10:00	+	–	–	+	–	+	–	+	+	–
8:27	–	–	+	–	+	+	–	+	+	+
6:33	+	–	+	–	+	–	–	+	–	–
7:48	–	+	–	–	–	–	+	–	–	+
5:05	–	–	+	+	+	–	+	+	–	–
2:16	–	+	–	–	–	+	–	+	+	+
9:42	+	–	–	+	+	+	–	–	–	+
12:55	–	+	–	–	–	–	+	–	+	+
10:08	–	+	–	+	–	+	–	–	–	–
1:05	+	–	+	+	–	+	–	–	+	–
11:18	+	–	–	+	–	–	–	+	+	–
3:40	–	–	+	–	+	–	–	–	+	+
4:49	+	+	–	–	+	–	+	+	–	–
6:11	–	+	–	–	–	–	+	+	–	+
8:20	+	–	+	–	+	+	–	+	–	–
2:30	–	–	–	+	+	–	+	–	+	+
5:50	–	+	–	+	–	–	+	–	–	–
9:28	+	+	–	–	–	+	+	–	+	+
7:43	–	+	+	+	–	+	–	–	–	–
1:59	+	–	–	+	–	+	–	+	–	–
Number correct	11/24	12/24	8/24	13/24	10/24	12/24	11/24	10/24	11/24	12/24
% correct	46%	50%	33%	54%	42%	50%	46%	42%	46%	50%

Key: Plus sign indicates correct response; minus sign indicates incorrect or no response.

Figure 1.2. Sample completed data sheet for Sample Instructional Program 2.

12") and give learners who make incorrect responses 5 seconds to correct their errors.

Nontargeted Information

- The instructor will make a statement about time (e.g., "There are 60 minutes in 1 hour. It's important to tell time so that you can be on time when you have a job") before proceeding to the next trial.

Data Collection

The instructor will scan the class during the response interval to see which learners make incorrect responses or fail to respond and quickly record a minus sign beside the names of those learners. When the lesson is finished, the instructor can go back and record a plus sign beside the names of learners who made correct responses. A sample completed data sheet can be found in Figure 1.2.

Maintenance

Once all learners have met the criterion of 100% correct responses for 1 day, the instructor will thin his praise statements for correct responses to every fifth trial until all students have met criterion for 5 days (i.e., FR5 schedule of reinforcement). Once learners have met criterion, the instructor will continue to find opportunities to ask them what time it is throughout the day until the end of the school year.

Generalization

The instructor will facilitate generalization by using a real clock during instruction. Throughout the school day, he also will find opportunities to ask students what time it is on various clocks (e.g., on their watches, on the clock in the cafeteria, on the clock in the office) on which the clock face may look different (e.g., square instead of round, fewer numerals, different font on numerals, different color on background).

Behavior Management

The instructor periodically will praise students for sitting in their seats, attending, and participating (e.g., "Telling time can be hard. I like the way you are paying attention and trying to get the right answers!").

Lesson Variations and Extension

Although it may be easy to teach lessons on telling time with direct instruction in a small group in a resource room, lessons on telling time also can be embedded within activities in inclusive general education classes to supplement massed trial practice in the resource room. For example, an instructor might give response cards to all of the learners in a math class and then present a problem involving time. The instructor can then show a beginning time on the clock and ask learners to hold up their response cards showing the time. (This serves as an instructional trial for students with moderate and severe disabilities and as an attentional cue for their peers without disabilities.) The instructor can then give feedback and present the problem (e.g., "That's right, it's 3:00 p.m. If you leave school at 3:00 in the afternoon, you live 5 miles from the school, and the school bus is traveling at 45 miles per hour, what time will you arrive at your home? Hold up your cards with the answer when you have worked the problem." Learners without disabilities can write the numbers in a formula on their worksheets. Those who are paired with a peer with a disability can assist the peer in entering the formula into a calculator (e.g., "Hit the number 45"). Once the answer is completed, the learners without disabilities can hold up their response cards to show the answer. The instructor can ask, "What time is this?" and, at the same time, scan the class for the correct answers and then enter the correct arrival time on a clock face for the learners to check their answers. Learners with disabilities can flip their response cards to the correct time shown on the clock and hold their cards up.

SUMMARY

This chapter described the basic components of systematic instruction that applies the principles of ABA. In particular, the chapter focused on response-prompting procedures, setting the foundation for the remainder of this book. ABA-based instruction is sometimes narrowly defined and misconstrued as a series of massed discrete trials. This chapter presented ABA-based instruction in a broader context that addresses all phases of learning and is based on the premise that systematic instruction can be presented in a number of formats across natural settings throughout the day. Additional resources for designing systematic instruction can be found in Appendix C.

QUESTIONS FOR REFLECTION

1. Write a task analysis for a chained task that you might teach to a learner with a moderate intellectual disability, making sure that each step is both observable and measurable. When you have finished, rewrite the chained task for a learner with a significant intellectual disability who might need to have steps broken down into smaller components.

2. List several general attentional cues and responses that you might use to begin an instructional session. Next, list specific attentional cues and responses that you might use when teaching a learner to spell a word, to work a simple addition problem, or to locate a web site on a computer.

3. Identify a discrete behavior that you might teach through massed trial instruction. Now, describe a way that you could embed an instructional trial on that same skill during different activities across three natural settings.

4. In both sample lesson plans, the instructors used response cards to increase and maintain attention and to keep learners actively engaged while also increasing the number of opportunities to respond. What other strategies might increase attention and keep learners actively engaged?

5. Identify a basic skill that is typically taught to younger learners without disabilities and that an older learner with disabilities might need to master. How might you teach that skill in an age-appropriate way? How might you embed it in daily activities?

REFERENCES

Alberto, P.A., & Troutman, A.C. (2009). *Applied behavior analysis for teachers* (8th ed.). Upper Saddle River, NJ: Prentice-Hall.

Berrong, A.K., Schuster, J.W., Morse, T.E., & Collins, B.C. (2007). The effects of response cards on active participation and social behavior of students with moderate and severe disabilities. *Journal of Developmental and Physical Disabilities, 19,* 187–199.

Collins, B.C. (2007). *Moderate and severe disabilities: A foundational approach.* Upper Saddle River, NJ: Pearson, Merrill, Prentice-Hall.

Grisham-Brown, J., Schuster, J.W., Hemmeter, M.L., & Collins, B.C. (2000). Using an embedded strategy to teach preschoolers with significant disabilities. *Journal of Behavioral Education, 10,* 139–162.

Horn, C., Schuster, J.W., & Collins, B.C. (2006). Use of response cards to teach telling time to students with moderate and severe disabilities. *Education and Training in Developmental Disabilities, 41,* 382–391.

Skibo, H., Mims, P., & Spooner, F. (2011). Teaching number identification to students with severe disabilities using response cards. *Education and Training in Autism and Developmental Disabilities, 46*(1), 124–133.

Spooner, F., Browder, D.M., & Mims, P.J. (2011). Evidence-based practices. In D.M. Browder & F. Spooner (Eds.), *Teaching students with moderate and severe disabilities* (pp. 92–122). New York, NY: Guilford.

Wolery, M., Ault, M.J., & Doyle, P.M. (1992). *Teaching students with moderate to severe disabilities.* New York, NY: Longman.

Wolery, M., & Gast, D.L. (1984). Effective and efficient procedures for the transfer of stimulus control. *Topics in Early Childhood Special Education, 4,* 52–77.

Wolery, M., & Schuster, J.W. (1997). Teaching students with moderate to severe disabilities. *Journal of Special Education, 31,* 61–79.

CHAPTER 2

Developing Data Sheets and Collecting Baseline Data

On completion of this chapter, the reader will be able to

- Describe how to conduct screening and assessment of prerequisite skills
- Describe how to assess individualized reinforcers that can be used to increase behaviors during instruction
- Distinguish between the function and the form of a behavior, and write behavioral objectives that address each
- Design a basic data sheet for assessing baseline performance of a behavior
- State the difference between a single-opportunity and multiple-opportunity format for collecting baseline data
- Provide guidelines for determining when to cease baseline data collection and proceed to instruction
- Construct and label a graph displaying formative instructional data
- Use multiple means of visual analysis to determine the effectiveness of instruction

TERMS USED IN THIS CHAPTER

screening	single-opportunity format	phase change lines
baseline condition	multiple-opportunity format	data paths
prerequisite skills	data points	therapeutic trend
reinforcer preference testing	formative data	contratherapeutic trend
form	summative data	aim star
function	ordinate	mean levels of performance
situational information	tic marks	overlap
performance data	abscissa	
summary information	condition change lines	

Data collection and analysis are crucial in systematic instruction. This chapter describes basic data collection and graphing, and future chapters elaborate on how to collect and graph data for specific response-prompting procedures.

SCREENING

Most instructors have an idea of possible targets for instruction when they first begin working with a learner. These targets have been identified through thorough assessment in compiling the individualized education program (IEP). Assessment data may have come from adaptive behavior scales, ecological inventories (Brown et al., 1979; Spooner, Browder, & Richter, 2011), functional behavior assessments (Horner, Albin, Todd, Newton, & Sprague, 2011; Horner & Carr, 1997), and assistive technology assessments (Parette, Peterson-Karlan, Wojcik, & Bardi, 2007); assessment reports of related services delivery personnel (e.g., occupational therapist, physical therapist, speech-language pathologist); and interviews with families (e.g., COACH assessment [Giangreco, Cloninger, & Iverson, 2011]) as well as with the learner. In addition, instructors will have a working knowledge of age-appropriate core content standards or goals developed for transition plans. All of these sources are taken into consideration when designing instructional programs. Before writing objectives for specific targeted skills, however, it is necessary to screen learners to identify skills that already have been mastered. For example, before targeting survival words (a discrete task), the instructor would want to know which words, if any, a student already can read, define, and apply. Before targeting food preparation (a chained task), the instructor would want to know what items, if any, a learner already can prepare.

Basic **screening** is a largely informal process. The instructor may sit down one-to-one with a learner and quickly go through a stack of flashcards, creating a pile of known words and a pile of unknown words. The instructor might show reading passages from simple to complex and ask the learner to read until repeated errors are made. The instructor might observe a learner during a morning routine to see whether the learner has difficulty completing any of the tasks (e.g., taking off and hanging up one's coat, locating one's desk, checking the schedule, getting out materials for class). The instructor might ask a learner to help prepare various snacks for the class (e.g., making sandwiches, heating an item in the microwave, preparing an item from a commercial mix) and observe which types of snacks the learner can and cannot prepare. If the learner makes an error in performing a chained task, the instructor can simply perform the steps the learner cannot complete. Once the instructor has spent time informally screening potential targets for instruction, behavioral objectives can be written, **baseline** data can be collected, and the instructional program can be developed.

PREREQUISITE ASSESSMENT

Once screening has been conducted, and before designing the instructional program, the instructor should identify the **prerequisite skills** the learner will need to participate in baseline and instructional sessions and to master the targeted behavior. Prerequisites may include, but are not limited to, visual and auditory acuity, gross or fine motor skills, ability to attend for a set amount of time, ability to imitate a model, verbal or augmentative communication skills, or letter or number recognition. The instructor can determine whether a learner has these prerequisite skills through informal observation, a survey of the learner's records, or direct testing. In some cases, adaptations will be needed, such as eyeglasses or an assistive device. In other cases, learners may need preliminary instruction on skills, such as identifying letter sounds or counting. Learners also may need to be taught how to sit and attend, how to wait for a prompt, or how to imitate a model.

Prerequisite assessment also should include **reinforcer preference testing** (Alberto & Troutman, 2009). This can be as simple as asking verbal students to state which reinforcers they prefer. This can be determined for nonverbal learners by 1) watching what they select when given a choice of potential reinforcers, 2) systematically assessing reinforcers through trials in which students are given paired choices (e.g., a sip of milk and a sip of water), or 3) measuring the duration of time a learner engages in various activities (e.g., listening to music, looking at a magazine). It is important that the instructor be prepared to provide these reinforcers because some learners might not respond to praise alone. For a more detailed description of how to conduct reinforcer preference testing, the reader may wish to consult other texts (e.g., Alberto & Troutman, 2009; Westling & Fox, 2009).

BEHAVIORAL OBJECTIVES

Chapter 1 discussed behavioral objectives and how they can be written to address specific phases of learning. Before a data collection system can be designed, it is important to consider whether objectives will be written for discrete or chained behaviors. It also is important to determine whether the **form** or the **function** is more important in determining how some behaviors will be measured.

Objectives for Discrete Behaviors

As defined in Chapter 1, a discrete behavior consists of a single step. Thus, data will indicate whether the learner performed a discrete behavior. The following is an example of a behavioral objective for a discrete behavior:

> When given a picture of an instructional material needed for a class activity, Brogan will pick up the item from an array of materials on the classroom shelf for 100% of the opportunities for 5 days.

The objective makes clear what Brogan is to do, what the stimulus will be for her to respond, and what criterion must be met for her to master the skill. Screening will have determined which items Brogan will select; for example, she already may be able to identify pencils, paper, glue, and scissors but not be able to distinguish between crayons or markers or specific colors of each. Once Brogan has mastered the criterion in the objective, the instructor may move on to identification of other instructional materials (e.g., workbooks, reading texts, science experiment materials).

Objectives for Chained Tasks

As defined in Chapter 1, chained tasks consist of a series of discrete behaviors or steps, each of which can be measured separately. In writing a behavioral objective for a chained task, the instructor will want to attach the task analysis, as follows:

> When told to do the laundry, Eve will independently complete the steps of the following task analysis with 100% accuracy at school, home, or the self-service laundry for three out of three opportunities.
>
> 1. Sort laundry
> 2. Put items in washer
> 3. Add correct amount of detergent
> 4. Set controls appropriate to the items being washed
> 5. Push button to begin wash cycle
> 6. Remove items from washer
> 7. Place items in dryer
> 8. Set controls appropriate to the items being dried
> 9. Remove items from dryer
> 10. Fold items

The IEP and transition team will have determined that doing her laundry is an important skill for Eve as she prepares to make the transition to adulthood. To facilitate generalization, the skill will be taught across settings. Screening may have indicated that Eve is able to complete some of the steps of the task analysis independently (i.e., putting in and removing items from washer and dryer), but she cannot perform the entire task; thus, it has been targeted for instruction.

Form versus Function

The function of a behavior is the outcome, and the form is how a behavior is performed (Collins, 2007). In the examples in the previous sections, the function or outcome of Brogan selecting instructional materials is that she will become more independent across her classes, and the function or outcome for Eve is that she will become more independent and also have clean clothing to wear each day and clean sheets and towels when she needs them. In both of these objectives, the form is important if the learners are to achieve the function. In collecting data for Brogan, a correct response would be marked each time she picked up the correct item. If the term *select* had been used in the objective, Brogan would have been free to use another form; instead of picking up an item, she could have indicated that she recognized it through her eye gaze toward the item or through pointing at it. This, however, would not have increased her independence. In collecting data for Eve, it is clear which form she should use for each step (e.g., pushing a button). If any one of these steps proves difficult for Eve, the task analysis can be broken down into even more specific steps (e.g., push button for cold water wash, open door to dryer). In addition, some steps could have adaptations, such as having Eve use premeasured packets of laundry detergent or dryer sheets if she does not know how to measure.

In certain cases, the instructor might determine that the form is not as important as the function; in these cases, the instructor may allow the learner to use a variety of forms as long as the function is accomplished. For example, there are a number of forms a learner can use to respond to the question, "What is your name?" Chase could verbally state his name, make a manual sign for his name, write his name, type his name, point to his name on a prepared card, or hit a key on a voice output device to provide his name. Regardless of the form, the function would be accomplished of giving the requested information, and data would be recorded to indicate a correct response. The speech-language pathologist, however, may have indicated that Chase is capable of verbal speech and has a goal of making his speech more intelligible. In that case, data only would be recorded to indicate a correct response if Chase verbally stated his name. In summary, the objective should clearly indicate whether form or function is the goal of instruction. If form is most important, the objective for this instructional program would be written as follows:

> When asked for personal information, Chase will verbally state the items requested with 100% accuracy for five out of five opportunities.

If the function is most important, the objective for this instructional program would be written as follows:

> When asked for personal information, Chase will respond with 100% accuracy for five out of five opportunities.

DATA SHEETS

Once the instructor has written the behavioral objective for an instructional program, a data collection system can be designed. Regardless of whether data sheets are designed to collect data during baseline, instructional, maintenance, or generalization sessions, all data sheets have three parts: 1) **situational information,** 2) **performance data,** and 3) **summary information.** Some data sheets may allow the instructor to record information for only one learner or one session, whereas others may allow the instructor to record data across multiple learners or across multiple sessions. It is easy for instructors to generate data sheets on a computer using a word processing table function or computer data management system (e.g., Excel). Some instructors also may record data electronically (e.g., using an electronic notebook). An advantage to recording data with a pencil and paper, however, is that the instructor can easily jot down notes about the instructional session (e.g., instruction interrupted midway by a series of announcements over the school intercom system; student behavior difficult to control because of altercation with another student). It is helpful to keep multiple hard copies of data sheets organized in a notebook with the instructional program and the graph. This allows any of the instructional staff to pick up the notebook, record data, and graph with ease while instruction takes place.

Situational Information

The situational information on a data sheet provides basic information about each session. This will include the name(s) of the learner(s) participating in the session, the name of the instructor conducting the session, the name of the behavior or skill that has been targeted for instruction, and the setting in which the instruction is taking place. Instructors also may want to record additional information, such as the condition (e.g., baseline, instruction, generalization, maintenance), the time of day the session is conducted, or the schedule of reinforcement that is to be delivered (e.g., every trial, every other trial).

Performance Data

The majority of each data sheet is devoted to recording the performance of the learner or learners on each instructional trial. The specific stimulus to be presented on each trial should be listed for discrete behaviors, and the steps of the task analysis should be listed for chained tasks. A key on the data sheet should indicate how to record accurate data for correct responses, incorrect responses, or failures to respond.

Summary Information

There should be a place to summarize data at the bottom of each data sheet. At minimum, this will consist of the number/percentage of correct responses, but it also could include the number of incorrect responses or failures to respond and the number of prompted responses during instruction.

BASELINE DATA COLLECTION

Baseline data differ from screening data in that they are acquired through a more formal process and are used as the basic measure for later comparison of data to determine whether a learner has made progress over time. Baseline data collection sessions are conducted in a one-to-one format and use the same materials and stimulus or task direction that will be used later during instruction. Baseline data collection sessions can be conducted in massed trial format or embedded across activities in natural settings throughout the day. If generalization is a goal, the baseline session should occur using natural materials in the same setting in which the learner will ultimately be expected to perform the behavior.

Discrete Behaviors and Chained Tasks

For a discrete task, the instructor will want to collect data from multiple trials per item during each baseline session. This provides a more accurate measure of a learner's ability. For example, if an instructor plans to teach five sight words, each word might be presented five times per session, for a total of 25 trials per session.

Although it is best to conduct multiple trials per session for chained tasks, the instructor only may have the opportunity to conduct one because some activities are performed just once in a session. For example, a session of preparing a snack may consist of a single opportunity to perform a task, such as making pudding. A session of consuming a snack, however, may provide multiple opportunities to perform the chained task of taking a spoon in hand, scooping pudding into the spoon, raising the spoon to the mouth, putting the spoon in the mouth, closing the lips to eat the pudding, removing the spoon from the mouth, and lowering the spoon to the table.

Single- and Multiple-Opportunity Formats

An instructor has two options for collecting baseline data on a chained task (Brown & Snell, 2011): 1) **single-opportunity format** and 2) **multiple-opportunity format.** In a single-opportunity format (Collins, Hager, & Galloway, 2011), the learner only has one opportunity to perform the task analysis, and the session ends when the first error is made. For example, the instructor can ask a learner to make the pudding. As soon as the first error is made, the instructor should thank the learner for helping and then complete the task for him or her. Although the learner is not permitted to watch the instructor complete the task, the learner does get to consume the pudding. In a multiple-opportunity format (e.g., Graves, Collins, Schuster, & Kleinert, 2005), the learner is permitted to attempt each step of the task analysis; if an error is made on a step, the instructor performs that step for the learner and then waits to see whether the learner can perform the step that follows. For example, the instructor can tell the learner to eat the pudding. The learner might pick up the spoon but begin to raise it to his or her lips without scooping. The instructor should interrupt the learner, take the spoon from the learner's hand, and scoop the pudding for the learner before putting the spoon back in the learner's hand and waiting to see what the learner does next.

Instruction never should occur during baseline sessions. That is why, if a multiple-opportunity format is used, the instructor attempts to perform the step for the learner without letting the learner observe. Prompting of any kind is never used during baseline sessions. The purpose of collecting baseline data is to determine exactly what learners can do correctly on their own without assistance.

It is up to the instructor to determine whether there will be a consequence for correct responses during baseline sessions. Although a more accurate picture of the learner's current ability will be obtained in the absence of encouragement, praising correct responses may allow learners to acquire skills through trial and error because they will get feedback on correct responses but not on incorrect responses. For example, a learner who guesses correctly when reading a sight word and does not get any feedback may guess differently on the next trial. A learner who guesses correctly in reading a sight word and receives praise, however, may remember the correct response and continue to make it during future trials.

Regardless of whether positive feedback on correct responses is given during baseline sessions, it is important to praise the learner's attempts to respond; doing so will help decrease frustration and maintain attending and appropriate behavior. Instructors should feel free to make statements that may be reinforcing, such as, "I like the way you are trying so hard when you don't know the answers," or "You are doing a great job sitting quietly and listening. As soon as I learn what you can already do by yourself, I'll begin teaching you."

It also is important to conduct more than one baseline session. It takes three **data points** to make a trend. If data are stable (the same across sessions, as shown in Figure 2.1) or decreasing (as shown in Figure 2.2), instruction can begin. If data, however, are increasing (as shown in Figure 2.3), this may indicate that learners are acquiring the ability to perform the targeted behavior through trial and error; in this case, there is no need to provide instruction until the learners quit making progress and data become stable.

SAMPLE FORMATS FOR BASELINE DATA COLLECTION SESSIONS

The following sections provide sample formats for sessions in which instructors will collect baseline data. One is for a discrete behavior, and one is for a chained task.

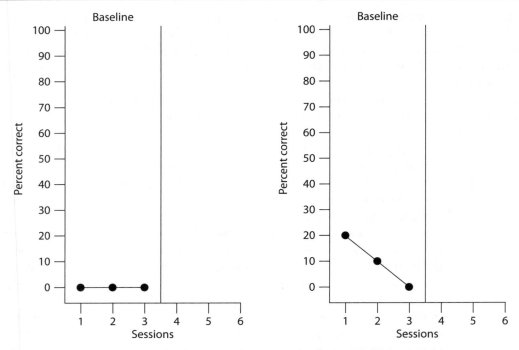

Figure 2.1. Graphed data showing stability in baseline responses.

Figure 2.2. Graphed data showing a decrease in baseline responses.

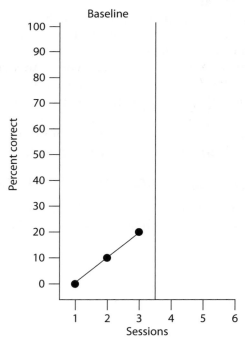

Figure 2.3. Graphed data showing an increase in baseline responses.

Sample Baseline Data Collection Session for a Discrete Behavior

The following section provides guidelines for conducting a baseline session as part of an instructional program to teach the discrete behavior of sight-word identification.

Behavioral Objective

When presented with products containing recipe words, Max will verbally state the word within 5 seconds of the task direction with 100% accuracy for 5 days.

Instructional Context

The baseline session will occur in a one-to-one format with Max facing the instructor.

Instructional Materials

Materials will consist of three packages of cooking mixes (e.g., cake mix, brownie mix, cookie mix) with the targeted cooking words on the back.

Assessment Procedure

There will be 3 trials per word for a total of 15 trials per session. Each instructional trial will proceed as follows.

Attentional Cue	• The instructor will begin the session by explaining that she wants to find out how many words Max can read on the back of cooking mixes so that he can learn to prepare them by himself. The instructor then will point to a word on the back of a boxed mix, give the specific attentional cue, "Max, tell me the name of the first letter of this word," and wait for Max to respond.
Task Direction	• The instructor will praise the attentional response and give the task direction, "Good looking, Max; the word begins with the letter *B*. What is the word?"
Response Interval	• The instructor will wait 5 seconds for Max to respond.
Consequence	• When Max reads a word correctly, the instructor will praise the response. The instructor will ignore all incorrect responses or failures to respond within the response interval.

Data Collection

The instructor will record a plus sign on the data sheet for each correct response and a minus sign on the data sheet for each incorrect response. A sample completed data sheet for collecting baseline data is shown in Figure 2.4.

Behavior Management

The instructor will praise Max periodically for sitting in his seat, attending, and participating (e.g., "I know these words are hard. I like the way you are paying attention and trying to read them!").

BASELINE DATA SHEET

Name: ___Max_____   Instructor: ___Ms. Smith_____

Skill: ___Cooking words_____   Setting: ___Consumer science class___

Words	Date		
	January 2	January 3	January 4
1. Bake	0	+	0
2. Mix	−	0	0
3. Preheat	0	0	0
4. Minutes	−	+	0
5. Stir	0	−	+
6. Mix	0	0	−
7. Preheat	+	0	0
8. Minutes	0	−	0
9. Stir	+	0	+
10. Bake	−	+	0
11. Preheat	0	0	0
12. Minutes	−	0	0
13. Stir	0	+	−
14. Bake	0	0	0
15. Minutes	0	−	+
Number correct	2/15	4/15	3/15
% correct	13%	27%	20%

Key: Plus sign indicates correct response; minus sign indicates incorrect response; zero indicates no response.

Figure 2.4.   Sample completed data sheet for a baseline data collection session for a discrete task.

Sample Baseline Data Collection Session for a Chained Task

The following section provides guidelines for conducting a baseline session as part of an instructional program to teach the chained task of computing a percentage on a calculator.

Behavioral Objective

When presented with word problems using percentages, Spenser will initiate working on each problem within 5 seconds of the task direction and will complete the task analysis for each problem with 100% accuracy within 20 seconds for 5 days. The task analysis will consist of the following steps:

1.   Enter the small amount.

2.   Hit *divide.*

3. Enter the large amount.
4. Hit *multiply.*
5. Enter 100.
6. State or write the answer.

Instructional Context

The baseline session will occur in a one-to-one format with Spenser sitting beside the instructor at a table.

Instructional Materials

Materials will consist of a calculator, a shopping list, various savings coupons, a list of the retail prices for the products on the shopping list, a list of calories for the food products on the list, a chart of daily caloric intake to maintain weight according to height, and recipes with preparation time or baking time.

Assessment Procedure

There will be five trials per session. Each instructional trial will proceed as follows.

Attentional Cue	• The instructor will begin the session by explaining that he wants to find out how well Spenser can work math problems using percentages. The instructor will then give the general attentional cue, "Are you ready?"
Task Direction	• When Spenser is attending, the instructor will explain the problem and then provide the task direction, as follows: "This ad says that you can get 10 cents off this brand of soap. The regular price for this brand of soap on your list is 2 dollars. Use your calculator to find what percent you will be saving if you use this coupon." In addition to problems about computing the percentage of savings, Spenser also will be presented with problems to compute the percentage of calories in a food item out of the daily caloric allowance for someone of Spenser's height, and the percentage of preparation time to prepare a food out of the number of minutes in the consumer science class.
Response Interval	• The instructor will wait 5 seconds for Spenser to begin working the problem. If Spenser begins working the problem, the instructor will wait 20 additional seconds for her to complete the problem.
Consequence	• The instructor will use a single-opportunity format. If Spenser fails to begin working the problem within the response interval or makes an error while working on the problem, the instructor will end the trial by saying, "You can stop now and try another problem," or "You can stop now, and we'll work on this another day." There will be no praise for correct responses other than "Thank you for working the problem."

Data Collection

The instructor will record a plus sign on the data sheet for each correct step of the task analysis. If Spenser fails to respond within the response interval or makes an error, the instructor will record a minus sign on the data sheet for that step and for every step that follows. A sample completed data sheet for a chained task is shown in Figure 2.5.

BASELINE DATA SHEET

Name: ___Spenser___   Instructor: ___Mr. Powell___
Skill: ___Percentages___   Setting: ___Math class___

Steps	Date		
	September 4	September 5	September 6
1. Enter small amount	0	0	0
2. Hit "divide"	0	0	0
3. Enter large amount	0	+	+
4. Hit "multiply"	0	–	0
5. Enter 100	0	0	0
6. State/write answer	–	0	–
Number correct	0/6	1/6	1/6
% correct	0%	17%	17%

Key: Plus sign indicates correct response; minus sign indicates incorrect response; zero indicates no response.

Figure 2.5.   Sample completed data sheet for a baseline data collection session for a chained task.

Behavior Management

The instructor will praise Spenser periodically for sitting in her seat, attending, and participating (e.g., "You're doing a great job trying to work these problems!").

GRAPHIC DISPLAYS

Formative data are data that are collected continuously across instructional sessions; **summative data** are collected only through assessment at the conclusion of an instructional program. In instructional programs, formative data are collected on daily progress, whereas summative data may be collected on generalization from a pretest to a posttest. The purpose of formative data collection is to monitor the progress of learners so that modifications can be made to the instructional procedure if adequate progress is not being made to enable a learner to reach criterion in a timely fashion. To make data-based decisions during instructional programs, instructors need to graph data on a continuous basis. A graph should be clear enough to allow instructors, learners, and others to determine the rate of progress through a simple visual analysis.

Components of Graphs

All graphs have standard components. As shown in Figure 2.6, two intersecting lines form the basis of a graph. The vertical line is the **ordinate** and shows the behavior being measured. Labeled **tic marks** are placed on the ordinate to indicate number correct or percent

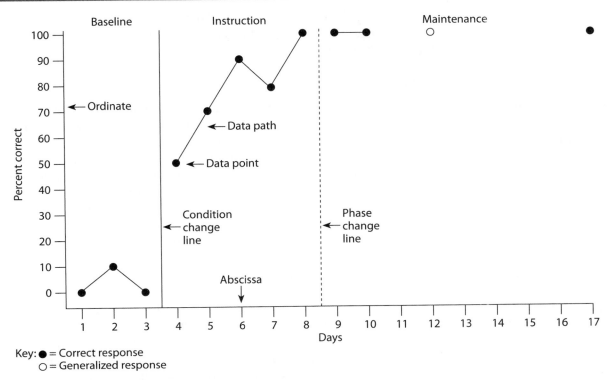

Figure 2.6.   Sample graph showing labeled components.

correct. (If number is used as the standard measure, then all instructional sessions must contain an equal number of trials.) The horizontal line is the **abscissa** and shows the measure of time used to collect data. Labeled tic marks are placed on the abscissa to indicate sessions or days. Both the ordinate and the abscissa should be clearly labeled. Solid **condition change lines** indicate the points at which conditions change (e.g., between baseline condition and instruction). Dashed **phase change lines** indicate the points at which phases of instruction change (e.g., modification made to instruction). All conditions and phases should be labeled.

Data points are placed to show the correct responses a learner has during each instructional session. These data points are connected by **data paths** unless there is a change in condition or phase or a break in planned instruction due to a holiday or an absence. Typically, correct responses are indicated by dark closed circles. Other symbols can be used to indicate other types of responses (e.g., open circles to indicate generalized responses, open triangles to indicate prompted responses). A key should be on every graph, indicating what each type of data point represents.

Although computer-generated graphs are attractive and can be easily generated using software (e.g., Excel, PowerPoint), an instructor may be more likely to record formative data if it is done with pencil and paper as soon as an instructional session ends. (Data can be transferred later to an electronic program if desired.) This method has the advantage of data being immediately available to the learner with statements of progress from the instructor (e.g., "Look, you did better today than yesterday," "I'm sorry you did not make progress today, but you can try harder tomorrow"). It also allows the instructor to write in notes to explain possible causes of fluctuating data (e.g., seizure prior to instruction, change in medication). Some learners can benefit from graphing their own progress as a reinforcer or as a targeted math skill. For easy access, it is helpful to keep hard copies of graphs in notebooks with instructional programs and data sheets.

Visual Analysis of Graphed Data

There are several ways to conduct a visual analysis of graphed instructional data (Alberto & Troutman, 2009; Gast, 2009). First, the instructor can eyeball the trend of data. For most instructional programs, increasing data indicate a **therapeutic trend,** and decreasing data indicate a **contratherapeutic trend.** If data remain stable and show no progress over baseline level or if there is a contratherapeutic trend, the instructor will want to make modifications to instruction. If data are too erratic (i.e., high degree of variability) to determine a trend, the instructor also needs to consider modifications to the instructional program. (Note that there are methods to determine the trend that are not described in this book because they would be more valuable to a researcher than to an instructor. For detailed examples, see Gast [2009].)

Second, the instructor may find it helpful to project the point at which the learner is expected to meet criterion (e.g., end of 6-week grading period, end of semester). If that is the case, the instructor can draw an **aim star** at that point on the graph and draw a line from the learner's mean baseline performance to the aim star. If the learner's data fall below this line over time, it is not likely that the learner will meet criterion at the desired point. Again, this is an indication that modifications in the instructional procedure are warranted.

Comparing **mean levels of performance** between baseline condition and instruction and computing the percentage of **overlap** between baseline condition and instruction are additional ways to visually analyze data, although these methods may not be as useful to instructors as looking at the trend or progress toward an aim star. They can be appropriate, however, for skills in which the instructor is anticipating an overall increase in a behavior even if a set target for criterion has not been specified. For example, an instructor who is teaching verbal communication skills might compare the mean level of intelligible utterances during the baseline condition with the mean level of intelligible utterances once an intervention has been implemented. The instructor also might draw a horizontal line extending from the highest data point in baseline into the intervention and then compute the percentage of data points that fall below that point during intervention. The less overlap, the more progress a learner is making.

Data Decision Rules

Instructors should conduct a visual analysis of graphed instructional data on a regular basis (e.g., daily or weekly). If a learner is not making progress or is not making progress at the desired rated, then the instructor needs to make decisions on how to modify instruction to facilitate progress. A lack of progress may indicate that a skill is too difficult for a learner. In this case, the instructor might decrease the number of behaviors being taught (e.g., teach 5 sight words at a time instead of 10), or the instructor might teach an easier version of the task (e.g., teach a different task analysis for tying shoes or teach the learner to fasten shoes with Velcro instead of tying them). Highly variable data may indicate that a learner has the ability to perform the correct response but is prevented from doing so by behavior issues (e.g., not paying attention) or medical issues (e.g., seizure activity). In the case of a behavioral issue, the instructor might try providing a stronger preferred reinforcer for correct responses (e.g., edible, sticker, activity) in addition to praise. If it is suspected that the learner has become dependent on prompting, the instructor might try differential reinforcement by providing reinforcement for independent responses and withholding reinforcement for prompted responses. If the learner is making progress but not at an adequate rate to reach criterion by the desired date, the instructor might try increasing the number of trials per session. Other modifications to instruction might include changing the instructional procedure, using more novel or interesting materials, making the instruction more meaningful or relevant for the learner by teaching it in an applied manner, changing from teaching in a group to teaching in a one-to-one format, using an admired peer as the instructor, changing the type of prompt to another that results in the correct response, increasing the response interval, or changing from a general to a specific attentional cue. The list is endless, but it is important to change only one variable in instruction at a time until the data indicate that the modification works or does not work. It also is important to try a modification long enough to give it time to work. For example, the instructor may have a decision rule that a modification in instruction will be made if the student has not exhibited the desired progress toward criterion after 10 instructional sessions and will implement a modification for 5 instructional sessions before trying another.

SUMMARY

This chapter described the importance of collecting screening data and baseline data before instruction. In addition, the importance of graphing formative data and conducting a visual analysis were stressed. Instructors who are anxious to begin instruction may find it tempting to bypass these steps. Collecting data on baseline performance, however, provides the justification for conducting instruction and the basis for determining progress. See Appendix A for a flowchart for collecting baseline data and Appendix B for a sample data sheet that can be used for collecting baseline data on both discrete and chained tasks.

QUESTIONS FOR REFLECTION

1. Identify a behavior that you might teach to a student with moderate or severe disabilities. What prerequisite skills are needed to perform the skill? What adaptations might be needed?

2. Design a data sheet you might use to teach the discrete skill of number identification. Design a data sheet you might use to teach the more complex skill of addition with regrouping. Be sure to include the task analysis.

3. What are the advantages and disadvantages of single-opportunity and multiple-opportunity formats during baseline sessions?

4. You are working with a student whose data during instruction fluctuate between 10% and 95%. What modifications might you try to stabilize the data?

REFERENCES

Alberto, P.A., & Troutman, A.C. (2009). *Applied behavior analysis for teachers* (8th ed.). Upper Saddle River, NJ: Prentice-Hall.

Brown, L., Branston, M.B., Hamre-Nietupski, S., Pumpian, I., Certo, N., & Gruenwald, L. (1979). A strategy for developing chronological-age-appropriate and functional curricular content for severely handicapped adolescents and young adults. *Journal of Special Education, 13*, 81–90.

Brown, F., & Snell, M.E. (2011). Measuring student behavior and learning. In M.E. Snell & F. Brown (Eds.), *Instruction of students with severe disabilities* (7th ed., pp. 186–223). Upper Saddle River, NJ: Pearson.

Collins, B.C. (2007). *Moderate and severe disabilities: A foundational approach.* Upper Saddle River, NJ: Pearson.

Collins, B.C., Hager, K.D., & Galloway, C.C. (2011). The addition of functional content during core content instruction with students with moderate disabilities. *Education and Training in Developmental Disabilities, 46*, 22–39.

Gast, D.L. (2009). *Single subject research methodology in behavioral sciences.* New York, NY: Routledge.

Giangreco, M.F., Cloninger, C.J., & Iverson, V.S. (2011). *Choosing outcomes and accommodations for children (COACH): A guide to educational planning for students with disabilities* (3rd ed.). Baltimore, MD: Paul H. Brookes Publishing Co.

Graves, T.B., Collins, B.C., Schuster, J.W., & Kleinert, H. (2005). Using video prompting to teach cooking skills to secondary students with moderate disabilities. *Education and Training in Developmental Disabilities, 40*, 34–46.

Horner, R.H., Albin, R.W., Todd, A.W., Newton, J.S., & Sprague, J.R. (2011). Designing and implementing individualized positive behavior support. In M.E. Snell & F. Brown (Eds.), *Instruction of students with severe disabilities* (7th ed., pp. 257–303). Upper Saddle River, NJ: Pearson.

Horner, R.H., & Carr, E.G. (1997). Behavioral support for students with severe disabilities: Functional assessment and comprehensive intervention. *Journal of Special Education, 31*, 84–104.

Parette, H.P., Peterson-Karlan, G.R., Wojcik, B.W., & Bardi, N. (2007). Monitor that progress? Interpreting data rends for assistive technology decision making. *Teaching Exceptional Children, 40*, 22–29.

Spooner, F., Browder, D.M., & Richter, S. (2011). Community and job skills. In D.M. Browder & F. Spooner (Eds.), *Teaching students with moderate and severe disabilities* (pp. 342–363). New York, NY: Guilford.

Westling, D.L., & Fox, L. (2009). *Teaching students with severe disabilities* (4th ed.). Upper Saddle River, NJ: Pearson.

CHAPTER 3

Using Graduated-Guidance, Most-to-Least Prompting, and System-of-Least-Prompts Procedures

On completion of this chapter, the reader will be able to

- Describe and perform the steps of the graduated-guidance, most-to-least prompting, and system-of-least-prompts procedures
- Design a data sheet for teaching a discrete behavior and a chained task with the graduated-guidance, most-to-least prompting, and system-of-least-prompts procedures
- Graph and analyze formative data collected from instruction with the graduated-guidance, most-to-least prompting, and system-of-least-prompts procedures
- State a rationale for pairing verbal prompts with more intrusive prompts

TERMS USED IN THIS CHAPTER

graduated-guidance procedure   response interval
most-to-least prompting procedure   variable ratio schedule of reinforcement
system-of-least-prompts (SLP) procedure

Three of the oldest systematic instructional procedures reported in the professional litera-ture as effective with students with moderate and severe disabilities include 1) **graduated-guidance procedure,** 2) **most-to-least prompting procedure,** and 3) **system-of-least-prompts (SLP) procedure.** Each of these procedures will be described in detail in this chapter within the framework of the principles described in Chapter 1. In addition, sample instructional programs based on investigations from the professional research, sample data sheets, and sample graphs will be provided.

GRADUATED GUIDANCE

The graduated-guidance procedure (Collins, 2007; Snell & Brown, 2011; Spooner, Browder, & Mims, 2011; Westling & Fox, 2009; Wolery, Ault, & Doyle, 1992) is perhaps the easiest of all of the response-prompting procedures to implement and has a long history of effective-ness (e.g., MacDuff, Krantz, & McClannahan, 1993). Because the procedure relies on a physical prompt, it is appropriate for teaching behaviors for which physical assistance will be needed, such as using utensils, writing, walking, using equipment, or performing a task that is potentially dangerous. The physical prompt is delivered according to the instructor's judgment as to how much assistance the learner needs on a moment-to-moment basis and is faded over time as assistance no longer is needed. Imagine walking alongside a toddler taking his or her first steps. The adult would have his or her hands ready to catch the child from falling and provide balance at any moment needed. As the child becomes able to bal-ance and take steps, the adult pulls away from touching the child but still shadows the child's movements, always ready to provide assistance.

In the graduated-guidance procedure, the prompt can be faded as the instructor feels appropriate on a moment-to-moment basis. The prompt also can be faded in a systematic fashion. For example, in teaching independent eating skills, the instructor might begin with a hand-over-hand physical prompt. As the instructor observes the learner becoming more competent, the instructor can move to gently guiding the learner's movements at the wrist. When the instructor feels the learner is ready, the instructor can move to the learner's fore-arm and then, later, to a nudge at the elbow. During this fading sequence, which may take days or weeks, the instructor always should be ready to jump in with a more intrusive physical prompt, if necessary, to keep the learner from making an error. Thus, the proce-dure is considered nearly errorless.

The steps for each trial when using the graduated-guidance procedure are as follows:

1. Secure the learner's attention.
2. Deliver the task direction.
3. Use a physical prompt, as needed, shadowing the learner's movements.
4. If the learner begins to make an error, immediately use a more intrusive physical prompt.

5. Praise prompted as well as unprompted behaviors performed by the student.

6. Fade the physical prompt over time as the student becomes more independent

The graduated-guidance procedure is appropriate for young learners or learners with significant intellectual disabilities who do not yet have the receptive language necessary to follow verbal directions or who are not yet sufficiently imitative to follow a model prompt. Instructors, however, may want to pair verbal directions with each behavior a learner performs to facilitate the learner acquiring the ability to understand verbal directions over time. For example, an instructor who is physically prompting a learner to scoop a spoonful of pudding from a bowl might, at the same time, say, "Scoop the pudding." The graduated-guidance procedure is also appropriate for students who have significant motor impairments and need physical guidance to perform motor behaviors.

Data collection, when using the graduated-guidance procedure, is simple. The instructor simply lists on the data sheet whether the learner can perform the behavior independently (e.g., record an I) or if the learner needs a physical prompt (e.g., record a P). The procedure can be used with either discrete behaviors or chained tasks. A sample completed data sheet for a discrete behavior taught with the graduated-guidance procedure can be found in Figure 3.1, and a sample completed data sheet for a chained task taught with the graduated-guidance procedure can be found in Figure 3.2. When graphing data from the graduated-guidance procedure, the instructor only indicates the correct unprompted (independent) behaviors.

MOST-TO-LEAST PROMPTING

Instead of relying on a single physical prompt, as in the graduated-guidance procedure, the most-to-least prompting procedure (Collins, 2007; Snell & Brown, 2011; Spooner et al., 2011; Westling & Fox, 2009; Wolery et al., 1992) relies on a hierarchy of prompts (as described in Chapter 1), beginning with the controlling prompt or the most intrusive prompt necessary for the learner to perform the correct response. Most often, this will be a physical prompt. This prompt is faded systematically by moving through a predetermined sequence of prompts, one at a time, until the learner can perform the desired behavior correctly and independently. The instructor moves through this sequence at a slow pace, only moving to a less intrusive prompt as the learner is ready. The procedure requires a minimum of three prompt levels (e.g., physical, model, independent). Thus, the procedure may take weeks for a learner to meet criterion. For example, the instructor may begin with a physical prompt for 1 week, move to a partial physical prompt for 1 week, move to a model prompt for 1 week, move to a verbal prompt for 1 week, and then allow the learner to perform the behavior independently. As with the graduated-guidance procedure, verbal prompts may be paired with more intrusive prompts from the beginning, thus exposing the learner to verbal language that may acquire meaning over time.

There are several ways to move from one prompt level to the next. The instructor may rely on personal judgment as to when the learner is ready. Another option is to have a predetermined, set number of sessions to use each prompt level with a student. In either case, the instructor can revert to the previous prompt level if the learner is unable to perform the response with a less intrusive prompt. The second way is more systematic. The instructor can conduct a probe session to assess whether a learner is ready to move to the next less intrusive prompt. For example, after 5 days of using a physical prompt, the instructor provides the opportunity for the learner to perform the behavior without a prompt, with a verbal prompt, and with a model prompt. On the basis of the learner's performance, the

GRADUATED-GUIDANCE DATA SHEET

Name: _Emory_   Instructor: _Mr. Brock_
Skill: _Activating switch to communicate yes/no_   Setting: _Primary classroom_

Steps	Date September 7	September 8	September 9
1. Yes	P	P	P
2. No	I	P	I
3. No	P	P	P
4. No	P	P	I
5. Yes	P	I	P
6. Yes	P	I	I
7. Yes	P	P	I
8. Yes	I	P	P
9. No	P	I	P
10. No	P	P	P
Number correct	2/10	3/10	4/10
% correct	20%	30%	40%

Key: I, independent response; P, physical prompt. Indicate whether student made *yes* or *no* response on each trial.

Figure 3.1.   Sample completed data sheet for using a graduated-guidance procedure with a discrete task.

instructor goes to that level of prompting next. Regardless of how an instructor decides to move from one prompt level to the next, the instructor always can return to a previous, more intrusive level of prompting if the learner requires that. In the most-to-least prompting procedure, the key is to change prompt levels across sessions and not within sessions.

The steps for using the most-to-least prompting procedure are as follows:

1. Secure the learner's attention.
2. Deliver the task direction.
3. Immediately use the most intrusive prompt necessary for the student to perform the correct response (e.g., physical), praising all correct responses.
4. After several sessions, move to the next less intrusive prompt level in the hierarchy (e.g., model), praising all correct responses.
5. After several sessions, move to the next less intrusive prompt level in the hierarchy (e.g., verbal), praising all correct responses.
6. Continue until the learner can perform the response independently across several sessions.

GRADUATED-GUIDANCE DATA SHEET

Name: ___Madigan___   Skill: ___Cutting with a knife___   Date: ___April 22___
Instructor: ___Ms. Smith___   Setting: ___Kitchen-consumer science___   Time: ___1:00___

Steps	Response
1. Place block of cheese on cutting board	P
2. Hold cutting board with left hand	I
3. Place knife blade on block of cheese 1˝ from end with right hand	P
4. Press down with right hand until blade cuts through cheese	P
5. Lay down knife on cutting board	P
6. Place slice of cheese on plate	P
Number correct	1/6
% correct	16%

Key: I, independent response; P, physical prompt.

Figure 3.2. Sample completed data sheet for using a graduated-guidance procedure with a chained task.

The most-to-least prompting procedure is appropriate for young learners or learners with significant intellectual disabilities who may need a lot of assistance during initial instruction on a new behavior (Summers & Szatmari, 2009). It also is appropriate for tasks that learners may find difficult during initial instruction (e.g., engaging a zipper, writing letters of the alphabet). As with the graduated-guidance procedure, the instructor may want to pair verbal prompts with more intrusive prompts to expose the learner to verbal language before using a verbal prompt, with the hope that the learner may acquire the receptive language skills necessary to follow directions over time.

When collecting data, the instructor records the level of prompt needed to perform the behavior correctly (e.g., FP = full physical, PP = partial physical, M = model, V = verbal, I = independent). A sample completed data sheet for a discrete task can be found in Figure 3.3, and a sample completed data sheet for a chained task can be found in Figure 3.4. Because the learner should be able to perform the behavior correctly at each prompt level, the graph should show him or her as always performing the response at criterion level with assistance until criterion is reached, as shown in Figure 3.5. Each phase of prompting should be labeled on the graph, and probe trials to determine whether a learner is ready to proceed to the next phase or level of prompting should be indicated.

SYSTEM OF LEAST PROMPTS

Whereas the graduated-guidance and most-to-least prompting procedures are appropriate for learners who need a lot of initial assistance or prompting to perform a behavior, some learners can respond with less intrusive prompts and, sometimes, independently (Demchak,

MOST-TO-LEAST PROMPTING DATA SHEET

Name: ___Zachary___ Instructor: ___Ms. Saylor___
Behavior: ___Engaging jacket zipper___ Activity: ___Recess___

	Week 1					Week 2					Week 3					Week 4				
Sessions	1	2	3	4	5	1	2	3	4	5	1	2	3	4	5	1	2	3	4	5
Trial 1	P	P	P	P	P	M	M	M	M	M	V	V	V	V	V	I	I	I	I	I
Trial 2	P	P	P	P	P	M	M	M	M	M	V	V	V	V	V	I	I	I	I	I
Trial 3	P	P	P	P	P	M	M	M	M	M	V	V	V	V	V	I	I	I	I	I
Trial 4	P	P	P	P	P	M	M	M	M	M	V	V	V	V	V	I	I	I	I	I
Trial 5	P	P	P	P	P	M	M	M	M	M	V	V	V	V	V	I	I	I	I	I
Number correct	S	S	S	S	S	S	S	S	S	S	S	S	S	S	S	S	S	S	S	S

Key: I, independent; M, model; P, physical; V, verbal.

Figure 3.3. Sample completed data sheet for using a most-to-least prompting procedure with a discrete task.

1989). The procedure (Collins, 2007; Snell & Brown, 2011; Spooner et al., 2011; Westling & Fox, 2009; Wolery et al., 1992) allows a learner to receive only the amount of assistance necessary to perform a correct response. Like the most-to-least prompting procedure, a prompting hierarchy is used. The instructor, however, begins by allowing the learner to perform a behavior independently before delivering prompts, starting with the least intrusive prompt and working through the hierarchy from least to most intrusive until the learner can perform the response correctly and independently. Thus, a learner may require a verbal prompt on one trial, a model prompt on another, and no prompt on another. The SLP procedure is easy to describe in layperson's terms: "If learners do not know what to do, tell them. If they still do not know what to do, show them. If they still do not know what to do, help them." (*Note:* The system-of-least-prompts procedure is typically abbreviated as SLP; the use of *SLP* in this text should not be confused with the common use of SLP as the abbreviation for speech-language pathologist.) Like the most-to-least prompting procedure, the SLP procedure requires a minimum of three levels of prompts (e.g., verbal, model, physical). Whereas the most-to-least prompting procedure employs the same level of prompt across one or more sessions, the prompt level used in the SLP procedure can vary from trial to trial within a session (discrete tasks) or from step to step within a trial (chained tasks). During each trial, the instructor waits a predetermined **response interval** (e.g., 3 seconds) for the learner to respond independently before beginning the prompting process, waiting the same response interval for the learner to perform the behavior between each prompt level and interrupting errors if the learner begins to make one instead of waiting for assistance.

MOST-TO-LEAST PROMPTING DATA SHEET

Name: _Whitney_   Instructor: _Ms. Smith_

Behavior: _Brushing teeth_   Setting: _Restroom_

	Sessions																			
	Week 1					Week 2					Week 3					Week 4				
	1	2	3	4	5	1	2	3	4	5	1	2	3	4	5	1	2	3	4	5
1. Turn on water	P	P	P	P	P	M	M	M	M	M	V	V	V	V	V	I	I	I	I	I
2. Wet brush	P	P	P	P	P	M	M	M	M	M	V	V	V	V	V	I	I	I	I	I
3. Put on tooth-paste	P	P	P	P	P	M	M	M	M	M	V	V	V	V	V	I	I	I	I	I
4. Brush front	P	P	P	P	P	M	M	M	M	M	V	V	V	V	V	I	I	I	I	I
5. Brush left side	P	P	P	P	P	M	M	M	M	M	V	V	V	V	V	I	I	I	I	I
6. Brush right side	P	P	P	P	P	M	M	M	M	M	V	V	V	V	V	I	I	I	I	I
7. Rinse mouth	P	P	P	P	P	M	M	M	M	M	V	V	V	V	V	I	I	I	I	I
8. Spit in sink	P	P	P	P	P	M	M	M	M	M	V	V	V	V	V	I	I	I	I	I
9. Turn off water	P	P	P	P	P	M	M	M	M	M	V	V	V	V	V	I	I	I	I	I
Number correct	9	9	9	9	9	9	9	9	9	9	9	9	9	9	9	9	9	9	9	9

Key: I, independent; M, model; P, physical; V, verbal.

Figure 3.4.   Sample completed data sheet for using a most-to-least prompting procedure with a chained task.

Although researchers have investigated variations on the procedure (e.g., Doyle, Wolery, Ault, & Gast, 1988; West & Billingsley, 2005), the typical steps for using the SLP procedure are as follows:

1. Secure the learner's attention.

2. Deliver the task direction.

3. Wait for a set number of seconds (i.e., response interval) for the learner to respond independently.

4. If the learner responds correctly, give praise; if there is no response or an error, give the least intrusive prompt in the hierarchy (e.g., verbal) and again wait a set number of seconds for a response.

5. If the learner responds correctly, give praise; if there is no response or an error, give the next least intrusive prompt in the hierarchy (e.g., model) and again wait a set number of seconds for a response.

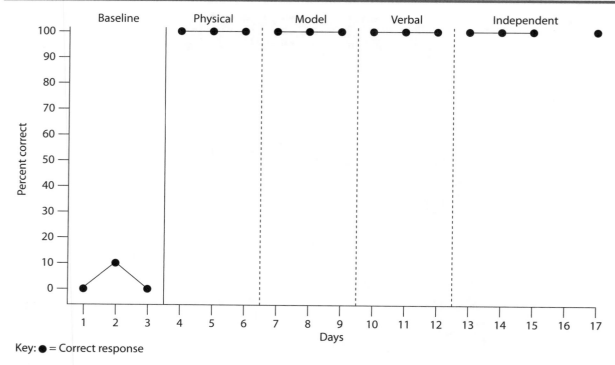

Key: ● = Correct response

Figure 3.5.   Sample graph for a most-to-least prompting procedure.

6. If the learner responds correctly, give praise; if there is no response or an error, continue to give the next least intrusive prompt (e.g., physical) in the hierarchy until the learner responds correctly.

7. Praise the correct response before going to the next trial for a discrete behavior or to the step of the task analysis for a chained task.

The SLP procedure has a long history of effectiveness in learners with moderate and severe disabilities across a variety of tasks (e.g., Collins, Branson, Hall, & Rankin, 2001; Collins, Hall, & Branson, 1997; Jones & Collins, 1997; Manley, Collins, Stenhoff, & Kleinert, 2008; Smith, Collins, Schuster, & Kleinert, 1999). Although the SLP procedure has the advantage of only allowing the learner to receive the amount of assistance necessary, this can be time consuming because the instructor may have to go through each prompt of the hierarchy on every single trial or step. The SLP procedure, however, allows learners who may never achieve independence to still make progress by only using the amount of assistance necessary, which may decrease over time. For example, a learner may not reach independence on performing a skill, but the assistance the learner needs may decrease from a physical prompt to a verbal direction.

When collecting data, the instructor has three options for recording the level of prompt needed to perform the behavior correctly. The instructor may 1) indicate the prompt level with a letter (e.g., I = independent, V = verbal, G = gestural, M = model, P = full physical), 2) circle the prompt level on a list of prompts, or 3) check off the prompt level under a labeled column. Sample data sheets accompany the sample instructional programs found later in this chapter. When graphing data from the SLP procedure, data points indicating independent responses are the ones that count toward criterion. The instructor, however,

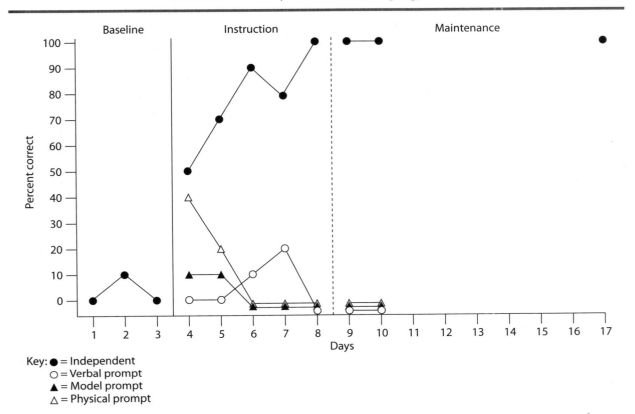

Figure 3.6. Sample graph for a system-of-least-prompts procedure. This shows an increase in the percentage of correct responses being generated independently as the learner relies less on prompts. Even when no longer used, all prompt levels are graphed until the learner reaches criterion; when a prompt level is not used, its value for that session is 0%.

also may want to graph other prompted responses by level of assistance. This can be done in two ways. The instructor may choose to 1) create a separate graph for each prompt level or 2) use different types of data points (e.g., open or closed circles or triangles) or different colors of data points to indicate different prompts on the same graph. A sample graph can be found with the sample instructional program in Figure 3.6.

SAMPLE INSTRUCTIONAL PROGRAMS

Because the SLP procedure is a natural procedure to use, and because it is cited in the professional literature more often than the graduated-guidance or most-to-least prompting procedures, the sample instructional programs presented in this chapter provide examples of using the SLP procedure to teach behaviors to learners with moderate and severe disabilities.

Sample Instructional Program 1

Making telephone calls is important for learners with moderate and severe disabilities for several reasons. For learners who may not communicate well through written expression (e.g., e-mail, texting), making telephone calls allows learners to convey and receive important information. For example, learners who might need assistance in the community can request help and provide information as to their location and whether there is a specific problem that needs attention. Telephone calls also can provide the opportunity to connect with peers and form friendships, which can be especially important for students who may be limited in mobility because of physical, sensory, or cognitive disabilities. The following instructional program is an example of how an elementary teacher used the SLP procedure to structure a daily lesson to teach the chained task of making a telephone call to a learner with a moderate to severe disability. The procedures are based on a research study conducted by Manley et al. (2008).

Core Content Standards

Practical Living/ Vocational
- Students will identify technology tools (e.g., electronic games, phones, computers) that are used in homes and schools.
- Students demonstrate skills that promote individual well-being and healthy family relationships.
- Students demonstrate strategies for becoming and remaining mentally and emotionally healthy.

Behavioral Objective

When presented with the task direction to make a telephone call at school or in the community, Taylor will make live and recorded telephone calls to friends by completing the following steps of the task analysis with 100% accuracy for 5 days.

1. Pick up telephone receiver or open phone.
2. Press the numbers listed on the telephone book page.
3. After a person says, "Hello," or a recorded message says, "Leave a message," state who is calling (e.g., "This is Taylor").
4. State the purpose of the call (e.g., "I'm calling to see what you are doing today").
5. After participating in a conversation or leaving a message, terminate the call (e.g., "Goodbye").
6. Hang up receiver or close telephone.

Instructional Context

Instruction will be in a one-to-one format and will occur in two settings. On most days, instruction will take place in the resource room at school with the teacher sitting across from Taylor. Instruction also will take place in various settings when Taylor is on community-based instruction each week with the teacher standing beside him. The friends listed in Taylor's telephone book will be aware that they may receive a telephone call from him within a specific window of time each day. Peers who are in school will have their teachers' permission to answer the classroom telephone at this time.

Instructional Materials

Materials will consist of a working landline telephone or cell phone and an individualized telephone book. The 8″ × 10″ laminated telephone book will contain one picture to a page of the student's family and friends with a telephone number printed in large black block letters underneath each picture.

Instructional Procedure

Each instructional trial will proceed as follows.

Attentional Cue	• The teacher will give the specific attentional cue, "Taylor, find someone in your telephone book to call today."
Task Direction	• Once Taylor has his telephone book open to the picture of the person he wants to call, the teacher will give the task direction, "Call [name of person]."
System-of-Least-Prompts Procedure	• The prompt hierarchy will be independent, verbal, model, physical. The teacher will wait for a 5-second response interval for Taylor to perform each step of the task analysis and for a 5-second delay interval between each prompt level per step.
	• Each session will consist of two trials of calling friends. Once Taylor has chosen a friend for the first call, the teachers will note whether the call was live or recorded and will select the next friend for Taylor to call to ensure that a different type of call results. In other words, if Taylor's first call is a live call, the teachers will select someone from his telephone book to call who will not answer so that he can experience a recorded call.
Consequence	• The teacher will praise all correct responses (e.g., "Nice job!"). The act of talking on the telephone to a friend should be a natural reinforcer for Taylor. If he makes an error while entering the telephone number, the teacher will terminate the call before using the next prompt level. When the teacher models entering the telephone number, she will not actually press the numbers.
Nontargeted Information	• After Taylor completes the task analysis, the teacher will add instructive feedback about other purposes for making telephone calls while praising him (e.g., "Nice job making the telephone call! Telephones can also be used to report emergencies by dialing *9-1-1*").

Data Collection

The teacher will place an *X* under the correct column to indicate the prompt level (i.e., independent, verbal, model, physical) used to make the call for each step of the task analysis. Each prompt level will be graphed. A sample completed data sheet is shown in Figure 3.7.

Maintenance

Once Taylor has met the criterion of 100% correct responses for 1 day, the teacher will thin her praise statements for correct responses to every third response (i.e., fixed ratio of 3, or FR3) until Taylor has met criterion for 5 days. During monthly probe sessions to monitor maintenance, Taylor will make calls with the natural reinforcement of talking with a friend only.

SYSTEM-OF-LEAST-PROMPTS DATA SHEET

Name: _Taylor_   Skill: _Making phone call_   Date: _May 8_
Instructor: _Ms. Elam_   Setting: _Primary classroom_   Time: _10:00_

Steps of task analysis	Live call				Recorded message call			
	I	V	M	P	I	V	M	P
1. Pick up receiver or open phone				X	X			
2. Press telephone numbers				X	X			
3. Leave message or state who is calling		X					X	
4. State purpose of call			X				X	
5. Terminate call		X				X		
6. Hang up or close phone				X			X	
Number/% independent	2/17%							
Number/% verbal	3/25%							
Number/% model	4/33%							
Number/% physical	3/25%							

Key: I, independent; M, model; P, physical; V, verbal.

Figure 3.7.   Sample completed data sheet for using a system-of-least-prompts procedure in Sample Instructional Program 1.

Generalization

The teacher will facilitate generalization by having Taylor alternate between making calls from a landline telephone and from a cell phone. Once he has reached criterion, she will ask him to make a phone call from a novel telephone (e.g., his home telephone, a public pay telephone). If he does not generalize, she will conduct review trials using the novel telephone.

Behavior Management

The teacher will periodically praise Taylor for paying attention (e.g., "I like the way you are working so hard to learn to make telephone calls!").

Lesson Variations and Extension

Once Taylor has mastered making telephone calls to convey information to friends, future lessons will consist of making other types of calls. One type of call could be to report emergencies (i.e., dialing 911). Another type of call could be to get information (e.g., find out movie times, find out whether a store carries a product). Yet another type of call could be to perform a function (e.g., make an appointment for a haircut, order a pizza). These could be taught through simulations using disconnected phones.

Sample Instructional Program 2

Although learners with moderate and severe disabilities can benefit from the social aspects of inclusion in general education classes and need to have access to the core content taught in those settings, providing sufficient support can be a challenge. In the following instructional program, a special education teacher collaborated with a general education teacher to develop a procedure to teach a learner with a moderate disability how to write a personal letter in an advanced English class. While peers without disabilities worked on pieces for their writing portfolios, Alex, the learner with a disability, worked on writing a letter with the support of a peer tutor. The procedures are based on a research study conducted by Collins et al. (2001).

Core Content Standards

Writing • Students will establish and maintain a focused purpose to communicate with an authentic audience by adhering to the characteristics of the form.

• Students will communicate clearly by using correct punctuation and correct capitalization.

Behavioral Objective

When told to write a personal letter, Alex will write a letter that includes the date, a greeting, a paragraph of content, and a closing with correct indentation, capitalization, and punctuation for 5 days.

Instructional Context

Each day, the special education teacher will complete a form with Alex that states the date, the person to whom Alex will write, and the content that Alex wants to convey. Alex will take this with her to an advanced English class in which students without disabilities are working independently on entries for their writing portfolios. When Alex is seated, the English teacher will read the form and provide the task direction. A peer tutor will sit beside Alex to provide support and assistance as Alex writes her letter. The English teacher will circulate during class and will provide feedback to Alex each time she stops by her desk. At the end of class, the English teacher will tell Alex how she did. Alex will then take her written work to the special education teacher to be included in her portfolio.

Instructional Materials

Alex will have a paper notebook and a pencil. In addition, she will have a form she completed with the special education teacher stating the date, the person to whom she will write a letter, and a list of content she will include in the letter. The peer tutor will have a data sheet on which to indicate the prompt levels that Alex needs as she writes her letter.

Instructional Procedure

Each instructional trial will proceed as follows.

Attentional Cue • The English teacher will give the specific attentional cue of asking Alex to state or point to the date, the person to whom she is writing, and the content she will include in her letter.

Task Direction	• Once Alex responds to the attentional cue, the English teacher will deliver the task direction, "Alex, write a letter to (name) about (content)."
System-of-Least-Prompts Procedure	• The prompt hierarchy will be independent, verbal, model, physical. The peer tutor will watch to see whether Alex can write the date, a greeting (e.g., "Dear Walden"), a paragraph of content (e.g., "I am coming to visit you on Saturday. Can we go swimming?"), and a closing (e.g., "Sincerely, Alex") using correct capitalization and correct punctuation. If Alex fails to perform one of these components or begins to make an error, the peer tutor will prompt from the hierarchy, allowing a response interval of 3 seconds between prompt levels. Because spelling is not part of the instructional objective, the peer tutor will tell Alex how to spell words when asked but will not prompt and record data on spelling.
Consequence	• The peer tutor will deliver general praise (e.g., "Good!") following all correct prompted or unprompted responses as Alex writes her letter. Whenever the English teacher stops by Alex's desk, she will deliver descriptive praise (e.g., "You did a good job starting 'Dear' and 'Walden' with capital letters and putting a comma after 'Dear Walden'"). At the end of class, the English teacher will read Alex's complete letter and tell her how she did ("Excellent work writing your letter today, Alex. I hope you have a good time at Walden's house on Saturday").
Nontargeted Information	• The nontargeted information included in this instructional program is spelling. Although not targeted for instruction, it is possible that Alex will learn to spell some of the words that the peer tutor spells for her.

Data Collection

On the data sheet, the peer tutor will indicate the most intrusive prompt level needed for each section of the letter by using the following key: 1) independent = I; 2) verbal = V; 3) model = M; or 4) physical = P. For example, Alex may independently put a period at the end of the first sentence in the content of her letter but need a model to put a question mark at the end of the second sentence. In this case, the peer tutor would write an *M* to indicate a model prompt because that was the most intrusive prompt Alex needed to make a correct response. Each prompt level will be indicated on the same graph. A sample completed data sheet is shown in Figure 3.8.

Maintenance

Once Alex has met the criterion of 100% correct responses for 1 day, the teacher will thin her praise statements for correct responses to an average of every third response (i.e., **variable ratio** of 3, or VR3, **schedule of reinforcement**) until Alex has met criterion for 5 days. Alex will continue to write a friendly letter once a month during English class.

Generalization

The special education teacher will facilitate generalization by having Alex write letters to different people each day and by sending different peer tutors to support her during English class. Once she has mastered writing a friendly letter, she will type it on the computer.

SYSTEM-OF-LEAST-PROMPTS DATA SHEET				

Name: _Alex_   Setting: _English class_   Date: _October 15_
Peer: _Hudson_   Skill: _Writing personal letter_   Time: _2:30_

	Part of letter			
Grammar	Date	Greeting	Body	Closing
Correct indentation	P	P	P	P
Correct capitalization	I	V	I	M
Correct punctuation	M	P	P	P
Number/% independent	2/17%			
Number/% verbal	1/8%			
Number/% model	2/17%			
Number/% physical	7/58%			

Key: I, independent; M, model; P, physical; V, verbal.

Figure 3.8.   Sample completed data sheet for using a system-of-least-prompts procedure in Sample Instructional Program 2.

Behavior Management

The English teacher and the peer tutor periodically will praise Alex for staying seated and working on her letter (e.g., "You are doing a nice job quietly working on your letter today").

Lesson Variations and Extension

Once Alex has mastered writing friendly letters, she can work on writing business letters. She also can work on sending and replying to e-mail messages at the computer. To extend this skill into other areas of core content, Alex can write or e-mail people for information about topics of study in core content classes (e.g., write letters to legislators about environmental policies).

SUMMARY

This chapter presented three response-prompting procedures that are backed by a wealth of evidence on their effectiveness in the professional literature. The graduated-guidance procedure relies on a physical prompt that is faded as it is no longer needed according to the instructor's judgment. The most-to-least prompting procedure uses a hierarchy of prompts from most to least intrusive that are faded systematically from one level of prompts to the next across sessions and over time. The SLP procedure uses a hierarchy of prompts from least to most intrusive that are faded by only offering the level of prompt that is needed from trial to trial or from step to step. Flowcharts for using the procedures described in this chapter can be found in Appendix A. Blank data sheets that can be used for each procedure can be found in Appendix B. Also, a list of additional resources describing and comparing the procedures presented in this chapter can be found in Appendix C.

QUESTIONS FOR REFLECTION

1. What are the similarities and differences between the most-to-least prompting and SLP procedures? What are the advantages and disadvantages of each?

2. Of the three procedures described in this chapter, which is the easiest or most natural to use? Why?

3. How can prompt levels be broken down into even smaller prompts?

4. Is one way of graphing SLP data better than another? Why or why not?

5. How might pictures be used in the SLP procedure? Should pictures be faded as a prompt level or kept permanently as part of the stimulus to respond? Why?

REFERENCES

Collins, B.C. (2007). *Moderate and severe disabilities: A foundational approach.* Upper Saddle River, NJ: Pearson, Merrill, Prentice-Hall.

Collins, B.C., Branson, T.A., Hall, M., & Rankin, S.W. (2001). Teaching secondary students with moderate disabilities in an inclusive academic classroom setting. *Journal of Developmental and Physical Disabilities, 13,* 41–59.

Collins, B.C., Hall, M., & Branson, T.A. (1997). Teaching leisure skills to adolescents with moderate disabilities. *Exceptional Children, 63,* 499–512.

Demchak, M. (1989). A comparison of graduated guidance and increasing assistance in teaching adults with severe handicaps leisure skills. *Education and Training in Developmental Disabilities, 24*(1), 45–55.

Doyle, P.M., Wolery, M., Ault, M.J., & Gast, D.L. (1988). System of least prompts: A systematic review of procedural parameters. *Journal of The Association for Persons with Severe Handicaps, 13*(1), 28–40.

Jones, G.Y., & Collins, B.C. (1997). Teaching microwave skills to adults with disabilities: Acquisition of nutrition and safety facts presented as non-targeted information. *Journal of Physical and Developmental Disabilities, 9,* 59–78.

MacDuff, G.S., Krantz, P.J., & McClannahan, L.E. (1993). Teaching children with autism to use photographic activity schedules: Maintenance and generalization of complex response chains. *Journal of Applied Behavior Analysis, 26,* 89–97.

Manley, K., Collins, B.C., Stenhoff, D.M., & Kleinert, H. (2008). Using a system of least prompts procedure to teach telephone skills to elementary students with cognitive disabilities. *Journal of Behavioral Education, 17*(3), 221–236.

Smith, R.L., Collins, B.C., Schuster, J.W., & Kleinert, H. (1999). Teaching table cleaning skills to secondary students with moderate/severe disabilities: Measuring observational learning during downtime. *Education and Training in Mental Retardation and Developmental Disabilities, 11,* 139–158.

Snell, M.E., & Brown, F. (2011). Selecting teaching strategies and arranging educational environments. In M.E. Snell & F. Brown (Eds.), *Instruction of students with severe disabilities* (7th ed., pp. 122–185). Upper Saddle River, NJ: Pearson.

Spooner, F., Browder, D.M., & Mims, P.J. (2011). Evidence-based practices. In D.M. Browder & F. Spooner (Eds.), *Teaching students with moderate and severe disabilities* (pp. 92–122). New York, NY: Guilford.

Summers, J., & Szatmari, P. (2009). Using discrete trial instruction to teach children with Angelman syndrome. *Focus on Autism and Other Developmental Disabilities, 24,* 216–226.

West, E.A., & Billingsley, F. (2005). Improving the system of least prompts: A comparison of procedural variations. *Education and Training in Developmental Disabilities, 40,* 131–144.

Westling, D.L., & Fox, L. (2009). *Teaching students with severe disabilities* (4th ed.). Upper Saddle River, NJ: Pearson.

Wolery, M., Ault, M.J., & Doyle, P.M. (1992). *Teaching students with moderate to severe disabilities.* New York, NY: Longman.

CHAPTER 4

Using Time-Delay and Simultaneous-Prompting Procedures

On completion of this chapter, the reader will be able to

- Explain why the time-delay procedure might be easier for an instructor to conduct than the most-to-least prompting or system-of-least-prompts procedures
- Explain why wait training might be necessary and how it should be conducted
- Describe and perform the steps of the progressive time-delay (PTD) procedure
- Design a data sheet for teaching a discrete behavior and a chained task with the PTD procedure
- Graph and analyze formative data collected from instruction with the PTD procedure
- State the difference between the constant time-delay (CTD) and PTD procedures
- Describe and perform the steps of the CTD procedure
- Design a data sheet for teaching a discrete behavior and a chained task with the CTD procedure
- Graph and analyze formative data collected from instruction with the CTD procedure
- State the difference between the time-delay and simultaneous-prompting (SP) procedures
- Describe and perform the steps of the SP procedure
- State why probe trials should precede training trials in the SP procedure
- Design a data sheet for teaching a discrete behavior and a chained task with the SP procedure
- Graph and analyze formative data collected from instruction with the SP procedure

TERMS USED IN THIS CHAPTER

time-delay procedure	wait training
progressive time-delay (PTD) procedure	delay interval
constant time-delay (CTD) procedure	probe trials
simultaneous-prompting (SP) procedure	training trials

This chapter describes two more procedures reported in the professional literature as being effective with students with moderate and severe disabilities: 1) **time-delay procedure (progressive time-delay [PTD] procedure** and **constant time-delay [CTD] procedure**) and 2) **simultaneous-prompting (SP) procedure.** Whereas the prompting procedures in Chapter 3 faded the prompt by intensity and intrusiveness, the procedures described in this chapter all fade the prompt by a dimension of time. This chapter also includes sample instructional programs based on investigations from the professional research, sample data sheets, and sample graphs.

TIME DELAY

The time-delay procedure has been established as an evidence-based procedure (Browder, Ahlgrim-Delzell, Spooner, Mims, & Baker, 2009; Schuster et al., 1998; Walker, 2008; Wolery, Holcombe, et al., 1992) that is easy to implement and often results in learners reaching criterion in a shorter period of time or a shorter number of instructional sessions. Like the procedures described in Chapter 3, the time-delay procedure has a long history of being effective with learners with moderate and severe disabilities across a variety of tasks (e.g., Branham, Collins, Schuster, & Kleinert, 1999; Collins, Hager, & Galloway, 2011; Falkenstine, Collins, Schuster, & Kleinert, 2009; Godsey, Schuster, Lingo, Collins, & Kleinert, 2008; Miracle, Collins, Schuster, & Grisham-Brown, 2001; Roark, Collins, Hemmeter, & Kleinert, 2002; Yilmaz, Birkan, Konukman, & Erkan, 2005; Yilmaz et al., 2010). In addition, it has been found to be more efficient than the system-of-least-prompts procedure (Doyle, Wolery, Gast, Ault, & Wiley, 1990; Godby, Gast, & Wolery, 1987). The time-delay procedure requires that the instructor select one single prompt that will be used across all instructional trials and sessions. This prompt must be a controlling prompt, which means that it must be likely to result in a correct response in the majority of instructional trials. In addition, the controlling prompt that is selected should be the least intrusive prompt necessary. The prompt that is selected will depend on the skill to be taught. For example, a physical prompt is not appropriate for teaching reading or verbal communication. In addition, the prompt that is selected will be dependent on the characteristics of the student. A verbal prompt would not be appropriate for a learner who has a hearing impairment or does not have the receptive language skills to follow verbal directions, a model prompt would not be appropriate for a learner who cannot imitate a model, and a physical prompt would not be appropriate for a learner who is tactilely defensive.

Before using a time-delay procedure, the instructor should check to see whether a learner has a wait response—the ability to wait a set number of seconds before responding to the stimulus or task direction in case the learner does not know the correct response. The time-delay procedure is nearly errorless when a learner knows how to wait for a prompt rather than guessing what the response should be and making an error. If a learner does not have a wait response, the instructor should conduct **wait training.** This is a common practice for learners who are young, who have a significant intellectual disability, or who are new to the procedure.

In wait training, the instructor selects a task in which it is impossible for the learner to guess and make the correct response. This might entail asking the student to read or define nonsense words (e.g., "What is a belly whomper?"), say the name of someone in a picture who is unknown (e.g., "Show me Willy"), point to an animal in a picture showing numerous animals, or perform some motor action the student does not know how to perform (e.g., "Raise your hand," without specifying which hand). Regardless of the response the learner may make, it will be incorrect if the learner does not wait for the prompt (e.g., "You raised your left hand, and you should have raised your right hand; next time, wait and I will show you what to do"). It also is important that the instructor select a valued reinforcer (e.g., social praise, small edible, access to a favorite object) so that the learner will be motivated to wait for the prompt. A trial of wait training would proceed as follows:

1. Get the attention of the learner.
2. Provide the reminder, "Wait if you do not know what to do, and I will help you."
3. State the task direction.
4. Wait a predetermined number of seconds (usually 3–5).
5. Deliver the controlling prompt.
6. Reinforce the learner if he or she makes a correct response, or restate the reminder to wait if the learner makes an incorrect response.

Once the instructor has determined that a learner has a wait response, instruction can begin. There are two types of time-delay procedures (Collins, 2007; Snell & Brown, 2011; Spooner, Browder, & Mims, 2011; Westling & Fox, 2009; Wolery, Ault, & Doyle, 1992): 1) the PTD procedure and 2) the CTD procedure. These two procedures will be described in the following sections.

Progressive Time Delay

The earliest references to the time-delay procedure in the professional literature described the PTD procedure, and the procedure continues to be effective in teaching behaviors to learners with moderate and severe disabilities. The underlying assumption of the PTD procedure is that the learner is being asked to perform a new behavior that is not in his or her repertoire, and this will have been established through screening and baseline sessions. Thus, the initial instructional session with the PTD procedure does not allow the opportunity for the learner to respond independently. Instead, the instructor secures the learner's attention, issues the task direction (e.g., "What word?"), and, using a 0-second **delay interval,** immediately delivers the controlling prompt (e.g., "The word is *tree*"). Praise is delivered if the learner responds correctly. On the basis of the learner's ability and the complexity of the target behavior, the instructor may choose to conduct more than one session using a 0-second delay interval.

After initial instruction using a 0-second delay interval, the instructor slowly increases the delay interval by waiting progressively larger increments of time across sessions, allowing the learner to respond independently if the correct response has been acquired and to wait for the prompt if the correct response has not yet been acquired. For example, the instructor may use a 1-second delay interval in the second instructional session, a 2-second delay interval in the third instructional session, and a 3-second delay interval in the fourth instructional session. The instructor will need to determine how fluently a student should be able to perform the correct response for the response to be useful in real-life applications. (See Chapter 1 for a discussion on fluency.) If the criterion for fluency is for the learner to perform a correct response within 3 seconds, then the instructor should continue to use a 3-second delay interval for all subsequent instructional sessions until the learner reaches criterion (e.g., 100% unprompted correct response for three sessions).

The steps for each trial when using the PTD procedure are as follows:

1. Secure the learner's attention.
2. Deliver the task direction.
3. Wait a predetermined set of seconds for the learner to respond (e.g., 0-second delay interval during first session, 1-second delay interval during second session, 2-second delay interval during third session, 3-second delay interval during all subsequent sessions).
4. Deliver the controlling prompt.
5. Wait the predetermined response interval (e.g., 3 seconds).
6. Praise correct responses or repeat the prompt for incorrect responses or failures to respond.

Although the PTD procedure can be effective with all learners, it may be especially helpful with learners who are young, who have significant intellectual disabilities, or who exhibit impulsive behaviors because it slowly teaches them to wait longer intervals of time before receiving assistance to make a correct response, thus decreasing the number of errors that might be made through guessing.

When using the PTD procedure, five types of data are collected: 1) correct response before the prompt (i.e., correct anticipation), 2) incorrect response before the prompt (i.e., incorrect anticipation, 3) correct response after the prompt (i.e., correct wait), 4) incorrect response after the prompt (i.e., incorrect wait), or 5) no response after the prompt. Data can be recorded in two ways. The instructor may record a plus sign (correct), a minus sign (incorrect), or a zero (no response) under a column header labeled *Before prompt* or *After prompt* as shown in Figure 4.1, or the instructor may indicate the type of response made under a column header as shown later in this chapter (see Sample Instructional Program 1). When data are graphed, a symbol (typically a closed circle) is used to indicate correct responses before the prompt, and a different symbol (typically an open triangle) is used to indicate correct responses after the prompt. Errors and failures to respond are not graphed. Graphed data will show an increase in correct responses before the prompt as there is a corresponding decrease in correct responses after the prompt. A sample graph for the PTD procedure can be found in Figure 4.2.

Constant Time Delay

The CTD procedure is just as effective as the PTD procedure and is easier to use because the instructor does not have to change delay intervals across sessions. There are only two delay intervals used with the CTD procedure. The first is a 0-second delay interval when initial instruction takes place in the first session, and the second is the final delay that the instructor has identified for fluency (e.g., 3 seconds) that is used in all subsequent sessions. Therefore, the steps for each trial when using the CTD procedure are as follows:

1. Secure the learner's attention.
2. Deliver the task direction.

PROGRESSIVE TIME-DELAY DATA SHEET

Name: _Joy_   Instructor: _Mr. Clark_

Steps	Date: September 7	Setting: School crosswalk	Delay interval: 0 seconds			Date: September 8	Setting: Main Street	Delay interval: 1 second		
	Before prompt		After prompt			Before prompt		After prompt		
	+	–	+	–	0	+	–	+	–	0
1. Stop			X					X		
2. Look left			X						X	
3. Look right			X			X				
4. Look left			X						X	
5. Cross			X			X				
Number	0/5	0/5	5/5	0/5	0/5	2/5	0/5	1/5	2/5	0/5
%	0%	0%	100%	0%	0%	40%	0%	20%	40%	0%

Key: Plus sign indicates correct response; minus sign indicates incorrect response; zero indicates no response.

Figure 4.1. Sample completed data sheet for using progressive time-delay procedure with a chained task.

3. Wait a predetermined set of seconds for the learner to respond (e.g., 0-second delay interval during first session, 3-second delay interval during all subsequent sessions).
4. Deliver the controlling prompt.
5. Wait the predetermined response interval (e.g., 3 seconds).
6. Praise correct responses or repeat the prompt for incorrect responses or failures to respond.

Data collection and graphing are done in the same manner as with the PTD procedure. A sample completed data sheet for the CTD procedure is included in Sample Instructional Program 1, later in this chapter.

SIMULTANEOUS PROMPTING

The SP procedure is the most recent to be reported in the professional literature and has been used long enough and in enough research studies to be established as an evidence-based practice (Morse & Schuster, 2004) in teaching a variety of skills across age levels to learners with moderate and severe disabilities (e.g., Birkan, 2005; Collins, Evans, Creech-Galloway, Karl, & Miller, 2007; Colozzi, Ward, & Crotty, 2008; Fetko, Schuster, Harley, & Collins, 1999; Palmer, Collins, & Schuster, 1999; Parrott, Schuster, Collins, & Gassaway, 2000; Rao & Mallow, 2009; Sewell, Collins, Hemmeter, & Schuster, 1998). It is a systematic

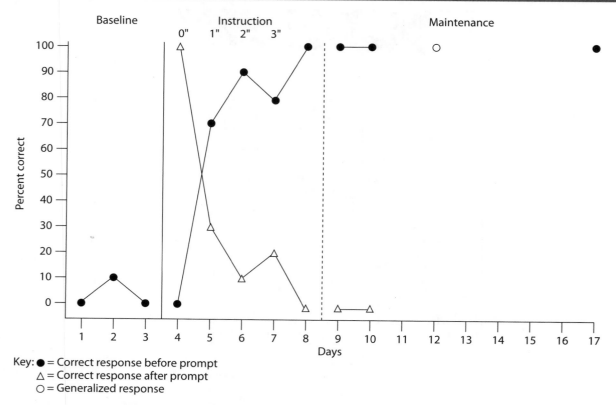

Key: ● = Correct response before prompt
△ = Correct response after prompt
○ = Generalized response

Figure 4.2. Sample graphed data for the progressive time-delay procedure. This shows an increase in the percentage of correct responses generated before prompting, with a corresponding decrease in correct prompted responses as the controlling prompt is needed less often. When there are no correct responses either before or after the prompt, the value for the session is 0%, and points for this data path continue to be graphed until the student has reached criterion.

form of an older procedure that was referred to as *antecedent prompt and test* in earlier studies (Ersoy, Tekin-Iftar, & Kircaali-Iftar, 2009; Singleton, Schuster, Morse, & Collins, 1999; Wolery, Ault, et al., 1992). The SP procedure is based on evidence that, in many of the studies using CTD, learners typically acquired behaviors in a minimal number of instructional sessions (Kurt & Tekin-Iftar, 2008; Schuster, Griffen, & Wolery, 1992). Thus, the SP procedure uses a 0-second delay interval only until learners reach criterion; there is no increase in the delay interval across sessions. Because learners do not have the opportunity to perform an independent response during instruction, it is necessary to conduct daily **probe trials** to determine when the learner has acquired a correct response at a criterion level of performance. These probe trials to assess behavior acquisition always occur before 0-second delay trials, and the 0-second delay trials only occur if the data from the probe trials indicate that they are necessary. In other words, SP is a simple procedure in which instructors conduct daily test or probe trials to assess learning followed by daily instructional or **training trials** to teach the target behavior. This sequence continues until the learner meets criterion during probe trials.

The steps for using the SP procedure are as follows (Collins, 2007; Snell & Brown, 2011; Spooner et al., 2011; Westling & Fox, 2009):

First, conduct probe trials.

1. Deliver the attentional cue.
2. Deliver the task direction.
3. Wait a predetermined number of seconds (i.e., response interval) for the learner to perform the correct behavior.
4. Whether the response is correct or incorrect, go to the next trial without prompting or correcting errors.

Second, conduct training trials.

1. Deliver the attentional cue.
2. Deliver the task direction.
3. Immediately use the least intrusive prompt necessary for the learner to perform the correct response (i.e., controlling prompt), praising all correct responses and correcting all errors.
4. Go to the next trial and repeat.

Training trials can immediately follow probe trials within the same session, or probe trials can occur early in the day with training trials naturally occurring in a distributed fashion throughout the remainder of the day. The only requirement is that probe trials precede training trials each day because this allows the instructor to measure whether a learner is maintaining a response over time (e.g., from one day to the next).

The only data that the instructor records during the SP procedure are probe trial data because these are the data that are counted toward criterion to determine whether a skill has been acquired; the collection of training trial data is optional, but such data may be collected if the instructor wants to monitor error rate. All the instructor needs to do is record after each trial whether a response is correct (+), if a response is incorrect (–), or if there is no response (0). All the instructor needs to graph are the probe data. A sample completed data sheet for the SP procedure is included in Sample Instructional Program 2, later in this chapter. Graphed data from the SP procedure would appear similar to the graph found in Figure 2.6 in Chapter 2.

SAMPLE INSTRUCTIONAL PROGRAMS

The following instructional programs illustrate how the time-delay and SP procedures can be implemented with students with moderate and severe disabilities. Although the first sample instructional program uses a CTD procedure, it easily could be implemented using a PTD procedure if the instructor wished to insert instructional trials using delay intervals with successively larger increments of time.

Sample Instructional Program 1

Learners typically acquire receptive language skills before expressive language skills. The first receptive skill to emerge may be the receptive identification of objects. This skill can be useful in that it allows the learner to begin making choices and using a daily schedule in which objects represent activities (e.g., tennis shoe = physical education class). Also, it is common for manual signs to be paired with verbal language to give learners a way to respond before they learn to use intelligible speech. In the following instructional program, a speech-language pathologist uses a CTD procedure to teach receptive identification of food items to a secondary learner with a significant cognitive disability in order to facilitate self-determination in the learner's life when the learner makes transitions by enabling him to make a choice of foods to eat at mealtime or when shopping with support in the grocery store. In addition, the speech-language pathologist includes manual signs in each instructional trial to facilitate the student making the connection between the sign and the verbal label for each object. The procedures are based on a research study conducted by Roark et al. (2002).

Core Content Standards

Practical Living/ Vocational
- Students evaluate consumer products and services and make effective consumer decisions.
- Students demonstrate the knowledge and skills they need to remain physically healthy and to accept responsibility for their own physical well-being.

Behavioral Objective

When presented with four food choices and the verbal task direction to point to a specific food, Jim will point to the correct food with 100% accuracy for 5 days.

Instructional Context

Instruction will be in a one-to-one format with the speech-language pathologist during scheduled sessions. The speech-language pathologist will collaborate with the special education teacher so that the teacher can conduct sessions in the absence of the speech-language pathologist; therefore, the term *instructor* will be used.

Instructional Materials

Materials will consist of three examples each (i.e., three brands) of the following food items: chocolate, fruit, eggs, spaghetti, peanut butter, tea, popcorn, jelly, and soup. The instructor has observed these to be foods that Jim enjoys eating, as indicated through lack of refusal and facial expressions. The instructor will teach three foods at a time to criterion and also will include foods that Jim has indicated he does not like through refusal and facial expressions. Empty packages will be used during instructional trials, although real foods will be used during generalization trials.

Instructional Procedure

Each instructional trial will proceed as follows.

Attentional Cue	• At the beginning of each session, the instructor will introduce the lesson (e.g., "Jim, I'm going to show you some foods that you might like to eat. When I tell you the name of a food, I want you to point to it. If you don't know which food to point to, wait and I will help you"). The instructor then gives the general attentional cue, "Jim, look."
Task Direction	• Once the instructor has Jim's attention, she will place three of the preferred food items and one nonpreferred food item on the table in front of Jim and give the verbal task direction to point to one of the items (e.g., "Jim, point to the chocolate") paired with the manual sign for the item.
Constant Time-Delay Procedure	• The controlling prompt will be a model (i.e., instructor will point to food item). During the first session, the instructor immediately will model the correct response (i.e., 0-second delay interval) after delivering the task direction along with the presentation of the stimulus. During all subsequent sessions, the instructor will wait a 5-second delay interval before modeling the correct response. Each session will consist of three trials per food item for a total of nine trials per session. Once Jim meets criterion on a set of three food items, the instructor will introduce three new food items.
Consequence	• The instructor will praise all correct prompted and unprompted responses (e.g., "Good job!"). If Jim makes an error before the prompt, the instructor will remind him to wait for help if he does not know the correct response and then will model the correct response for him. If Jim makes an incorrect response or fails to respond after the prompt, the instructor will use a physical prompt to assist him in making the correct response (i.e., point to the correct food item).
Nontargeted Information	• The nontargeted information included in this instructional program is the manual sign for each food item. The instructor will demonstrate each manual sign when she delivers the task direction (e.g., "Show me the chocolate"). This is done to facilitate Jim learning the manual signs for the food items as well as the verbal labels.

Data Collection

The instructor will record a plus sign for each correct response, a minus sign for each incorrect response, or a zero for no response in the columns indicating *before* or *after* the prompt. Correct prompted and unprompted responses will be graphed daily. A sample completed data sheet is shown in Figure 4.3.

Maintenance

Once Jim has met the criterion of 100% correct responses for 1 day, the instructor will thin her praise statements for correct responses to every third response (i.e., fixed ratio of 3, or FR3) until Jim has met criterion for 3 days. The instructor will continue to monitor maintenance once per week for the remainder of the school year.

Generalization

The instructor will facilitate generalization by varying the brand of food items that Jim is asked to identify during each instructional trial per session. For example, Jim will be asked to

CONSTANT TIME-DELAY DATA SHEET

Name: _Jim_   Instructor: _Ms. Metcalfe_

Food item	Date: September 15 / Setting: Speech / Delay: 0 seconds Before	After	Date: September 16 / Setting: Speech / Delay: 5 seconds Before	After	Date: September 17 / Setting: Speech / Delay: 5 seconds Before	After
Chocolate		+	−		+	
Popcorn		+	+			−
Fruit		+		−	+	
Popcorn		+	+			+
Fruit		+		0		0
Popcorn		+		+	+	
Chocolate		+		−		+
Fruit		+	+		+	
Chocolate		+	+		+	
Total correct	0/0	9/9	4/9	1/9	5/9	2/9
% correct	0%	100%	44%	11%	56%	22%

Key: Plus sign indicates correct response; minus sign indicates incorrect response; zero indicates no response.

Figure 4.3.   Sample completed data sheet for using a constant time-delay procedure with a discrete task in Sample Instructional Program 1.

identify Hershey's chocolate, Nestle's chocolate, and Cadbury's chocolate during each instructional session. Once each week, Jim's teacher will take him to a grocery store during community-based instruction and ask him to identify the targeted food items.

Behavior Management

The instructor will periodically praise Jim for paying attention (e.g., "You are doing a nice job sitting up straight and listening!").

Lesson Variations and Extension

Although this instructional program uses a format in which the speech-language pathologist uses direct instruction with discrete trials to work with Jim during their regularly scheduled sessions, she also will collaborate with Jim's teacher, who will take the opportunity to embed instructional trials in a distributed trial format whenever possible each day. For example, the teacher will use the same CTD procedure to ask Jim to identify chocolate during school breaks, during lunch, when baking brownies in consumer science class, or when on community-based instruction in the grocery store and will record the data in the same manner as the speech-language pathologist.

Sample Instructional Program 2

In the next instructional program, a paraprofessional who supports an elementary student with moderate and severe disabilities in the restroom throughout the school day uses an SP procedure to teach hand washing. Although hand washing is an important functional skill for maintaining good hygiene and preventing illnesses, the paraprofessional takes the opportunity to embed core content within the skill that will be useful to the student. The procedures are based on a research study conducted by Parrott et al. (2000).

Core Content Standards

Practical Living/ Vocational	• Students will identify strategies (e.g., diet, exercise, rest, immunizations) and good hygiene practices (e.g., hand washing, brushing teeth, using tissues) that promote good health and prevent diseases.
Math	• Students are able to use basic communication and mathematics skills for purposes and situations they will encounter throughout their lives.
Reading	• Students will know that some words have multiple meanings and identify the correct meaning as the word is used. • Students will apply knowledge of synonyms, antonyms, or compound words for comprehension.

Behavioral Objective

When told to wash her hands in the restroom, Sara will perform the steps of the task analysis for washing hands with 100% accuracy for 5 days. The task analysis will consist of the following steps:

1. Walk to sink
2. Turn on cold water
3. Turn on hot water
4. Squirt soap from dispenser into hand
5. Place hands under running water
6. Rub hands together until all suds are gone
7. Turn off hot water
8. Turn off cold water
9. Pull paper towel from wall dispenser
10. Dry hands with paper towel
11. Throw paper towel in trashcan

Instructional Context

On the daily schedule compiled by the special education teacher, each member of the staff is assigned to accompany students who need assistance to the restroom throughout the day. In this case, the teacher will work with the classroom paraprofessional on the procedure to systematically teach hand washing to Sara while also teaching her how to embed core content in the task analysis that has been targeted for Sara on her individualized education program (IEP).

Instructional Materials

The paraprofessional only will need the materials typically available in the school restroom: 1) a sink with handles for turning hot and cold water on and off, 2) soap from a wall dispenser, 3) paper towels from a dispenser, and 4) a trashcan.

Instructional Procedure

Each instructional trial will proceed as follows.

Attentional Cue	• The paraprofessional will give the general attentional cue of stating Sara's name to get her attention after she has finished her toileting procedures.
Task Direction	• Once Sara responds to the attentional cue by looking at the paraprofessional, the paraprofessional will deliver the task direction, "It's time to wash your hands."
Simultaneous-Prompting Procedure	• The first hand-washing session of the day will serve as the probe trial in the SP procedure. The paraprofessional will wait 5 seconds for Sara to initiate each step of the task analysis. If Sara fails to initiate a step, the paraprofessional will perform that step and then ask, "What's next?" • Training trials using a 0-second delay interval will occur during all subsequent hand-washing sessions of the day. During these trials, the paraprofessional immediately will use a physical prompt to assist Sara in performing the correct response. She will pair physical assistance with verbal directions (e.g., "Turn on the cold water" while physically assisting Sara in turning on the cold water).
Consequence	• During probe sessions, the paraprofessional will not give any feedback on performance. During training sessions, she will give descriptive praise.

Nontargeted Information

When the paraprofessional praises Sara's correct response during training trials, she will add nontargeted information on reading (i.e., antonyms, homonyms), math (i.e., counting in sequence), and health (i.e., concept of germs) that have been targeted on her IEP as follows:

"Good Job! You turned *on* (or turned *off*) the cold water with your *right* hand."

"Nice job. You turned *on* (or turned *off*) the hot water with your *left* hand."

"Excellent. You got *1, 2, 3* squirts of soap."

"Great job washing your hands—*washing with soap and water kills germs so you won't get sick.*"

"Excellent. You counted out *1, 2, 3* paper towels."

Data Collection

The paraprofessional only will collect data during the probe trial that occurs during the first session of hand washing each day. On the data sheet, she will record a plus sign for correct responses, a minus sign for incorrect responses, and a zero for failure to respond. A sample completed data sheet is shown in Figure 4.4.

SIMULTANEOUS-PROMPTING DATA SHEET

Name: _Sara_   Skill: _Washing hands_   Date: _April 22_

Instructor: _Ms. Carruba_   Setting: _Restroom_   Time: _9:00_

Steps	Probe response
1. Walk to sink	+
2. Turn on cold water	−
3. Turn on hot water	−
4. Squirt soap from dispenser into hand	−
5. Place hands under running water	+
6. Rub hands together until all suds are gone	+
7. Turn off hot water	−
8. Turn off cold water	0
9. Pull paper towel from wall dispenser	+
10. Dry hands with paper towel	0
11. Throw paper towel in trashcan	0
Number correct	4
% correct	36%

Key: Plus sign indicates correct response; minus sign indicates incorrect response; zero indicates no response.

Figure 4.4. Sample completed data sheet for using a simultaneous-prompting procedure with a chained task in Sample Instructional Program 2.

Maintenance

Once Sara has met the criterion of 100% correct responses for 1 day, praise will be thinned to the end of the task (fixed ratio of 11, or FR11). Her independent hand washing will continue to be monitored for the remainder of the school year.

Generalization

The paraprofessional will facilitate generalization by having Sara wash her hands in the same restroom and with the same materials as her peers. Once Sara has mastered the task, she will wash her hands with the support of a peer without disabilities under the supervision of the paraprofessional.

Behavior Management

The paraprofessional periodically will praise Sara's behavior in the restroom (e.g., "You are such a big girl using the restroom like all of the other big kids").

Lesson Variations and Extension

Because the materials in restrooms in public schools and in bathrooms in homes vary, the special education teacher will collaborate with the parents on facilitating independent hand washing at home using the same procedures with an altered task analysis. For example, the home bathroom may have a bar of soap and a cloth towel. During core content classes, links can be made to hand washing. For example, the health teacher might say, "This is a picture of the germs that cause infections. That's why it's so important to wash our hands every time we finish using the restroom. Germs are spread by people who do not wash their hands."

SUMMARY

This chapter presented two response-prompting procedures that fade prompts through a dimension of time: 1) time delay and 2) SP. These procedures are backed by a wealth of evidence on their effectiveness in the professional literature. The time-delay procedure begins with an immediate delivery of a controlling prompt (0-second delay interval). There are two types of time delay. In the PTD procedure, the delay interval before providing a controlling prompt is increased by small increments over time. In the CTD procedure, the delay interval before prompting remains at a predetermined set of seconds throughout instruction. The SP procedure consists of daily probe trials that are followed by daily training trials using a 0-second delay interval. Flowcharts for using the procedures described in this chapter can be found in Appendix A. Blank data sheets that can be used for each procedure can be found in Appendix B. Also, a list of additional resources describing and comparing the procedures presented in this chapter can be found in Appendix C.

QUESTIONS FOR REFLECTION

1. Which procedure in this chapter seems easiest to implement? Why?

2. What is the difference between the CTD and PTD procedures?

3. What is the advantage of conducting probe sessions before rather than after training trials with the SP procedure?

4. Why is it important to monitor errors with a time-delay procedure? What might an instructor do if a learner is making more than 20% errors per session?

5. Why would the instructor expect errors to be high with an SP procedure during probe trials and low during training trials?

REFERENCES

Birkan, B. (2005). Using simultaneous prompting for teaching various discrete tasks to students with mental retardation. *Education and Treatment in Developmental Disabilities, 40,* 68–79.

Branham, R., Collins, B.C., Schuster, J.W., & Kleinert, H. (1999). Teaching community skills to students with moderate disabilities: Comparing combined techniques of classroom simulation, videotape modeling, and community-based instruction. *Education and Training in Mental Retardation and Developmental Disabilities, 33,* 170–181.

Browder, D., Ahlgrim-Delzell, L., Spooner, F., Mims, P.J., & Baker, J.N. (2009). Using time delay to teach literacy to students with severe developmental disabilities. *Exceptional Children, 75,* 343–363.

Collins, B.C. (2007). *Moderate and severe disabilities: A foundational approach.* Upper Saddle River, NJ: Pearson.

Collins, B.C., Evans, A., Creech-Galloway, C.G., Karl, A., & Miller, A. (2007). A comparison of the acquisition and maintenance of teaching functional and core content in special and general education settings. *Focus on Autism and Other Developmental Disabilities, 22,* 220–233.

Collins, B.C., Hager, K.D., & Galloway, C.C. (2011). The addition of functional content during core content instruction with students with moderate disabilities. *Education and Training in Developmental Disabilities, 46,* 22–39.

Colozzi, G.A., Ward, L.W., & Crotty, K.E. (2008). Comparison of simultaneous prompting procedure in 1:1 and small group instruction to teach play skills to preschool students with pervasive developmental disorder and developmental disabilities. *Education and Training in Developmental Disabilities, 43,* 226–248.

Doyle, P.M., Wolery, M., Gast, D.L., Ault, M.J., & Wiley, K. (1990). Comparison of constant time delay and the system of least prompts in teaching preschoolers with developmental delays. *Research in Developmental Disabilities, 11*(1), 1–22.

Ersoy, G., Tekin-Iftar, E., & Kircaali-Iftar, G. (2009). Effects of antecedent prompt and test procedure on teaching simulated menstrual care skills to females with developmental disabilities. *Education and Training in Developmental Disabilities, 44,* 54–66.

Falkenstine, K.J., Collins, B.C., Schuster, J.W., & Kleinert, K. (2009). Presenting chained and discrete tasks as nontargeted information when teaching discrete academic skills through small group instruction. *Education and Training in Developmental Disabilities, 44,* 127–142.

Fetko, K.S., Schuster, J.W., Harley, D.A., & Collins, B.C. (1999). Using simultaneous prompting to teach a chained vocational task to young adults with severe intellectual disabilities. *Education and Training in Mental Retardation and Developmental Disabilities, 34,* 318–329.

Godby, S., Gast, D.L., & Wolery, M. (1987). A comparison of time delay and system of least prompts in teaching object identification. *Research in Developmental Disabilities, 8*(2), 283–305.

Godsey, J.R., Schuster, J.W., Lingo, A.S., Collins, B.C., & Kleinert, H.L. (2008). Peer-implemented time delay procedures on the acquisition of chained tasks by students with moderate and severe disabilities. *Education and Training in Developmental Disabilities, 43,* 111–122.

Kurt, O., & Tekin-Iftar, E. (2008). A comparison of constant time delay and simultaneous prompting with embedded instruction on teaching leisure skills to children with autism. *Topics in Early Childhood Special Education, 28,* 53–64.

Miracle, S.A., Collins, B.C., Schuster, J.W., & Grisham-Brown, J. (2001). Peer versus teacher delivered instruction: Effects on acquisition and maintenance. *Education and Training in Mental Retardation and Developmental Disabilities, 36,* 375–385.

Morse, T.E., & Schuster, J.W. (2004). Simultaneous prompting: A review of the literature. *Education and Training in Developmental Disabilities, 39*(2), 153–168.

Palmer, T., Collins, B.C., & Schuster, J.W. (1999). The use of a simultaneous prompting procedure to teach receptive manual sign identification to adults with disabilities. *Journal of Developmental and Physical Disabilities, 11,* 179–191.

Parrott, K.A., Schuster, J.W., Collins, B.C., & Gassaway, L.J. (2000). Simultaneous prompting and instructive feedback when teaching young children with moderate and severe mental retardation. *Journal of Behavioral Education, 10,* 3–19.

Rao, S., & Mallow, L. (2009). Using simultaneous prompting procedure to promote recall of multiplication facts by middle school students with cognitive impairment. *Education and Training in Developmental Disabilities, 44,* 80–90.

Roark, T.J., Collins, B.C., Hemmeter, M.L., & Kleinert, H. (2002). Including manual signing as nontargeted information when using a constant time delay procedure to teach receptive identification of packaged food items. *Journal of Behavioral Education, 11,* 19–38.

Schuster, J.W., Griffen, A.K., & Wolery, M. (1992). Comparison of simultaneous prompting and constant time delay procedures in teaching sight words to elementary students with moderate mental retardation. *Journal of Behavioral Education, 2*(3), 305–325.

Schuster, J.W., Morse, T.E., Ault, M.J., Doyle, P.M., Crawford, M., & Wolery, M. (1998). Constant time delay with chained tasks: A review of the literature. *Education and Treatment of Children, 21,* 74–106.

Sewell, T.J., Collins, B.C., Hemmeter, M.L., & Schuster, J.W. (1998). Using simultaneous prompting to teach dressing skills to preschoolers with developmental delays. *Journal of Early Intervention, 21,* 132–145.

Singleton, D.K., Schuster, J.W., Morse, T.E., & Collins, B.C. (1999). A comparison of antecedent prompt and test and simultaneous prompting procedures in teaching grocery sight words to adolescents with mental retardation. *Education and Training in Mental Retardation and Developmental Disabilities, 34,* 182–199.

Snell, M.E., & Brown, F. (2011). Selecting teaching strategies and arranging educational environments. In M.E. Snell & F. Brown (Eds.), *Instruction of students with severe disabilities* (7th ed., pp. 122–185). Upper Saddle River, NJ: Pearson.

Spooner, F., Browder, D.M., & Mims, P.J. (2011). Evidence-based practices. In D.M. Browder & F. Spooner (Eds.), *Teaching students with moderate and severe disabilities* (pp. 92–122). New York, NY: Guilford.

Walker, G. (2008). Constant and progressive time delay procedures for teaching children with autism: A literature review. *Journal of Autism and Developmental Disorders, 38*(2), 261–275.

Westling, D.L., & Fox, L. (2009). *Teaching students with severe disabilities* (4th ed.). Upper Saddle River, NJ: Pearson.

Wolery, M., Ault, M.J., & Doyle, P.M. (1992). *Teaching students with moderate to severe disabilities.* New York, NY: Longman.

Wolery, M., Holcombe, A., Cybriwsky, C., Doyle, P.M., Schuster, J.W., & Ault, M.J. (1992). Constant time delay with discrete responses: A review of effectiveness and demographic, procedural, and methodological parameters. *Research in Developmental Disabilities, 13*(3), 239–266.

Yilmaz, I., Birkan, B., Konukman, F., & Erkan, M. (2005). Using a constant delay procedure to teach aquatic play skills to children with autism. *Education and Training in Developmental Disabilities, 40,* 171–182.

Yilmaz, I., Konunkman, F., Birkan, B., Ozen, A., Yanardag, M., & Gamursoy, I. (2010). Effects of constant time delay procedure on the Halliwick's methods of swimming rotation skills for children with autism. *Education and Training in Autism and Developmental Disabilities, 45,* 124–135.

CHAPTER 5

Increasing the Efficiency of Instruction Through the Addition of Nontargeted Information and Through Instruction in Small-Group Formats

CHAPTER OBJECTIVES

On completion of this chapter, the reader will be able to

- State the difference between effectiveness and efficiency in terms of instruction
- Explain how the addition of nontargeted information increases the efficiency of systematic instruction
- Describe three ways in which nontargeted information can be added to an instructional trial
- Describe ways in which observational learning can be facilitated
- List the advantages of providing systematic instruction in a small-group format
- Explain why heterogeneous grouping might be beneficial to learners
- List and describe models for organizing small-group instruction, including presenting stimuli and identifying responses
- Provide examples for using individual and group attentional cues and responses when teaching in a small-group format
- Design a lesson for delivering systematic instruction with response-prompting procedures in a small-group format
- Design a data sheet for monitoring the progress of learners taught in a small-group format

TERMS USED IN THIS CHAPTER

efficiency	heterogeneous group	tandem model
nontargeted information	universal design	one-to-one supplemental
observational learning	intrasequential model	instruction
instructive feedback	intersequential model	

The previous chapters in this book described how to provide effective instruction for students with moderate and severe disabilities. If a procedure is effective, then a learner will acquire a new behavior or skill. There also are ways to make instruction more efficient. **Efficiency** can be defined by several outcomes of instruction and can refer to how quickly a learner acquires new information in terms of the amount of time or the number of instructional sessions to criterion (Collins, 2007; Wolery, Ault, & Doyle, 1992). Although all of the procedures described in this book have been shown to be effective, some are slightly more efficient than others (e.g., Demchak, 1989; Godby, Gast, & Wolery, 1987; Schuster, Griffen, & Wolery, 1992). For example, it takes less time to implement a procedure that uses a single prompt than it does to implement a procedure that uses a hierarchy of prompts. Efficiency also can refer to the number of errors learners make in responding with a procedure. Typically, the fewer errors a learner makes, the more efficient a procedure is because the instructor will not have to spend time correcting errors. Another way to increase efficiency is to add **nontargeted information** (i.e., content in addition to the stated objectives for the lesson) whenever possible during instruction (Collins, Hendricks, Fetko, & Land, 2002; Werts, Wolery, Holcombe, & Gast, 1995). Finally, instruction can be more efficient when it is conducted in a small-group format rather than a one-to-one format. When taught in a small-group format, the instructor can teach more than one learner at the same time, and each learner can acquire skills by observing the instruction provided to other members of the group.

This chapter will focus on increasing the efficiency of instruction by describing ways to facilitate the acquisition of nontargeted information within instructional sessions (Collins et al., 2002; Werts, Hoffman, & Darcy, 2011; Werts et al., 1995) and ways to use systematic instruction in small-group formats (Collins, Gast, Ault, & Wolery, 1991; Wolery et al., 1992). Sample instructional programs based on investigations from the professional research as well as sample data sheets will be included.

NONTARGETED INFORMATION

One of the ways in which instruction can be more efficient is to expose students to content in addition to what already has been targeted for instruction. There are two ways to do this. The first is through adding content to the instructional trial (e.g., Cromer, Schuster, Collins, & Grisham-Brown, 1998; Falkenstine, Collins, Schuster, & Kleinert, 2009; Fiscus, Schuster, Morse, & Collins, 2002; Roark, Collins, Hemmeter, & Kleinert, 2002; Smith, Schuster, Collins, & Kleinert, 2011; Taylor, Collins, Schuster, & Kleinert, 2002; Wolery, Schuster, & Collins, 2000), and the second is through facilitating **observational learning** (e.g., Falkenstine et al., 2009; Fickel, Schuster, & Collins, 1998; Smith, Collins, Schuster, & Kleinert, 1999; Stonecipher, Schuster,

Collins, & Grisham-Brown, 1999). In both scenarios, learners may acquire additional content, thus saving instructional time because this content will not have to be taught separately or in the future. Even if the content is not acquired at a criterion level, instructors may find that learners acquire content more quickly when they have had prior exposure to it (Wolery et al., 2000).

Nontargeted Information Added to an Instructional Trial

Nontargeted information can be added to an instructional trial in three ways. First, it can be added to the stimulus or task direction (e.g., Roark et al., 2002). Second, it can be added when delivering a prompt (e.g., Jones & Collins, 1997). Third, it can be added when providing a consequence or **instructive feedback** on performance (e.g., Smith et al., 2011). The nontargeted information may be related or unrelated to the content being presented (e.g., Werts et al., 1995).

Nontargeted Information Added to the Stimulus

Once the instructor has secured the attention of the learner, the stimulus or task direction is provided, as described in Chapter 1. In presenting the stimulus, the instructor can insert nontargeted information in addition to the content that has been targeted for instruction. For example, the instructor may point to the letters of a vocabulary word while naming them before asking the learner to read the word (e.g., *"P-H-O-T-O-S-Y-N-T-H-E-S-I-S.* What word is this?"). Once the learner has met criterion on reading the word, the learner also may have learned to spell it. (See Sample Instructional Program 1 in Chapter 4 for another example of nontargeted information inserted in the stimulus.)

Nontargeted Information Added to the Prompt

Another way to add nontargeted information to an instructional trial is in the delivery of the prompt that is used to elicit a correct response. For example, a prompt hierarchy used in the system-of-least-prompts (SLP) procedure might proceed as follows:

1. The instructor asks, "What word is this?" and waits for response.
2. If no correct response, the instructor delivers the first prompt, "The word begins with *P-H,* which makes the *F* sound," and waits for response.
3. If no correct response, the instructor delivers the second prompt, "The word refers to what happens when a plant is exposed to sunlight," and waits for response.
4. If no correct response, the instructor delivers the final (controlling) prompt, "The word is photosynthesis," and waits for response.

Once the learner has met criterion on reading the word, the learner also may be able to respond correctly when asked, "What letter sound does *P-H* make?" and "What happens when a plant is exposed to sunlight?"

Nontargeted Information Added in the Consequence

Nontargeted information presented in the consequence that follows a response is known as instructive feedback. Whether a response is correct or incorrect, feedback is provided. For example, the instructor may say, "You are correct," or "No, the word is photosynthesis," followed by the statement, "Photosynthesis is the process in which carbohydrates are produced from light and chlorophyll in plants." This is an example of nontargeted information that is related to the targeted vocabulary word for instruction, but students also may acquire unrelated, nontargeted information, as in, "Correct! The word is photosynthesis. Most plants are green; blue and yellow combine to make green" (nontargeted information that the student may need for art class).

Observational Learning

Observational learning occurs when learners acquire content through the observation of others (Collins et al., 1991). For example, when learners in a small group each have different content targeted for instruction during a lesson, each member of the group may acquire the information taught to the other members of the group whether it is targeted or nontargeted (e.g., Falkenstine et al., 2009). Instructors can facilitate this by ensuring that all learners are attending to each other as instructional trials are conducted. This might be done by giving a general attentional cue (e.g., "Everyone, look") while showing the stimulus to the entire group (e.g., presenting a vocabulary word or a math problem) before calling on a specific learner to respond. The instructor can then provide feedback on the response to the entire group (e.g., "Yes, this word is *photosynthesis*. Did everyone hear Hudson say this word? Photosynthesis. Nice job paying attention and listening!"). Information on how to structure small-group instruction is presented in the following section.

SMALL-GROUP INSTRUCTION

A misconception in special education is that individually designed instruction to teach individually identified goals and objectives for learners with moderate and severe disabilities must be provided in a one-to-one instructional format. Although a one-to-one format may sometimes be necessary, as when teaching personal management skills, there are a number of advantages to teaching in a small-group format (Collins et al., 1991) that have been reported in the professional literature describing small-group instruction with students with moderate and severe disabilities (e.g., Colozzi, Ward, & Crotty, 2008; Falkenstine et al., 2009; Fickel et al., 1998; McDonnell et al., 2006; Stonecipher et al., 1999; Tekin-Iftar & Birkan, 2010). The first advantage is that learners in a small group can learn from observing each other. Observational learning can result in quicker acquisition if the same content is being presented to all learners in the group, but it is possible for learners to acquire even more content when the objectives for each learner are different. The second advantage is that learners in a small group have the opportunity to practice social skills. They can learn to take turns, to raise a hand and wait to be acknowledged before making a response, and to sit in close proximity to other learners without touching or instigating an inappropriate behavioral incident. The third advantage is that teaching learners in a small group is an efficient use of the instructor's time. For example, it takes less time to teach a lesson one time to six learners than to teach six separate lessons. The fourth advantage is that teaching learners in a small group requires fewer instructional personnel. For example, two staff could divide a class of 12 learners in half to conduct instruction, or one instructor could conduct instruction with 10 learners, thus freeing two staff to work one-on-one with two learners who require extra attention (e.g., hand-over-hand assistance) or who have not yet acquired the appropriate behaviors to work in a group format. The final advantage is that teaching in a small-group format prepares learners to function in larger, more inclusive settings. Although small-group instruction in a school setting may take place in a general education classroom or in a resource room, the goal is that learners will learn to function in larger groups found in some educational (e.g., lecture-based college class), community (e.g., first aid class at health center), vocational (e.g., cooking or carpentry class at community center), or recreation/leisure (e.g., yoga class at health club) settings.

Considerations in Delivering Small-Group Instruction

An instructor who is planning to use systematic instruction in a small-group format will want to address a number of considerations in planning the lesson. These include the way in which the small group will be composed, the manner in which instructional procedures will be implemented, and the measurement and evaluation procedures that will make up the assessment component of the lesson (Collins et al., 1991). These are described in the following sections.

Group Composition

The professional literature has defined small-group instruction as consisting of a single instructor delivering instruction to a group of 2 to 10 learners. The learners may be homogeneous in that they all are the same age, have the same learning characteristics, or are at the same level of learning, but this is not necessary. Teaching a **heterogeneous group** of learners who are working at different levels may allow learners at beginning levels to learn from those at more advanced levels (e.g., Fickel et al., 1998). If instruction for each member of the group is on the same content, then the use of **universal design** (Spooner, Browder, & Mims, 2011; Westling & Fox, 2009) can address the needs of all learners in the group (i.e., provide adaptations so that all learners can participate in a lesson regardless of ability).

In determining the content, the instructor will want to decide the skill or skills that learners are to be taught as well as the stimulus or stimuli to which they will respond (Collins et al., 1991). The instructor has the following options. First, the instructor may decide to teach the same skill to all learners in the group using the same stimulus (e.g., material). For example, the instructor may teach sight word reading by presenting the same vocabulary words on flashcards to each member of the group. Second, the instructor may decide to teach the same skill to all members of the group but with a different stimulus. For example, the instructor may teach sight word reading by presenting different vocabulary words on flashcards to each member of the group. Third, the instructor may decide to teach different skills to all learners in the group while presenting the same stimuli. For example, the instructor may present the same vocabulary words on flashcards to all members of the group. The objective for one or more learners may be to read the words, the objective for one or more learners may be to define the words, and the objective for one or more learners may be to identify the letters in each word. Finally, the instructor may decide to teach different skills to all learners in the group using different stimuli. For example, the instructor may ask some learners to read vocabulary words from flashcards, the instructor may ask some learners to match vocabulary words to their definitions on a worksheet, and the instructor may ask some learners to spell vocabulary words orally or through writing them on a sheet of paper. If this model is used, the content does not have to center on the same or related academic skills. The instructor could be teaching reading to one or more learners and math to the others. For example, one learner may be asked to read a word problem while another is asked to work the problem.

The next component to be considered when working with learners in small groups is the way in which instruction will be organized. The instructor has four options (Collins et al., 1991). First, the instructor may use an **intrasequential model** in which each learner receives one-to-one instruction within the group setting. The instructor would give task directions to a group of learners and then rotate around the group giving feedback and working with each learner individually. An example would be asking the learners to write a sentence and then delivering instruction individually to each learner on spelling, writing letters of the alphabet, using punctuation, and using correct grammar, depending on the level at which each student is working. Second, the instructor may use an **intersequential model** in which all learners in the group work together to perform a skill. In a science lesson, the instructor may have all of the learners work together to perform an experiment, such as attempting to dissolve different ingredients in a liquid. The instructor could ask individual learners to respond to directions and questions as they work, and different learners may perform different roles in the task (e.g., measuring, pouring, stirring, completing a table of results), but all would be praised for working together and paying attention to each other. If the instructor is teaching learners to work within a small-group format, a **tandem model** is a third option. In this model, the instructor begins instruction with a small number of learners and slowly increases the size of the group over time. For example, the instructor may begin by teaching a small group of two learners. As these learners acquire the skills to take turns and exhibit appropriate behavior during instruction, the instructor would add a third learner to the group. Additional learners can be added until the instructor reaches the desired number of learners in the group. For example, a group that begins with two learners could increase by one learner each week to a maximum of six learners. When the instructor believes that all students are benefiting from small-group instruction but that one or more learners need additional instruction to acquire the content of the lesson, there is a fourth option for conducting group instruction. This would be to conduct small-group instruction with **one-to-one supplemental instruction.** For example, the instructor may teach a science lesson to a small group of five learners but pull out one or two learners for direct, massed trial instruction on basic vocabulary used in the lesson. In another example, the instructor may pull out learners from a math lesson who need additional flashcard instruction on basic math facts to keep up with the group lessons.

Instructional Procedures

Once the composition of the small group is determined, the next step is to focus on the instructional procedures that will be used to teach the content of the lesson. Chapters 3 and 4 described a variety of response-prompting procedures that are supported by the professional research base as being effective in teaching students with moderate and severe disabilities. These include the graduated-guidance, most-to-least prompting, system-of-least-prompts, constant time-delay, progressive time-delay, and simultaneous-prompting procedures. It should be noted that, although it may be easier for the instructor if all learners are taught with the same procedure, this is not necessary. For example, the instructor may use a graduated-guidance procedure to physically assist one learner in writing a vocabulary word while using a time-delay procedure with a verbal model prompt to teach another student to read and define the same word. Regardless of the instructional strategy selected, instructional trials in small-group instruction should begin with an attentional cue, provide the opportunity for students to respond to a task direction, and end with an appropriate consequence (i.e., feedback on performance), as described in Chapter 1.

The instructor will first need to determine whether to use general or specific attentional cues to determine whether all learners in the small group are ready to learn. Attentional cues should be individually determined on the basis of each learner's needs. Attentional cues, whether general or specific, can be delivered individually or to the entire group. For example, the instructor may say, "Everyone, look at me" (general group cue), and wait for all eyes to signal attention (general group response) before beginning instruction; or, the instructor may say, "Everyone, put your finger on the first word at the top of the page of your book" (specific group cue), and wait for all learners to comply with this request (specific group response) before beginning instruction. If desired or necessary, the types of attentional cues and responses can be combined. In this case, the instructor may say, "Everyone, look at me [general group cue]. Hudson, what did I ask everyone to do?" (specific individual cue) and then wait until all learners have their eyes on the instructor (general group response) and Hudson says, "Look at the teacher" (specific individual response), before beginning instruction.

Once the learners in the group have indicated their readiness to attend and learn, the instructor will need to decide how to proceed with instruction. First, the task direction must be delivered. As with attentional cues, this may be delivered to the entire group (e.g., "Read the word") and result in a choral response (e.g., Everyone states, "Photosynthesis"), or this may be delivered to an individual in the group (e.g., "Hudson, read the word") and result in an individual response (e.g., Hudson states, "Photosynthesis"). Again, these can be combined, as when the instructor asks for a choral response in reading the word and then asks for an individual response in defining the word (e.g., "Good, the word is photosynthesis. Hudson, what does this word mean?").

Regardless of the manner in which instruction is structured, the instructor needs to decide in advance how many instructional trials (e.g., opportunities to respond and receive feedback) will be delivered to each learner in the group and how many instructional trials each learner will receive per turn. For example, the instructor may ask each learner to read one word per turn or may ask each learner to read five words per turn before moving to the next learner. The sequence of instructional trials may be delivered in a predictable fashion (e.g., round robin) or in an unpredictable fashion. An unpredictable sequence of calling on students may promote attending.

As described in Chapter 1, there are three basic trial formats for conducting instruction. Massed trials occur when one instructional trial immediately follows the last in rapid succession. For example, the instructor may ask Hudson to read a word more than once before moving to the next learner in the group (e.g., "What word?"…"Good! What word again?"…"Great! Tell me what word one more time"…"Excellent!"). Spaced trials occur when a learner has the opportunity to stop and listen to the instruction of others within the group before being asked again to respond. This also facilitates the social skill of taking turns. For example, the instructor would ask Hudson to read a word, then ask other students to read the same or different words before returning to Hudson and asking him to read the word again. The final format of distributed trials occurs when a learner has instructional trials on one target of instruction interspersed with instructional trials on other targets of instruction. Distributed trials are more natural in that opportunities to use learned skills in the real world are interspersed with other skills. As an example, the instructor may ask each learner in the group to read and define the word *photosynthesis* at the beginning of a lesson. The group would then do a science activity of watering and rotating their plants on a windowsill, of measuring and recording data on the growth of plants in sunny or dark areas of the classroom, and of discussing the hours of sunshine and darkness in a typical day along with the meaning of *a.m.* and *p.m.* before concluding the lesson by again reading and defining the word *photosynthesis.*

After each instructional trial delivered in a small-group lesson, it is important for the instructor to provide feedback as to whether the learners' responses were correct or incorrect. In the event that a learner makes an incorrect response or fails to respond, the instructor may want to provide the correct response to increase the likelihood that the learner will respond correctly in the future. On the basis of individual and group data, the instructor will need to decide whether to repeat a lesson to mastery by the entire group before moving forward to new content (i.e., group criterion) or whether to let each learner in the group advance at his or her own pace within the group (i.e., individual criterion). Although a group criterion is easier for the instructor to manage and allows the opportunity for overlearning (which can facilitate maintenance), an individual criterion allows learners who quickly acquire new content to master more content over a period of time and decreases the risk that learners who master content will grow bored and begin to demonstrate inappropriate behaviors within the small-group lesson.

Measurement and Evaluation

As with all instruction, data on the performance of learners in a small-group format must be monitored and analyzed to make ongoing instructional decisions and to determine when criterion has been met. When systematic instruction is used, trial-by-trial data are collected and graphed. In most cases, the instructor will collect and graph individual data, but it is acceptable to collect and graph group data when a group criterion is used.

If nontargeted information is being presented during instruction, then the instructor will want to conduct a pretest before a unit of instruction and a posttest once criterion on the targeted content is reached to determine whether learners also have acquired the nontargeted information. For example, an instructor may give pre- and posttests on spelling or definitions when teaching learners to read a series of vocabulary words. Learners who have been exposed to spelling on flashcards or to definitions provided during feedback statements (e.g., "Good job! The word is photosynthesis, and that is the process in which carbohydrates are produced from light and chlorophyll in plants"). If the instructor is teaching different content across students in the group, a posttest will verify whether learners have acquired each other's content through observation. For example, three learners who have been taught to read *photosynthesis*, *carbohydrates*, and *chlorophyll*, respectively, may have acquired the ability to read, spell, and/or define the vocabulary words taught to each other.

Instructors also may want to collect pre- and posttest data to determine whether learners are generalizing content. In this case, pre- and posttests would be conducted to see whether learners respond correctly 1) to novel people (e.g., classroom paraprofessionals, related services delivery personnel, peers without disabilities, members of the community), 2) in novel settings in which skills will be needed (e.g., counting money in the lunchroom, on a job site, or while shopping in the community), or 3) across novel materials (e.g., reading vocabulary words typed in different font style or color, on a computer monitor, in a book). If learners do not generalize, then further instruction across individuals, settings, or materials is indicated.

Permanent products are another way to verify the acquisition of content. Instructors may collect work samples (e.g., worksheets of completed math problems, written or typed sentences or paragraphs) periodically throughout instruction to document that progress is being made or learning is occurring.

Regardless of how acquisition in a small group is documented, data on the performance of learners should be collected to assess learning and to assist instructors in making instructional decisions (e.g., when to change an ineffective procedure, when to expand the exemplars used during instruction, when to pull learners out of a small group for individual instruction, when to discontinue instruction and move to an easier or more difficult skill). Once instructors have determined that everyone in a group has met the established criterion, procedures for facilitating maintenance can be implemented (e.g., waiting until the end of the lesson to provide feedback on performance).

SAMPLE INSTRUCTIONAL PROGRAMS

The following instructional programs illustrate how nontargeted information can be inserted during instruction with students with moderate and severe disabilities. The first sample program takes place in a one-to-one instructional format, and the second sample program takes place during small-group instruction, taking advantage of the possibility that observational learning will occur.

Sample Instructional Program 1

Learners in elementary school often prepare snacks that can be shared with the class. This gives the opportunity for students with moderate and severe disabilities to learn a functional skill. It also provides a good forum for embedding instruction in core content (e.g., using one-to-one correspondence in preparing enough for the class, measuring ingredients, practicing fine motor skills used in cutting and stirring, identifying sight words used in recipes, sequencing and following directions). In the following instructional program, an instructor (i.e., the paraprofessional, Mr. Dick) adds both related and unrelated nontargeted information when implementing a constant time-delay (CTD) procedure to teach learners to make snacks. The procedures are based on a research study conducted by Fiscus et al. (2002).

Core Content Standards

Practical Living/ Vocational	• Students will identify strategies (e.g., diet) and good hygiene practices (e.g., hand washing) that promote good health and prevent diseases.
Math	• Students will choose and use appropriate tools for specific measurement tasks.
Reading	• Students will interpret specialized vocabulary (words and terms specific to understanding the content).
	• Students will identify the correct sequence.

Behavioral Objective

When presented with 1 of 3 snacks to prepare and the verbal task direction to fix the snack, Dylan will follow a picture recipe to prepare the snack with 100% accuracy for 5 days.

Instructional Context

Instruction will be in a one-to-one format in Dylan's elementary education classroom. Snacks will be prepared to share with peers after recess.

Instructional Materials

Materials will consist of the foods (i.e., cheese slices, crackers, frozen waffles, syrup, milk, flavored drink mix), utensils and dishes (i.e., knife, spoon, fork, glass, plate), and appliances (i.e., microwave, refrigerator) that will be needed to prepare the snacks. When needed, the instructor will use a second set of materials to model for Dylan (e.g., glass and spoon to make flavored milk). In addition, Dylan will use a laminated picture recipe book. The instructor has selected snacks to be prepared through a survey of elementary learners across three classrooms to determine which snacks they most often enjoy preparing at home. The instructor also has ensured that the learners in the class do not have any known food allergies to the snacks that have been selected. The instructor will have a box of novel kitchen utensils/items to be used in presenting nontargeted information. These will consist of a potholder, measuring cups and spoons, spatula, can opener, strainer, wooden spoon, ice cream scoop, and bottle opener (see Fiscus et al., 2002, p. 58).

Instructional Procedure

Each instructional trial will proceed as follows.

Attentional Cue	• At the beginning of each session, the instructor will tell Dylan that it is time to wash his hands and prepare a snack for the class. The instructor will then secure Dylan's attention with the specific attentional cue, "Point to the snack in the recipe book that you would like to prepare today."
Task Direction	• Once Dylan has indicated his attention by selecting the snack to be prepared, the instructor will give the task direction (e.g., "Dylan, fix flavored milk for the class").
Constant Time-Delay Procedure	• The controlling prompt will be a verbal direction plus a model (i.e., instructor will say, "Get the flavored milk mix," while showing Dylan how to do this). During the first session, the instructor will immediately model the correct response while stating the verbal directions (i.e., 0-second delay interval) after giving the task direction. During all subsequent sessions, the instructor will wait a 5-second delay interval before giving verbal directions and modeling the correct response for each step of the task analysis. Once Dylan meets criterion across the three snacks, the instructor will select three new snacks from the survey completed with elementary learners.
Consequence	• The instructor will praise all correct prompted and unprompted responses (e.g., "Good job!") for each step of the task analysis completed within 20 seconds. If Dylan makes an error before the prompt, the instructor will remind him to wait for help if he does not know the correct response and then will model the correct response for him. If Dylan makes an incorrect response or fails to respond after the prompt, the instructor will use a physical prompt to assist him in making the correct response.

Nontargeted Information

Two types of nontargeted information will be presented during each step of the task analysis. First, the instructor will present nontargeted information related to the task by pointing to the corresponding words underneath each picture presented for each step of preparing the snack in the recipe book as the verbal directions are delivered as part of the prompt to complete the step (e.g., "This says, 'Get out the flavored milk mix'"). Second, the instructor will provide instructive feedback that contains information unrelated to the task during the consequence. This will consist of presenting and labeling common kitchen utensils/items that are used to prepare meals and stating the function of each (e.g., "Good job getting out the flavored milk mix. This is a potholder. We use it to handle foods that might be hot so we do not get burned").

Data Collection

The instructor will record a plus sign for each correct response or a minus sign for each incorrect or no response in the columns indicating *before* or *after* the prompt. Both correct prompted and unprompted responses will be graphed daily. Once Dylan has met criterion, the instructor will conduct a session in which he is asked to read the words in the recipe book without the pictures and in which he is asked to label and give the function of the kitchen utensil/items that were presented to him as he learned to prepare snacks. A sample completed data sheet is shown in Figure 5.1.

Maintenance

Once Dylan has met the criterion of 100% correct responses for 1 day, the instructor will thin praise statements for correct responses to every third response (i.e., fixed ratio of 3, or FR3) until Dylan has met criterion for 3 days. On the final day of instruction, the instructor will not provide praise statements until Dylan has finished preparing the snack for the entire class. The instructor will continue to monitor maintenance for the remainder of the school year by occasionally asking Dylan to prepare a previously learned snack.

Generalization

The instructor will facilitate generalization by varying the types of food items that Dylan uses to prepare snacks. For example, Dylan will use white and wheat crackers, Swiss and American cheese, waffles with and without fruit, different brands of syrup, and strawberry and chocolate milk mix. In addition, multiple examples of kitchen utensils/items that are presented as nontargeted information will be used that vary in size, color, and/or shape.

Behavior Management

Appropriate behavior will be facilitated by allowing Dylan to select the snacks to be prepared and allowing him to consume them with the peers in his class. In addition, the instructor will use the standard classroom behavior management program in which students receive tokens at the end of lessons that can be accumulated and then traded for identified preferred reinforcers (e.g., classroom activities).

Lesson Variations and Extension

In addition to the nontargeted information presented in this instructional program, instructors may consider adding core content as nontargeted information. This could be science or health information on nutrition (e.g., calories, fat grams, vitamin content, basic food groups), math (e.g., cost of each ingredient and total cost of snack), and social studies (e.g., the geographic origin of each ingredient in the snack, the climate needed to produce the ingredient).

CONSTANT TIME-DELAY DATA SHEET

Name: _Dylan_   Skill: _Follow recipe for flavored milk_   Date: _May 8_
Instructor: _Mr. Dick_   Setting: _Classroom_   Time: _2:00_

Steps	Before prompt	After prompt
1. Get out drink mix	+	
2. Get out milk	+	
3. Get out glasses for class	−	
4. Get out spoon	+	
5. Open drink mix		+
6. Open milk		0
7. Put scoop mix in each glass	+	
8. Pour milk in each glass	+	
9. Stir milk in each glass		+
10. Put spoon in sink		−
11. Close drink mix	−	
12. Put away drink mix	+	
13. Close milk	+	
14. Put away milk		−
15. Put away recipe book	−	
Number/% correct	7/47%	2/13%
Number/% incorrect	3/20%	2/13%
Number/% no response	0/0%	1/7%

Key: Plus sign indicates correct response; minus sign indicates incorrect response; zero indicates no response.

Figure 5.1.   Sample completed data sheet for using a constant time-delay procedure to teach a chained task in Sample Instructional Program 1.

Sample Instructional Program 2

In the next instructional program, an instructor in a high school resource room uses a CTD procedure to conduct small-group instruction. The skills are individualized for each of the three students in the group. Virginia is taught to tell time to enable her to be more independent in attending general education classes and extracurricular activities with her peers without disabilities. Alexandra is taught to read vocabulary words used in her arts and humanities class. William is taught to recognize the abbreviations used for states on maps in his social studies class. To maximize the amount of content acquired by the learners during instruction, the instructor also adds nontargeted information that will be beneficial to the learners. Thus, each

learner has the opportunity to acquire both the targeted content and the nontargeted information taught to the other learners in the group. The procedures are based on a research study
conducted by Falkenstine et al. (2009).

Core Content Standards

Practical Living/ Vocational	• Students demonstrate skills and work habits that lead to success in future schooling and work (Virginia).
Arts and Humanities	• Students make sense of ideas and communicate ideas with the visual arts (Alexandra).
Social Studies	• Students will use a variety of geographic tools (e.g., maps, globes) to explain and analyze the reasons for the distribution of physical and human features on Earth's surface (William).

Behavioral Objectives

When shown a clock and asked to state the time, Virginia will state the correct time with 100%
accuracy for 5 days.

When shown a flashcard containing an arts and humanities vocabulary word, Alexandra
will state the word with 100% accuracy for 5 days.

When shown a flashcard containing an abbreviation for the name of a state, William will
say the state's name with 100% accuracy for 5 days.

Instructional Context

The instructor will conduct small-group instruction around a small table in the resource room
in which life skills are taught. When it is a learner's time to receive instruction, the learner will
move to the middle seat facing the instructor.

Instructional Materials

The instructor will use an analog clock to teach telling time and hand-lettered 3″ × 5″ index
cards to teach reading vocabulary words and abbreviations. In addition, the instructor will
use a wristwatch and a dictionary while presenting nontargeted information.

Instructional Procedure

Each instructional trial will proceed as follows.

Attentional Cue	• The instructor will announce, "It is time for our group lesson," and then wait for the learners to sit down at the table and give eye contact to show that they are attending before proceeding.
Task Directions	• The instructor will work with one learner at a time. The task direction for each learner will be as follows: 1) Virginia—"What time is it?" 2) Alexandra —"What is this word?" and 3) William—"What is this state name?"
Constant Time-Delay Procedure	• The learners will receive two trials each on two stimuli per instructional session for a total of 10 massed trials per learner. The stimuli for each learner will be presented in random order. Specifically, Virginia will receive trials on 9:45, 12:45, 6:15, 7:30, and 5:45; Alexandra will receive trials

on *artist, canvas, sculpture, frame,* and *palette*; and William will receive trials on the abbreviations *KY, SC, NC, OR,* and *NJ* (see Falkenstine et al., 2009, pp. 130–131). Each time learners reach criterion on each of their sets of stimuli, they will begin instruction on five new stimuli. Each learner will be taught individually in a massed trial format within the group, and the order in which learners receive instruction will vary from day to day.

- During the first instructional session, the learners immediately will be prompted to make the correct response (i.e., 0-second delay interval). During all subsequent sessions, the instructor will wait 4 seconds for learners to make a correct response before providing a prompt. The controlling prompt for all learners will be a verbal model.

Consequence

- After each instructional trial, the instructor will provide praise if the response was correct before or after the prompt, will correct all errors that occur before or after the prompt, or will repeat the prompt for failures to respond after the prompt.

Nontargeted Information

The instructor will present two types of nontargeted information after the consequence (i.e., praise or error correction) of each instructional trial. One type of nontargeted information will be a discrete skill, and the other will be a chained task. Learners will not be expected to respond but will simply attend as the instructor presents this information. After the trial consequence for Virginia, the teacher will provide the discrete nontargeted information of an alternate way to state the time (e.g., "9:45 is the same as a quarter until 10") and the chained nontargeted information of demonstrating the task analysis for setting a wristwatch to show the stated time (e.g., 9:45). After the trial consequence for Alexandra, the instructor will provide the discrete nontargeted information of the definition of the vocabulary word (e.g., "An artist is someone who paints") and the chained nontargeted information of demonstrating the task analysis for locating and reading the definition of the word (e.g., *artist*) in a dictionary. After the trial consequence for William, the instructor will provide the discrete nontargeted information of the capital of the state (e.g., "The capital of Kentucky is Frankfort") and the chained nontargeted information of spelling the state name (e.g., "*K-E-N-T-U-C-K-Y*").

Data Collection

The instructor will collect data after each instructional trial for each learner in the group. On the data sheet, she will record a plus sign for correct responses before or after the prompt, a minus sign for incorrect responses before or after the prompt, and a zero for failure to respond after the prompt. A sample completed data sheet is shown in Figure 5.2. As learners meet criterion on each set of stimuli, the instructor will assess learning by asking each learner to state or demonstrate all nontargeted information presented to each member of the group.

Maintenance

Once learners meet the criterion of 100% correct responses before the prompt for 1 day, the instructor will thin praise to follow every third response (i.e., FR3) for 4 days.

SMALL-GROUP DATA SHEET

Instructor: __Ms. Williams__   Date: __October 10__   Time: __9:00__

Virginia: Telling time			Alexandra: Arts/humanities words			William: State abbreviations		
Stimuli	Before	After	Stimuli	Before	After	Stimuli	Before	After
9:45	–		Artist		–	KY	+	
7:30	+		Frame		0	OR	+	
12:45	+		Canvas	+		SC	+	
5:45	+		Palette	–		NJ		+
6:15		+	Sculpture	+		NC		–
9:45		–	Artist	+		KY	+	
12:45		0	Canvas	+		SC	–	
6:15	+		Sculpture		+	NC	+	
7:30	–		Frame		–	OR		0
5:45	+		Palette	+		NJ	+	
No./% correct	5/50%	1/10%	No./% correct	5/50%	1/2%	No./% correct	6/60%	1/10%

Key: Plus sign indicates correct response; minus sign indicates incorrect response; zero indicates no response.

Figure 5.2.   Sample completed data sheet for small-group instruction using a constant time-delay procedure in Sample Instructional Program 2.

Generalization

Once learners meet the criterion of 100% correct responses before the prompt for 5 days, the instructor will assess generalization. Virginia will be asked to tell time on a digital clock, Alexandra will be asked to read a passage from her arts and humanities book containing the targeted vocabulary words, and William will be asked to identify the state name abbreviations on a map of the United States.

Behavior Management

The instructor periodically will praise the learners in the group for attending and observing each other during small-group instruction.

Lesson Variations and Extension

Conducting supplemental small-group instruction in a resource room is a good way to provide extra instruction on content that learners may not grasp when taught in a large group in a general education class. It also is a good way to teach prerequisite skills that learners may need in order to more fully participate in general education classes. For example, vocabulary and definitions for units of study can be taught, or additional practice can occur on working math problems. It also is an appropriate place to teach and practice skills that same-age peers already possess (e.g., telling time, counting money, using a dictionary) without stigmatizing a learner. It should be noted, however, that small-group instruction does not have to occur in a resource room, and instructional groups do not have to consist solely of learners who have disabilities. Coteachers can divide learners in a general education classroom and tailor the skills taught to the needs of the learners. For example, a teacher in a chemistry class may ask one learner in a small group to identify the elements of the periodic table based on their abbreviations, another learner to name the properties of the elements, and another to identify valences. It is possible that these learners will acquire the content taught to all members of the group. In another example, a teacher in a calculus class may ask one learner to state the number on rolls of dice, another to work a formula for probability based on the dice rolls, and another to compile a corresponding table.

SUMMARY

This chapter presented two ways to increase the efficiency of instruction. The first is to add nontargeted information or content to instructional trials, and the second is to provide instruction in a small-group setting in which learners can acquire content through observational learning. It is possible for learners to acquire nontargeted information regardless of whether it is related to the targeted content being presented and for learners to acquire both targeted content and nontargeted information presented to other learners in a small-group setting through observation. A flowchart for conducting small-group instruction can be found in Appendix A, and a blank data sheet can be found in Appendix B.

QUESTIONS FOR REFLECTION

1. What is nontargeted information? What are three ways that this can be presented during an instructional trial?

2. What is the difference between instructive feedback and observational learning?

3. Provide examples of nontargeted information that is and is not related to the targeted content of a lesson.

4. What are some general guidelines for conducting small-group instruction?

5. Why can heterogeneous groups be desirable? Provide an example of skills that might be taught in a heterogeneous group.

6. How and when is the acquisition of nontargeted information assessed? How can the inclusion of nontargeted information be used to increase the efficiency of future instruction?

7. How might small-group instruction be used to supplement core content taught in a general education class?

REFERENCES

Collins, B.C. (2007). *Moderate and severe disabilities: A foundational approach.* Upper Saddle River, NJ: Pearson, Merrill, Prentice-Hall.

Collins, B.C., Gast, D.L., Ault, M.J., & Wolery, M. (1991). Small group instruction: Guidelines for teachers of students with moderate to severe handicaps. *Education and Training in Mental Retardation, 26,* 18–32.

Collins, B.C., Hendricks, T.B., Fetko, K., & Land, L. (2002). Student-2-student learning in inclusive classrooms. *Teaching Exceptional Children, 34*(4), 56–61.

Colozzi, G.A., Ward, L.W., & Crotty, K.E. (2008). Comparison of simultaneous prompting procedure in 1:1 and small group instruction to teach play skills to preschool students with pervasive developmental disorder and developmental disabilities. *Education and Training in Developmental Disabilities, 43,* 226–248.

Cromer, K., Schuster, J.W., Collins, B.C., & Grisham-Brown, J. (1998). Teaching information on medical prescriptions using two instructive feedback schedules. *Journal of Behavioral Education, 8,* 37–61.

Demchak, M. (1989). A comparison of graduated guidance and increasing assistance in teaching adults with severe handicaps leisure skills. *Education and Training in Developmental Disabilities, 24*(1), 45–55.

Falkenstine, K.J., Collins, B.C., Schuster, J.W., & Kleinert, K. (2009). Presenting chained and discrete tasks as nontargeted information when teaching discrete academic skills through small group instruction. *Education and Training in Developmental Disabilities, 44,* 127–142.

Fickel, K.M., Schuster, J.W., & Collins, B.C. (1998). Teaching different tasks using different stimuli in a heterogeneous small group. *Journal of Behavioral Education, 8,* 219–244.

Fiscus, R., Schuster, J.W., Morse, T., & Collins, B.C. (2002). Teaching elementary students with cognitive disabilities food preparation skills while embedding instructive feedback in the prompt and consequent event. *Education and Training in Mental Retardation and Developmental Disabilities, 37,* 55–69.

Godby, S., Gast, D.L., & Wolery, M. (1987). A comparison of time delay and system of least prompts in teaching object identification. *Research in Developmental Disabilities, 8,* 283–306.

Jones, G.Y., & Collins, B.C. (1997). Teaching microwave skills to adults with disabilities: Acquisition of nutrition and safety facts presented as non-targeted information. *Journal of Physical and Developmental Disabilities, 9,* 59–78.

McDonnell, J., Johnson, J.W., Polychronis, S., Riesen, T., Jameson, J., & Kercher, K. (2006). Comparison of one-to-one embedded instruction in general education classes with small group instruction in special education classes. *Education and Training in Developmental Disabilities, 41,* 125–138.

Roark, T.J., Collins, B.C., Hemmeter, M.L., & Kleinert, H. (2002). Including manual signing as nontargeted information when using a constant time delay procedure to teach receptive identification of packaged food items. *Journal of Behavioral Education, 11,* 19–38.

Schuster, J.W., Griffen, A.K., & Wolery, M. (1992). Comparison of the simultaneous prompting and constant time delay procedures in teaching sight words to elementary students with moderate mental retardation to select lower priced grocery items. *Education and Training in Mental Retardation, 27,* 219–229.

Smith, B.R., Schuster, J.W., Collins, B.C., & Kleinert, H. (2011). Using simultaneous prompting to teach restaurant words and classifications as non-target information to secondary students with moderate to severe disabilities. *Education and Training in Autism and Developmental Disabilities, 46*(2), 251–266.

Smith, R.L., Collins, B.C., Schuster, J.W., & Kleinert, H. (1999). Teaching table cleaning skills to secondary students with moderate/severe disabilities: Measuring observational learning during downtime. *Education and Training in Mental Retardation and Developmental Disabilities, 34,* 342–353.

Spooner, F., Browder, D.M., & Mims, P.J. (2011). Evidence-based practices. In D.M. Browder & F. Spooner (Eds.), *Teaching students with moderate and severe disabilities* (pp. 92–122). New York, NY: Guilford.

Stonecipher, E.L., Schuster, J.W., Collins, B.C., & Grisham-Brown, J. (1999). Teaching gift wrapping skills in a quadruple instructional arrangement using constant time delay. *Journal of Developmental and Physical Disabilities, 11*, 139–158.

Taylor, P., Collins, B.C., Schuster, J.W., & Kleinert, H. (2002). Teaching laundry skills to high school students with disabilities: Generalization of targeted skills and nontargeted information. *Education and Training in Mental Retardation and Developmental Disabilities, 37*, 172–183.

Tekin-Iftar, E., & Birkan, B. (2010). Small group instruction for students with autism. *Journal of Special Education, 44*, 50–63.

Werts, M.G., Hoffman, E.M., & Darcy, C. (2011). Acquisition of instructive feedback: Relation to target stimulus. *Education and Training in Autism and Developmental Disabilities, 46*(1), 134–149.

Werts, M.G., Wolery, M., Holcombe, A., & Gast, D.L. (1995). Instructive feedback: Review of parameters and effects. *Journal of Behavioral Education, 5*(1), 55–75.

Westling, D.L., & Fox, L. (2009). *Teaching students with severe disabilities* (4th ed.). Upper Saddle River, NJ: Pearson.

Wolery, M., Ault, M.J., & Doyle, P.M. (1992). *Teaching students with moderate to severe disabilities.* New York, NY: Longman.

Wolery, T.D., Schuster, J.W., & Collins, B.C. (2000). Effects of future learning of presenting non-target stimuli in antecedent and consequent conditions. *Journal of Behavioral Education, 10*, 77–94.

Using Naturalistic Language Strategies

CHAPTER 6

CHAPTER OBJECTIVES

On completion of this chapter, the reader will be able to

- Describe the characteristics of naturalistic language strategies
- List and provide examples of strategies to enhance to the environment to facilitate communication
- Describe and perform the steps of a naturalistic modeling procedure to facilitate communication
- Describe and perform the steps of a naturalistic mand-model procedure to facilitate communication
- Describe and perform the steps of a naturalistic incidental-teaching procedure to facilitate communication
- Describe and perform the steps of a naturalistic time-delay procedure to facilitate communication
- Design a data sheet for facilitating communication with a naturalistic modeling, mand-model, incidental-teaching, or time-delay procedure
- Graph and analyze formative data collected when facilitating communication with a naturalistic modeling, mand-model, incidental-teaching, or time-delay procedure
- Discriminate between the various purposes for using each of the four naturalistic language strategies

TERMS USED IN THIS CHAPTER

naturalistic language strategies	mand-model procedure
milieu strategies	incidental-teaching procedure
modeling procedure	naturalistic time-delay procedure

So far, the chapters in this book have focused on strategies to increase the acquisition of functional skills and core content using systematic response-prompting procedures. This chapter presents additional response-prompting strategies, but the focus is on instruction to increase communication skills in students with moderate and severe disabilities. These strategies are considered naturalistic because they occur when opportunities arise within ongoing activities throughout the day. Although it is best for naturalistic strategies to be used across settings by school personnel, families, and others involved in the lives of learners, the examples presented in this chapter focus on implementing **naturalistic language strategies** in school settings.

NATURALISTIC LANGUAGE STRATEGIES

Naturalistic language strategies also are known as **milieu strategies.** These strategies have several characteristics (Browder, Spooner, & Mims, 2011; Collins, 2007; Downing, 2011; Westling & Fox, 2009; Wolery, Ault, & Doyle, 1992). First, they occur in natural activities in natural environments. Next, they are embedded through the day whenever opportunities arise to use language. Trials are delivered according to the interests of the learner rather than being dictated by the instructor. Each trial is brief in length and is followed by a natural consequence that is reinforcing to the learner. To increase the number of opportunities for trials, the environment can be set up or arranged to facilitate the need for communication. The form of communication is open and can include verbal language, manual signing, or the use of augmentative communication technology. Finally, there are several types of naturalistic strategies, each with a different purpose, but all can be interchanged from trial to trial, if desired. The following sections describe how to implement naturalistic language strategies.

Environmental Arrangement

The more reasons that a learner has to communicate, the more opportunities there are for the instructor to deliver instructional trials. There are several ways to arrange the environment to create opportunities to communicate (Downing, 2011). Enhanced milieu teaching consists of the combination of environmental arrangements with naturalistic or milieu response-prompting strategies and communicative partners (Hemmeter & Kaiser, 1994). One environmental arrangement is to limit the necessary materials for an activity. During snack, the instructor can have too few cookies for the class, creating an opportunity for the learner to have to ask for a cookie. Likewise, the instructor could have too few crayons or balls of clay during an art activity or too few toys during recess. If there are enough materials, these can be within eyesight but out of reach of the learner who is targeted to communicate, thus creating another opportunity for the learner to communicate. Novel materials can create the desire to communicate. Adding a new art material, such as a marker in a neon color or with a scent, can create an opportunity for the learner to ask for the material. Rotating the toys available for recess also can create the desire to request the new item. When possible, instructors can provide choices for learners and allow them to communicate their choices in the desired way. Examples might include making selections from three entrees available for lunch or making selections when given opportunities in daily schedules (e.g., "Would you like to do math or reading first?" "Would you like to work on addition or subtraction?" "Would you like to count bears or monkeys?" "Would you like to write your answers on a worksheet or type them on the computer?"). Another way to provide an opportunity to communicate is to interrupt an ongoing activity. For example, the instructor may be playing ball with a learner at recess (a preferred activity) and stop the activity after several tosses of the ball until the learner communicates the desire for the activity to continue. Finally, the instructor can create "silly opportunities" for communication to occur, such as putting the learner's gloves on the wrong hands or the learner's jacket on backwards until the learner communicates the error. Two or more of these strategies for arranging the environment can be used in together, as illustrated in the following scenario.

At snack time, Charles's instructor adds pink lemonade as a new option for a drink and places the container on a shelf where it can be seen. When Charles communicates that he would like a drink, he is given a choice between yellow and pink lemonade. When the choice is made, the instructor makes the lemonade, places a cup upside down in front of Charles, and waits to pour until Charles communicates what is wrong. With the cup right side up, the instructor only pours a small amount into the cup, creating the need for Charles to request more. The instructor lays several brightly colored curly-shaped straws on the table out of Charles's reach. If Charles wants a straw, he must request it as well as indicate which color. Once Charles has the cup, the straw, and enough lemonade, he is reinforced by getting to consume the drink.

Milieu Strategies

There are four specific milieu or naturalistic language strategies (Browder et al., 2011; Collins, 2007; Downing, 2011; Westling & Fox, 2009; Wolery et al., 1992). These are described in the following sections.

Modeling

The **modeling procedure** is appropriate when an instructor is teaching a new form of communication to a learner. For example, the goal may be to teach a learner to ask for a drink rather than crying to indicate being thirsty. The instructional trial is simple:

1. Wait until the learner's focus indicates the need to communicate (e.g., Learner is looking at a new ball on a high shelf before going outside for recess).

2. According to the learner's interest, model the response that the learner should make. (e.g., Instructor takes the ball from the shelf and models the word *ball*).

3. Wait a set number of seconds for the learner to imitate the target response (e.g., 5 seconds).

4. Reinforce the learner for making the target response (e.g., Instructor says, "Yes! This is a ball!" while handing the ball to the learner).

Note that the instructor will give the ball to the learner even if the attempt to verbally communicate is only an approximation of the target response (e.g., "Baaa") or even if the child fails to verbally communicate. There will be many opportunities to repeat the procedure,

MODELING DATA SHEET

Name: ___Carolyn___   Instructor: ___Mr. Morris___
Target skill: ___Greeting peers___

Trials	Date				
	September 14	September 15	September 16	September 17	September 18
1. Homeroom	+			+	+
2. Language arts	+	+	+	+	+
3. Science		+		+	+
4. Math				+	+
5. Lunch		+	+		
6. P.E.			+		+
7. Art	+	+			+
8. Community-based instruction	+	+			+
9. Social studies		+		+	+
10. Departure			+	+	+
Total/%	4/40%	6/60%	4/40%	6/60%	9/90%

Key: Plus sign indicates correct response.

Figure 6.1.   Sample completed data sheet for the modeling procedure.

and the intent is not to punish a learner by withholding the ball for failure to communicate but, rather, to reinforce all forms of communication, including eye gaze. Over time, communication can be shaped by praising successive approximations of the desired response and continuing to model the response for the learner.

Data collection is simple with the modeling procedure. The instructor records a plus sign if the learners imitates an acceptable response. If desired, the instructor also can record a minus sign if the response is not acceptable and a zero if the learner fails to make any response. A sample completed data sheet is shown in Figure 6.1. The number or percent of correct responses is recorded on the graph.

Mand-Model

The **mand-model procedure** (e.g., Bourett, Vollmer, & Rapp, 2004; Hemmeter, Ault, Collins, & Meyer, 1996; Mobayed, Collins, Strangis, Schuster, & Hemmeter, 2000; Murphy & Holmes, 2009) builds on the model procedure by facilitating independent communicative initiations by the learner. Note that *mand* is the term used for telling a learner what is expected and can be perceived as a basic form of a command or demand; an example of a simple mand is, "Tell me what you want." The steps include the following:

1. Wait until the learner's focus indicates the need to communicate (e.g., Learner is waiting for a drink to be served at snack time).

2. If the learner initiates a correct response, reinforce the learner (e.g., Instructor says, "Yes! You can have a drink!" while pouring a cup of lemonade for the learner).

3. If the learner's focus signals an opportunity for an instructional trial and the learner has failed to initiate a response, provide a mand to cue the learner to communicate (e.g., Instructor holds a pitcher of lemonade in front of the learner and says, "Tell me what you want").

4. Wait a set number of seconds for the learner to provide the target response (e.g., 3 seconds).

5. Reinforce the learner if the target response is made (e.g., Instructor says, "Yes! You can have a drink!" while pouring a cup of lemonade for the learner).

6. If the learner fails to respond or responds incorrectly, model the response for the learner (e.g., "Tell me 'drink'").

7. Wait a set number of seconds for the learner to imitate the target response (e.g., 3 seconds).

8. Reinforce the learner if the target response is made (e.g., Instructor says, "Yes! Drink!" while pouring a cup of lemonade for the learner).

As with the modeling procedure, the instructor gives a drink to the learner after the model regardless of whether the correct response has been made. By pouring small amounts of lemonade in the cup at a time, there can be several opportunities to repeat trials of either the model or the mand-model procedures.

Data are recorded by indicating beneath a labeled column on the data sheet whether the learner initiated a response, responded following a mand, or responded following a model. A sample completed data sheet is shown in Figure 6.2. The number or percent of correct initiations is recorded on the graph. If desired, the number or percent of correct response to mands and models also can be recorded on the graph.

Incidental Teaching

The **incidental-teaching procedure** (e.g., Hemmeter et al., 1996) is used when a learner is communicating in a basic way (e.g., single words or signs), and the goal is to expand the breadth of communication. For example, the goal may be to go from a single word utterance to linking together several words in a sequence. This may include adding adjective, verbs, or nouns. This can done through the following steps:

1. Wait until the learner initiates the desired form of communication (e.g., during lunch, learner says, "Apple").

2. Model the desired expansion (e.g., Instructor says, "Red apple").

3. Wait a set number of seconds for the learner to imitate the response (e.g., 3 seconds).

4. Reinforce the learner if the target response is made (e.g., Instructor says, "Yes! Red apple!" and gives learner a slice of apple).

Once the learner is independently using the desired expansion (e.g., "Red apple"), the instructor can slowly expand the desired response (e.g., "Want red apple"; "Want red apple, please"; "I want red apple, please") over time. Note that numerous trials can occur during

MAND-MODEL DATA SHEET

Name: ___Judy_____   Date: ___September 20_____
Instructor: ___Mr. and Mrs. Wilder___   Target response: ___More___

Opportunities to respond	Imitation	Mand	Model
1. Play			–
2. Play			0
3. Play		+	
4. Play		+	
5. Play			–
6. Snack			+
7. Snack	+		
8. Snack			0
9. Snack			+
10. Snack	+		
11. Play	+		
12. Play			–
13. Play			0
14. Play	+		
15. Play	+		
Number correct	5	2	2
Number incorrect			3
Number no response			3

Key: Plus sign indicates correct response; minus sign indicates incorrect response; zero indicates no response.

Figure 6.2.   Sample completed data sheet for the mand-model procedure.

a single activity and that the learner receives the reinforcer (e.g., slice of apple) regardless of whether the response is made.

The instructor will record data throughout the day on the expansions on initiations made by the learner. The instructor will record a plus sign under a column to show if the learner initiated an expansion before a model or imitated an expansion after a model. The instructor also can record a minus sign if the learner made an incorrect expansion or a zero if the learner failed to imitate an expansion after a model. A sample completed data sheet is shown in Figure 6.3. Initiated expansions will be recorded on the graph. Graphing correct imitations is optional.

Naturalistic Time Delay

The final milieu procedure, **naturalistic time delay** (e.g., Grunsell & Carter, 2002; Miller, Collins, & Hemmeter, 2002), combines a naturalistic procedure for communication with the time-delay procedure previously described in Chapter 4. This procedure can be effec-

INCIDENTAL-TEACHING DATA SHEET

Name: _Danny_   Instructor: _Ms. Prater_

Target skill: _Adding an adjective to a request_

Trials	April 8 B	April 8 A	April 9 B	April 9 A	April 10 B	April 10 A	April 11 B	April 11 A	April 12 B	April 12 A
1. Homeroom	+			+	+		+		+	
2. Language arts		+	+			+		+	+	
3. Science	+		+		+		+			+
4. Math		+	+		+			+		+
5. Lunch	+			+		+	+		+	
6. P.E.		+	+			+		+		+
7. Art	+			+	+		+		+	
8. Community-based instruction		+		+		+		+	+	
9. Social studies	+			+		+	+			+
10. Departure		+		+	+		+		+	
Total	5	5	4	6	5	5	6	4	6	4
%	50%	50%	40%	60%	50%	50%	60%	40%	60%	40%

Key: Plus sign indicates elaboration on response before or after model.

Figure 6.3. Sample completed data sheet for the incidental-teaching procedure.

tive in facilitating a generalized response because it requires the learner to practice using acquired communicative responses during ongoing activities when communication is needed. The steps are as follows:

1. Interrupt an ongoing activity when there is an opportunity to require the learner to communicate (e.g., Instructor closes sketch book or removes crayons when learner is coloring a picture during art class).

2. Insert a delay interval by waiting a set number of seconds for the learner to make a communicative response (e.g., 3 seconds).

3. Reinforce the learner if the target response is made (e.g., Instructor says, "Good job requesting! Here are the crayons you need").

4. If no response, provide a model prompt (e.g., Instructor says, "Tell me, 'I need my crayons'").

5. Reinforce the learner if the target response is made (e.g., Instructor says, "Excellent! Here are your crayons").

In selecting a delay interval, the instructor may use a progressive time-delay (PTD) procedure, beginning with a 0-second delay interval and slowly increasing the delay interval over time (e.g., 0, 1, 2, and 3 seconds). The instructor also may choose to use a constant time-delay (CTD) procedure, beginning with a 0-second delay interval and then moving to a set delay interval (e.g., 3 seconds). As with the other milieu procedures, the instructor provides the reinforcer after a set number of seconds regardless of whether the learner has made the desired communicative response (e.g., Instructor gives crayons to learner and allows learner to continue coloring).

Data are collected in the same manner as with the CTD or PTD procedures. A plus sign is recorded for correct responses, a minus sign is recorded for incorrect responses, or a zero is recorded for no response after the prompt under a column marked *before* or *after* the prompt. In addition, the data are graphed in the same manner at time-delay data (see Figure 4.2 in Chapter 4). A sample completed data sheet is shown with the second instructional program in this chapter.

SAMPLE INSTRUCTIONAL PROGRAMS

Increasing communication skills may be an appropriate target of instruction for learners of all ages with moderate and severe disabilities. The following examples illustrate how milieu strategies can be used with young learners as well as with adolescents nearing transition to adulthood. The examples also illustrate how milieu strategies can be implemented by professionals as well as by parents. It is important to remember that implementing strategies to increase communication is most effective when the strategies are implemented consistently across settings.

Sample Instructional Program 1

The first sample instructional program employs a mand-model procedure implemented by parents of a preschool child and monitored by a home interventionist. The procedures are based on a research study conducted by Mobayed et al. (2000).

Core Content Standards

Practical Living/ Vocational

- Students will identify effective social interaction skills (e.g., identifying emotions, listening, cooperation, etiquette, politeness, communication, sharing, empathy, following directions, and making friends) that promote responsible and respectful behavior.
- Students will identify strategies for stress management, problem solving, conflict resolution, and communication (e.g., self-control, work and play collaboration, caring, reconciling, asking for help, active listening).

Behavioral Objective

Across activities in the home, Judy will independently initiate a verbal request for *more* when appropriate opportunities arise for 5 days.

Instructional Context

Whereas the parent may implement the milieu strategy to facilitate verbal requests across activities in the home, the following activities will be designated for creating opportunities to communicate and for collecting data on the number of independent initiations: 1) when playing with toys in the living room and 2) when eating a snack or meal in the dining area (e.g., kitchen, dining room).

Instructional Materials

The play area in the living room will be equipped with a variety of preferred age-appropriate toys that are made up of several parts (e.g., a train with several cars, a set of blocks, a Mr. Potato Head game, a jar of bubbles). The dining area will be stocked with a variety of preferred food items that can be served in small portions (e.g., raw vegetables, crackers, milk or juice, macaroni, pieces of fruit).

Instructional Procedure

Each instructional session will proceed as follows.

Attentional Cue	• The parent will begin the play session or meal by presenting toys or food to gain Judy's attention. Once Judy is attending, the parent will allow Judy to sample the materials (e.g., play with a toy for a few seconds or take a small bite of the food).
Mand-Model Procedure	• If the parent sees Judy looking at the material or trying to access the material (e.g., opening mouth for more food, reaching for toy) and Judy does not initiate a verbal request for *more,* the parent will provide a mand (i.e., "Tell me what you want"). If Judy does not request *more* within 3 seconds of the mand, the parent will provide a model (i.e., "Tell me, 'More'"). If Judy does not request *more* within 3 seconds of the model, the parent will provide access to the material and then wait a few minutes for Judy to initiate another trial by looking at or trying to access more of the material.

Consequence

The natural consequence of requesting *more* is to receive access to the material. This can be accompanied by parental feedback, such as smiling, hugging, and/or saying, "Good job!" If Judy makes an error by making an inappropriate verbal response, the parent will correct the response (e.g., "No, this is not a dog—tell me, 'More'"). If Judy indicates that more is not desired (e.g., pushes away food or toy), the parent can try a new material or end the session. If necessary, the parent can choose to shape a response of "more" by reinforcing successive approximations (e.g., "mmm…," "mo…," "more") over time.

Nontargeted Information

Although nontargeted information is not required, the parent may model an expanded response during the consequence. For example, the parent might say, "Good job saying 'more'! Here is 'more cracker.'"

Data Collection

The parent will record a plus sign for correct initiations and correct responses to mands or models under the appropriate column on the data sheet. If there is an incorrect or no response following a model, the parent will record a zero under the appropriate column. A sample completed data sheet is shown in Figure 6.2.

Maintenance

Once Judy consistently initiates *more* across opportunities for 1 day, the parent will fade praise for responses to an average of every three initiations (i.e., variable ratio of 3, or VR3) for 4 days.

Generalization

Generalization is facilitated by using a variety of toys and foods during instructional sessions in the natural environments of the living room and the dining area. Once Judy is consistently initiating requests during these activities, the parent can provide novel toys or foods. In addition, the parent can provide opportunities to make requests in other activities, such as playing with bath toys in the bathroom or playing with outdoor play equipment (e.g., swings, balls, sandbox toys) in the backyard. The parent also might embed opportunities to make requests during rough and tumble play that Judy enjoys.

Behavior Management

Appropriate behavior will be facilitated by providing preferred items Judy desires during sessions. If behavior indicates that Judy is no longer reinforced by these items (e.g., spits out food, throws toy), the session can be terminated.

Lesson Variations and Extension

The mand-model procedure described in this instructional program also can be implemented by others in the home, including siblings and other caregivers. For older learners, the procedure can be implemented in school settings. Appropriate activities might include snack time or lunchtime or playtime in the classroom (e.g., playing games, reading stories, listening to music) or on the playground (e.g., jumping rope, riding seesaw). The procedure also can be implemented during instructional activities (e.g., art activity, science experiment, computer work). The key is to identify activities in which a learner prefers to engage and to embed as many trials as possible by limiting the amount of materials or the length of access to a material.

Sample Instructional Program 2

The second sample instructional program for facilitating communication with a milieu strategy is conducted in a high school across activities and settings. In this program, the instructor is preparing a learner without verbal communication skills to make the transition to a vocational facility at which a standard intelligible form of communication will be needed. Thus, the instructor has decided to teach the learner several manual signs that will be of use in the vocational facility as well as in the home setting. The learner currently has a repertoire of several basic manual signs (e.g., EAT, PLEASE, SORRY, SWIM, DRINK) but most often communicates through behavior (e.g., tugging at person's arm) and gestures (e.g., pointing). The instructor has selected a naturalistic time-delay procedure in which both mands and models will be delivered across selected activities to facilitate the use of specific manual signs. The procedures are based on a research study conducted by Miller et al. (2002).

Core Content Standards

Practical Living/   •   Students demonstrate skills and work habits that lead to success in
Vocational   future schooling and work.

Behavioral Objective

Across activities and school settings, Leon will use targeted manual signs to communicate basic needs for 5 days.

Instructional Context

The instructor has identified activities across school settings in which Leon uses behavior or gestures to communicate basic needs. The instructor has targeted three manual signs for initial instruction. These include 1) making the manual sign for TICKET to request the tickets that are given on completion of independent classroom assignments in the token economy that is part of Leon's behavior management program, 2) making the manual sign for MONEY to request money to pay for his lunch in the cafeteria, and 3) making the manual sign for FREE TIME to request leisure time in the resource room when he cashes in his tickets at the end of the day. Once Leon is using these manual signs consistently to indicate basic needs, the instructor will add three additional manual signs and will continue in this pattern throughout the school year.

Instructional Materials

Instruction on requesting tickets will take place across the classes (both in the general education classroom and in the resource room) that Leon attends. Instruction on requesting money will take place in the cafeteria. Instruction on requesting free time will take place in the resource room at the end of the day.

Instructional Procedure

Each instructional session will proceed as follows.

Attentional   •   When there is an opportunity for Leon to communicate a request with
Cue   one of the targeted manual signs, the instructor will interrupt the activity and establish eye contact with Leon to initiate each instructional trial.

Naturalistic   •   The instructor will conduct trials in the following manner. When Leon
Time-Delay   completes an independent assignment and turns it in to the instructor, he
Procedure   will stand in front of Leon with the ticket in hand and will wait 4 seconds for him to make the manual sign to request the ticket. If Leon fails to make the manual sign, the instructor will give the mand, "What do you want?" and will wait 4 more seconds for a response. If Leon still fails to make the manual sign, the instructor will model the response and will wait 4 more seconds for a response. If Leon still fails to make the manual response, the instructor will give him the ticket. This will be repeated each time Leon is

to receive a ticket for completed work across settings. The same trial sequence will happen at lunch in the cafeteria; when Leon goes through line, selects his lunch items, and then goes to the cashier, the instructor will stand in front of the cashier and wait for Leon to make the manual sign to request money to pay for his lunch. The trial sequence will be repeated on each occasion that Leon needs money to pay for food (cafeteria, school store, community). The same trial sequence will be repeated again at the end of the day in the resource room when Leon turns in his tickets for leisure activities and the instructor takes a ticket but waits for Leon to make the manual sign to request free time. The trial sequence will be repeated each time he turns in a ticket to engage in a different leisure activity for a set number of minutes.

Consequence • Although the natural consequence for making the correct manual sign will be to receive access to the item requested (i.e., ticket, money, or leisure activity), the instructor also will provide praise for correct responses. Even if Leon does not make the correct sign, he will receive access to the item because the procedure is not meant to be punitive.

Nontargeted Information

The inclusion of nontargeted information is not part of the procedure in this instructional program.

Data Collection

Data will be collected as in the time-delay procedure with a plus sign for a correct response before or after the prompt, a minus sign for an incorrect response before or after the prompt, and a zero for no response after the prompt. In the instructional program, the prompt is the mand model. A sample completed data sheet is shown in Figure 6.4.

Maintenance

Once Leon consistently initiates the targeted manual signs across opportunities for 5 days, the instructor will discontinue instruction but continue to monitor use of manual signs at periodic intervals for up to 6 weeks.

Generalization

Generalization is facilitated by teaching the use of manual signs in natural settings within ongoing activities. The instructor will monitor generalization by checking to see whether Leon also is using the manual signs across settings (e.g., at home, during community-based instruction, at the YMCA), across activities (e.g., vocational work jobs, lunch, swimming, cooking), and across people (e.g., general education teachers, peers, family members, paraprofessionals).

Behavior Management

Appropriate behavior will be facilitated by teaching Leon to use manual signs as an appropriate form of communication in place of the inappropriate form of behavior (e.g., pushing, shoving, hitting) that he currently uses to communicate.

NATURALISTIC TIME-DELAY DATA SHEET

Name: Leon   Instructor: Mr. Davis   Date: January 3

Trials	Setting: Classes — Before	Response: Ticket — After	Setting: Cafeteria — Before	Response: Money — After	Setting: Resource room — Before	Response: Free time — After
1.	+		+			0
2.		0	+			+
3.		+		−	+	
4.		−		0	+	
5.	+			+		−
6.	−			−	+	
7.	+		+			+
8.	+		−			−
9.		−	+		+	
10.	−		+		−	
	Data summary for day					
	Total/% correct before	13/43%		Total/% correct after	4/13%	

Key: Plus sign indicates correct response; minus sign indicates incorrect response; zero indicates no response.

Figure 6.4. Sample completed data sheet for the naturalistic time-delay procedure.

Lesson Variations and Extension

The naturalistic time-delay procedure described in this instructional program also can be implemented by others in the home, including siblings and caregivers. In particular, it should be taught to supervisors in the vocational setting in which the learner is preparing to transition following school. The number of manual signs taught can be expanded over time. In addition, manual signs can be added to create more complex communication, such as using PLEASE, indicating the specific amount of money (e.g., FIVE DOLLARS), or providing the name of the leisure activity (e.g., PLAY GAME, WORK ON COMPUTER). The same procedure can be used for younger learners during ongoing activities, such as snack time, recess, or special classes (e.g., art, music, physical education). Although this instructional program used manual signing as the targeted mode of communication, the procedure is appropriate with any desired form of communication, such as verbal speech or the use of a low-tech or high-tech augmentative and alternative communication device. Again, the key is to identify activities that are reinforcing to the learner and in which the learner is likely to want to communicate to continue the activity.

SUMMARY

This chapter presented naturalistic (milieu) strategies to facilitate communication that included 1) modeling, 2) mand-model, 3) naturalistic time delay, and 4) incidental teaching. Each of these procedures can be enhanced by manipulating the environment in which the learner is to communicate. Although specific periods for data collection may be identified, the procedures should be embedded in activities throughout the day to increase the number of opportunities a learner has to respond. The procedures should be learner directed according to the interests of the learner, and responses should be naturally reinforced within activities. To maximize learning, procedures can be combined as appropriate. Flowcharts for using the four naturalistic language strategies can be found in Appendix A. Sample blank data sheets for each procedure can be found in Appendix B.

QUESTIONS FOR REFLECTION

1. Describe the four naturalistic prompting procedures. What is the purpose of each?

2. Describe ways that the environment can be enhanced to increase opportunities to respond.

3. What are some forms of communication that might be targeted for intervention?

4. How does teaching appropriate forms of communication decrease inappropriate behavior?

REFERENCES

Bourett, J.A., Vollmer, T.R., & Rapp, J.T. (2004). Evaluation of a vocal mand assessment and vocal mand training procedures. *Journal of Applied Behavior Analysis, 37*, 129–144.

Browder, D.M., Spooner, F., & Mims, P. (2011). Communication skills. In D.M. Browder & F. Spooner (Eds.), *Teaching students with moderate and severe disabilities* (pp. 262–282). New York, NY: Guilford.

Collins, B.C. (2007). *Moderate and severe disabilities: A foundational approach.* Upper Saddle River, NJ: Pearson, Merrill, Prentice-Hall.

Downing, J.E. (2011). Teaching communication skills. In M.E. Snell & F. Brown (Eds.), *Instruction of students with severe disabilities* (7th ed., pp. 461–491). Upper Saddle River, NJ: Pearson.

Grunsell, J., & Carter, M. (2002). The behavior chain interruption strategy: Generalization to out-of-routine contexts. *Education and Training in Mental Retardation and Developmental Disabilities, 37*, 378–390.

Hemmeter, M.L., Ault, M.J., Collins, B.C., & Meyer, S. (1996). The effects of teacher-implemented language instruction within free-time activities. *Education and Training in Mental Retardation and Developmental Disabilities, 31*, 203–212.

Hemmeter, M.L., & Kaiser, A.P. (1994). Enhanced milieu teaching: Effects of parent-implemented language intervention. *Journal of Early Intervention, 18*, 269–289.

Miller, C., Collins, B.C., & Hemmeter, M.L. (2002). Using a naturalistic time delay procedure to teach nonverbal adolescents with moderate-to-severe mental disabilities to initiate manual signs. *Journal of Developmental and Physical Disabilities, 14*, 247–261.

Mobayed, K.L., Collins, B.C., Strangis, D., Schuster, J.W., & Hemmeter, M.L. (2000). Teaching parents to employ mand-model procedures to teach their children requesting. *Journal of Early Intervention, 23*, 165–179.

Murphy, C., & Holmes, D.B. (2009). Derived more-less relational mands in children diagnosed with autism. *Journal of Applied Analysis, 42,* 253–268.

Westling, D.L., & Fox, L. (2009). *Teaching students with severe disabilities* (4th ed.). Upper Saddle River, NJ: Pearson.

Wolery, M., Ault, M.J., & Doyle, P.M. (1992). *Teaching students with moderate to severe disabilities.* New York, NY: Longman.

CHAPTER 7

Facilitating Maintenance and Generalization

On completion of this chapter, the reader will be able to

- Describe strategies that facilitate maintenance when using systematic instruction
- Explain the difference between a fixed ratio and a variable ratio schedule for delivering reinforcement during systematic instruction
- Explain the difference between stimulus and response generalization and provide examples of each
- List conditions across which generalization might be facilitated and assessed
- Describe consecutive and concurrent models of instruction and identify which might be more likely to result in generalization
- Describe strategies that facilitate generalization when using systematic instruction
- Distinguish between a multiple-exemplar approach and general case programming in facilitating generalization

TERMS USED IN THIS CHAPTER

natural reinforcers	multiple-exemplar approach	indiscriminable contingency
stimulus generalization	general case programming	concurrent model of instruction
response generalization	simulations	community-based instruction (CBI)
consecutive model of instruction	community-referenced instruction	in-vivo instruction

It does not matter how many skills learners acquire during instruction if the skills do not maintain or generalize. It never can be assumed that, just because a learner is able to perform a skill to criterion level under instructional conditions in the presence of the instructor, the learner also will be able to perform that skill over time once instruction has ended or that the learner will be able to perform that skill under novel conditions, such as in the presence of a different person, in a different setting, or with different materials.

As noted in Chapter 1, maintenance is the performance of a skill over time, and generalization is the performance of a skill under untrained conditions. At minimum, all instructors should ensure that skills maintain and generalize once criterion has been met and instruction has ended. Maintenance can be assessed by periodically requiring that a learner perform a skill over time. For example, vocabulary words that were mastered in a span of 3 weeks can be reassessed 1 week later, 3 weeks later, and then 6 weeks after that. If the learner is not maintaining the ability to read the words, then the words can be taught again. To assess generalization of the same vocabulary words, the special education teacher might ask the general education teacher to assess whether the learner can read the same words within the context of a general education class, this time as they appear in written text versus on the flashcards that were used for instruction in the resource room. If the learner does not demonstrate the ability to generalize, the general education teacher will need to take time to reteach the words as they appear in the text in the general education setting.

To decrease the need to reteach to ensure maintenance and generalization, instructors can apply several strategies during instruction that facilitate these phases of learning. The following sections describe those strategies.

STRATEGIES TO FACILITATE MAINTENANCE

There are a number of strategies that have been shown to have a positive effect on the maintenance of skills in learners with moderate and severe disabilities (Alberto & Troutman, 2009; Collins, 2007; Snell & Brown, 2011; Westling & Fox, 2009). The first strategy is to teach skills that are required in a learner's life across environments. In other words, there should be a functional or useful link to the real world. Skills should be taught in a way that learners will need to use them in the real world once instruction has ended. Likewise, learners should acquire knowledge that can be applied in real life once instruction has ended. For example, instruction on addition is a functional skill that can be used to count money to make purchases, to add deposits to a bank account, to determine how many people will be attending a meeting so that adequate materials and refreshments can be planned, to measure enough materials for a sewing or carpentry project, or to double a recipe when cooking for guests. Functional knowledge from science can be applied to functional life skills. For example, learning that the Earth rotates every 24 hours provides the basis for telling time and applying *a.m.* and *p.m.* in a correct manner, learning that genes are inherited from parents provides the basis for taking health precautions when a family has a history of diabetes or high blood pressure, and learning that plants require sunlight to thrive through photosynthesis provides the basis for placing house plants in a window and rotating them at intervals.

Another strategy for facilitating maintenance is to allow overlearning to occur. An instructor never should teach to criterion for 1 day and then stop. Requiring a minimum of three sessions of performance of a skill at criterion decreases the likelihood that a learner met criterion through guessing and builds a strong case that the learner has acquired the ability to perform the skill each and every time it is needed. One of the advantages of using a group criterion for learners before advancing to new units of instruction is that this provides the opportunity for overlearning by those who meet criterion ahead of other members of the group.

Continuing instruction on skills for several sessions once learners have met criterion also provides time for the instructor to thin the reinforcement provided during the consequence of each trial (Alberto & Troutman, 2009; Collins, 2007; Snell & Brown, 2011; Westling & Fox, 2009). The rationale for this is simple: When learners are required to use acquired skills in natural settings, it is rare that they will receive reinforcement. It is important to provide constant feedback on every single trial as a skill is being acquired because positive reinforcement, such as praise, increases the likelihood that a learner will again perform a skill correctly, and error correction decreases the likelihood that a learner will repeat an error. Thus, during the acquisition phase of learning, feedback should be provided at the end of every instructional trial. Once the learner meets criterion, maintenance can be facilitated by fading feedback to a more natural rate that reflects what is likely to occur in natural environments. This can be done in several ways: 1) through delivering a fixed ratio schedule of reinforcement or 2) through delivering a variable ratio schedule of reinforcement. For example, when a learner has met 100% criterion for 1 day, the instructor may decide to praise every other correct response for 2 days; this could be every other trial when presenting discrete tasks or every other step when presenting chained tasks. This schedule of reinforcement would be described as a fixed ratio of 2 (i.e., FR2). If the instructor then decides to delay reinforcement until the end of a session consisting of 10 trials or the end of a chained task consisting of 10 steps, the schedule of reinforcement would be described as a fixed ratio of 10 (i.e., FR10). Although a fixed ratio of reinforcement is simple for the instructor to remember, a variable ratio of reinforcement is a better reflection of the real world because it is likely that reinforcement in natural environments will be intermittent and sporadic. Thus, the instructor who decides to change to a variable schedule of reinforcement for 2 days once a learner meets criterion might decide to provide reinforcement on the average of every three trials for discrete tasks or every three steps for chained tasks (i.e., VR3). The instructor can provide a visual reminder to thin reinforcement by circling the trials to be reinforced in advance on the data sheet.

Just as it is important to use more natural schedules of reinforcement to facilitate maintenance, the instructor also should consider using **natural reinforcers** that are likely to be found in natural settings. Although the instructor may find it necessary to use tangible reinforcers during the acquisition phase of learning in order to motivate learners, these always should be paired with more natural reinforcers. The tangible reinforcers then can be faded when criterion is met. For example, an instructor who provides an edible, such as a piece of candy or cracker or a sip of a drink, always should pair this with natural reinforcers, such as praise, smiles, pats on the back, thumbs up, or high fives, because it is more likely that learners will encounter this type of feedback in natural settings when they perform an acquired skill.

Another way to manipulate reinforcement to facilitate maintenance in natural environments over time is to delay reinforcement. For example, instructors who provide points or tokens for correct performance during instruction and later allow learners to trade these for preferred items (e.g., colored pencils, fancy erasers) or activities (e.g., free time to look at a book or play a game) are mimicking the real world, in which most people receive pay for working that they can then spend in a way that they choose.

Although there are a number of ways to facilitate maintenance of skills, the only way to ensure that learners are maintaining what they have been taught is to conduct periodic probes over time in which learners are asked to perform targeted skills. If skills do not maintain, then the instructor can conduct review trials until learners again demonstrate criterion performance. As noted in Chapter 4, the simultaneous-prompting procedure requires that probe sessions occur before instruction rather than immediately after instruction to measure what learners maintain over time before determining whether further instruction is needed (Singleton, Schuster, Morse, & Collins, 1999). An example of a behavioral objective written to reflect maintenance is as follows:

> When it is time for lunch, Doug will prepare a sandwich by accurately performing the steps of the task analysis with 100% accuracy for 6 months once criterion has been met.

STRATEGIES TO FACILITATE GENERALIZATION

In considering the generalization phase of learning, the instructor needs to be aware of two types of generalization that may be the desired outcomes of instruction. **Stimulus generalization** occurs when a learner performs a consistent correct response to a class of stimuli (Alberto & Troutman, 2009; Collins, 2007; Snell & Brown, 2011; Westling & Fox, 2009). For example, if the teacher (Stimulus 1), the paraprofessional (Stimulus 2), or a peer (Stimulus 3) greets Jerry in the morning by saying, "Hello," Jerry would respond with a consistent correct response of replying, "Hello." If the instructor has taught Jerry to respond to each of these stimuli in the same manner over time, generalization can be ensured by exposing him to a novel untrained stimulus and waiting to see whether the correct response is performed. In this case, Jerry might demonstrate generalized responding by saying, "Hello," in response to a greeting of "Hello" from the school's principal (novel stimulus).

Response generalization occurs when a learner responds to a single stimulus with a group of correct responses, all within the same response class (Alberto & Troutman, 2009; Collins, 2007; Snell & Brown, 2011; Westling & Fox, 2009). For example, if the teacher says, "Hello," Jerry could respond by saying, "Hello" (Response 1), "Hi" (Response 2), or "How are you?" (Response 3). If the instructor has taught Jerry that it is appropriate to use any of these responses, generalization is ensured when the instructor hears him use a novel, untrained response from the same response class, such as saying, "Good morning" or "Good afternoon."

In the best of all worlds, learners will learn that a class of stimuli can result in a class of correct responses. Thus, the learner in the previous examples might use a variety of appropriate responses when greeted by a variety of people. Although it is clear that generalization is what makes a response functional or useful to learners across a variety of natural conditions, most learners with moderate and severe disabilities have difficulty acquiring generalized responses; thus, it is necessary for instructors to use strategies to facilitate generalization during instruction or at least to test to determine whether generalization has occurred before discontinuing instruction.

It is important that generalization be assessed and facilitated across a number of conditions. These include generalization across 1) individuals (e.g., reading the same words presented by a teacher, a paraprofessional, a peer, a school administrator, or a parent), 2) materials (e.g., reading the same words written in different fonts, colors, or sizes), 3) settings (e.g., reading the same words in the general education setting, the resource room, the school office, the community, or at home), 4) times of day (e.g., reading the same words when arriving at school and when leaving school), and 5) activities (e.g., reading the same words presented during story time, a game, or an experiment).

Rather than use instructional strategies to facilitate generalization, instructors often employ a sequential or **consecutive model of instruction** that is known as "train and hope." In other words, they provide instruction in the educational setting until a learner reaches criterion and then move on, assuming that the learner will be able to apply what has been taught across activities in natural settings. Often, no one even assesses the skill for generalization once it has been taught.

The best way to facilitate generalization is through careful selection of instructional materials and through careful planning of instruction. The professional research has shown that teaching with multiple exemplars is more likely to result in generalization than teaching with a single exemplar (e.g., Collins & Griffen, 1996; Dogoe, Banda, Lock, & Feinstein, 2011; Smith, Collins, Schuster, & Kleinert, 1999; Taylor, Collins, Schuster, & Kleinert, 2002). The simplest model for using multiple exemplars is to teach in a sequence, presenting a single example until a learner reaches criterion and then assessing for generalization. If generalization fails to occur, the instructor teaches with another exemplar until the learner reaches criterion and again assesses generalization. This sequence of "teach, test, teach, test, teach, test" continues until the learner finally demonstrates generalization under a novel condition. For example, the instructor may present community words written on flashcards to criterion and then ask the learner to identify the same words in the natural environment. If the learner fails to generalize, the instructor would return to the classroom and teach with a new set of flashcards, possibly from photographs of the words as they appear in the community; when criterion is reached with the new set of flashcards, the instructor would again assess the ability of the learner to identify the words in the community. It is obvious that this sequential model could take a long time before the learner finally demonstrates generalization under natural conditions.

A better method is to use a **multiple-exemplar approach,** or to teach with more than one exemplar at a time. For example, the instructor might vary the way words or math facts appear on flashcards. The flashcards can vary in color or size. The letters or numbers on the flashcards can vary in font, color, and size. Math facts can be written horizontally or vertically. This variation in materials teaches the learner to attend to the relevant characteristics of the stimulus, such as the sequence of the letters in the word or the sequence of the numbers in the problem, rather than on the characteristics of the stimulus that are not relevant. To ensure that generalization has occurred, the instructor tests with novel stimuli once criterion has been reached (e.g., words or math facts written on a worksheet). Although teaching with multiple exemplars may cause initial instruction to criterion to take longer, the resulting generalization causes this strategy to be more efficient than teaching with one exemplar at a time in sequence. It should be noted that the use of multiple exemplars is not limited to materials but also can include teaching across settings, instructors, activities, and times of day.

Whereas the use of multiple exemplars is likely to result in generalization, the selection of the exemplars for instruction can determine the extent to which a learner generalizes. **General case programming** (Alberto & Troutman, 2009; Collins, 2007; Lerman, 1996; Snell & Brown, 2011; Westling & Fox, 2009) is a strategy designed to increase the likelihood that a learner will be able to perform a skill under a broader array of conditions. Although general case instruction may be more time consuming to design, the outcome for learners who have difficulty with generalization can make it worthwhile. In general case programming, stimuli or instructional conditions are selected that sample the range that the learner may encounter when performing a skill. Once the instructor identifies the entire universe of possible exemplars, a minimum number that sample the range are selected for instruction. The effectiveness of teaching with a general case approach has been validated in classic research investigations by Horner and colleagues. In one study (Day & Horner, 1986), the researchers found that a learner who was taught to put on examples of shirts that sampled the range of possibilities (i.e., v-neck, crew neck, turtleneck; long sleeve, short sleeve, no sleeve; heavy weight, light weight) could put on an array of novel shirts not used in training. In another study (Horner, Jones, & Williams, 1985), the researchers found that learners who were taught to cross streets on a route that sampled the range of possibilities (i.e., two-lane, four-lane; stop light, crosswalk; one-way, two-way) could safely cross an array of novel streets not used in training. In the classroom, the instructor might employ general case programming by considering the range of stimuli of sight words that may be possible in selecting instructional materials (e.g., flashcards, community signs, books; dark letters, brightly colored letters; standard font, boldfaced, italics). In teaching core content, the instructor might teach the life cycles of amphibians, mammals, and insects or mix solutions made of sugar, salt, and powder. In building concepts, the instructor might provide a range of shades from the spectrum to teach the colors red, blue, or yellow. The instructor also may find it necessary to throw in nonexamples, such as teaching that pink and orange are not shades of red.

In addition to teaching with multiple exemplars, another way to facilitate generalization during classroom instruction is to teach in **simulations** with natural cues and materials that reflect the conditions in which the learner will be expected to perform the tasks that have been taught (Branham, Collins, Schuster, & Kleinert, 1999; Collins, Stinson, & Land, 1993; Mechling & Gast, 2003; Nietupski, Hamre-Nietupski, Clancy, & Veerhusen, 1986). The use of realistic items in conjunction with natural cues when teaching skills is known as using *common stimuli* because they reflect what the learner will encounter in the community. This type of format is known as **community-referenced instruction** because, although it occurs in a classroom setting, it reflects community variables to the extent possible (e.g., Colyer & Collins, 1996). For example, community-referenced instruction might consist of using real coins and bills to teach money, real price tags to determine prices and compute sales tax, real labels to teach the identification of words found on products, or real foods that can be divided into halves, thirds, or quarters. In providing cues, the instructor should attend to how stimuli are presented in the community. For example, an instructor who is teaching the next dollar strategy in the classroom might provide Beverly with a wallet or purse containing dollar bills. The instructor would stand in front of Beverly and ask her to select an item to order from a fast food menu ("Can I take your order, please?"). When Beverly has indicated a choice, the instructor would state the price as it would be heard in the community (e.g., "That will be three twenty-five"). While standing, Beverly would remove dollars bills from the wallet or purse and count them while laying them on the table in front of the instructor (i.e., "One, two, three dollars and one for change"). The instructor would thank Beverly, take the money, and return the change to her. Beverly would then put the change in the wallet or purse to end the instructional trial. If more than one learner is involved in the instruction, both would stand in line, one behind the other, as they awaited their turns. In other words, it is important to teach in what is known as an **indiscriminable contingency,** a type of instruction in which the variables in instruction are so similar to the variables in the natural environment that the learner cannot discriminate the difference.

Ideally, realistic simulations will take place in a **concurrent model of instruction,** in which learners are receiving instruction in the classroom as well as in the community. When classroom simulations are the only option for instruction, however, it is imperative that the instructor test for generalization in the natural setting (e.g., fast food restaurant) once criterion in the classroom simulation has been met. If generalization does not occur, then **community-based instruction (CBI)** or **in-vivo instruction** (i.e., teaching in the natural environment) may be necessary for learners to generalize (Branham et al., 1999; Brown et al., 1986; Collins et al., 1993; Spooner, Browder, & Richter, 2011; Walker, Uphold, Richter, & Test, 2010). For example, if Beverly can use the next dollar strategy correctly to count out enough dollar bills to pay for a purchase in the classroom but cannot perform the same skill at a cash register when making a purchase in the community, she may require in-vivo instruction in the environment in which the skill is needed.

A final way to facilitate generalization is to address it when determining the consequences that follow a correct response (Alberto & Troutman, 2009; Westling & Fox, 2009). First, the instructor can facilitate generalization by reinforcing a generalized response whenever it occurs, especially when it occurs naturally during a novel activity or across a novel environment. The use of natural reinforcers (e.g., getting to consume a selected food after purchasing it) facilitates generalization because they are likely to be available outside of the instructional setting. Fading to a natural schedule of reinforcement (i.e., praise on a variable schedule) facilitates generalization because a learner is not likely to receive verbal feedback each time a generalized response occurs in the natural environment. Delaying reinforcement facilitates generalization because reinforcement is not always readily available in the natural environment (e.g., receiving compensation for work delayed until payday). Teaching learners to practice self-reinforcement facilitates generalization because learners can reinforce themselves (e.g., take a 5-minute coffee break after working on a task without interruption for 30 minutes) when no one else is available to do this in the natural environment.

One way to ensure that generalization is an outcome of instruction is to include it in the individualized education program (IEP; Billingsley, Burgess, Lynch, & Matlock, 1991). Adding a measure of fluency also will facilitate generalization because a fluent response is more likely to be functional and naturally reinforced in natural settings (e.g., entering information into an automated teller machine before it shuts down). The following example shows how an IEP objective might address generalization in the criterion.

When presented with the opportunity to use the next dollar strategy, Beverly will count out the appropriate number of dollars with 100% accuracy within 10 seconds for 3 days across at least three of the following activities: 1) when purchasing at school or in the community, 2) when purchasing a ticket for an activity at school or in the community, 3) when simulating making purchases in the classroom, 4) when purchasing a personal item in the community, or 5) when making a purchase for school staff or parents in the community.

SAMPLE INSTRUCTIONAL PROGRAMS

Although all of the instructional programs presented thus far in this text have included maintenance and generalization components, the following instructional programs offer additional examples as to how these crucial phases of learning can be addressed. Both of the instructional programs demonstrate how secondary teachers of students with moderate and severe disabilities plan to address maintenance and generalization in teaching transition skills that their students will need in future environments, bearing in mind that, if a learner acquires a skill that does not maintain or generalize, instruction has little meaning.

Sample Instructional Program 1

The first sample instructional program employs a system-of-least-prompts procedure with multiple exemplars to teach a secondary student with moderate and severe disabilities to do laundry. The procedures are based on a research study conducted by Taylor et al. (2002).

Core Content Standards

Reading · Students will interpret the meaning of jargon, dialect, or specialized vocabulary found in a passage.

· Students will identify essential information from a passage needed to accomplish a task.

· Students will apply the information contained in a passage to accomplish a task/procedure or to answer questions about a passage.

Behavioral Objective

When presented with laundry items, Andrea will independently complete the steps of the task analysis to wash and dry the items for 5 days in either the consumer science classroom or a community self-service laundry.

Instructional Context

Andrea is 16 years of age, and the transition plan that she has developed with her family and support team contain goals to make the transition to a supported living apartment and work in local business in her community. Laundry skills will be needed for Andrea to independently maintain an appearance suitable to the workplace, and it is anticipated that she will launder her clothing in a local self-service laundry. The high school's consumer science class has a washer and dryer that she can use to learn to launder her clothing. In addition, she participates in CBI on a weekly basis, making it feasible for her to engage in probes for generalization at the local self-service laundry. To facilitate generalization, instruction in the consumer science room will be conducted on alternate days by the consumer science teacher, the special education teacher, a paraprofessional, and a peer tutor. Generalization probes in the community will be conducted in the community by Andrea's job coach, as being a self-service laundry attendant is a possible future occupation and maintaining a clean and neat appearance is an employability skill.

Instructional Materials

The laundry area of the consumer science classroom will be adapted to facilitate generalized reading because reading for comprehension of specialized vocabulary to perform tasks is part of the age-appropriate core content Andrea is to master as well as a way for her to become more independent in that targeted task. In addition, multiple exemplars of laundry materials will be used to increase the likelihood that Andrea can use a variety of laundry products. Thus, instructional materials will include the following: 1) an assortment of items to be laundered, 2) a minimum of three brands (i.e., multiple exemplars) of liquid laundry detergents and fabric softener sheets for instruction in the consumer science classroom, 3) a novel brand (i.e., novel exemplar) of laundry detergent and fabric softener sheets to be used in the community self-service laundry, and 4) functional laundry words (i.e., detergent, fabric softener, cycle, normal, permanent press, cotton, pastels, delicates, soiled, recommended, presoak, rinse, capacity, irritant) printed in black letter on white 5″ × 7″ cards to be placed on the washer and dryer during instruction (see Taylor et al., 2002, p. 175).

Instructional Procedure

Each instructional session will proceed as follows.

Attentional Cue	•	The instructor will ask, "Are you ready to wash and dry clothes?" and wait for an affirmative response.
System-of-Least-Prompts Procedure	•	The task direction will be, "Wash and dry the clothes." The instructor will wait 5 seconds for Andrea to initiate the first step of the task analysis and, if appropriate, an additional 15 seconds for Andrea to complete the step. If Andrea fails to perform the correct response or fails to complete the correct response within the given response interval, the instructor will provide a verbal prompt and then a model prompt, waiting the appropriate response interval between the prompts in the hierarchy. Instruction will continue in this manner for each step of the task analysis.
Consequence	•	Verbal praise will follow each prompted or unprompted correct response.

Nontargeted Information

After each step of the task analysis, the instructor will present a laundry word either on as flashcard, on a product, or on an appliance. For example, instructive feedback after one step of the task analysis might consist of the instructor pointing to the word *cycle* on a flashcard and saying, "Good job! You placed the clothing in the washer. This word is *cycle,* and you will need to remember to select the heavy load cycle for washing heavy jeans." Instructive feedback on another step of the task analysis might consist of the instructor pointing to the word *cycle* on the washer and saying, "Nice work! This word is *cycle.* You selected the heavy load cycle for washing jeans."

Data Collection

For each step of the task analysis, the instructor will record *I* for each independent response, *V* for each correct response after a verbal prompt, and *M* for each correct response after a model prompt. A sample completed data sheet is shown in Figure 7.1.

SYSTEM-OF-LEAST-PROMPTS DATA SHEET

Name: _Andrea_   Skill: _Laundry_
Instructor: _Ms. Pratt_   Setting: _Consumer science room_

Task analysis	May 8	May 9	May 10	May 11	May 12
1. Carry laundry to washer	P	I	I	I	I
2. Open washer lid	P	M	M	M	V
3. Put clothes in washer	V	V	V	V	I
4. Remove detergent lid	P	V	V	V	I
5. Measure liquid detergent	P	P	M	M	V
6. Pour detergent in washer	I	M	I	I	I
7. Close washer lid	M	M	M	V	V
8. Select water temperature	V	V	V	V	I
9. Select load size	V	V	V	V	I
10. Select cycle	P	M	M	V	I
11. Start washer	M	I	I	I	I
12. Open lid at end of cycle	M	M	M	I	I
13. Take clothes out of washer	P	V	V	V	I
14. Open dryer door	P	V	V	I	I
15. Put clothes in dryer	I	I	I	I	I
16. Close dryer door	I	I	I	I	I
17. Select heat cycle	M	M	I	I	I
18. Select minutes for drying	V	V	V	I	I
19. Start dryer	V	V	V	V	V
20. Open door at end of cycle	M	V	V	V	I
21. Remove clothes	P	V	V	I	I
22. Put clothes in basket	P	P	P	M	V
Number/% independent	3/14%	4/18%	6/27%	10/45%	17/77%

Key: I, independent; M, model; P, physical; V, verbal.

Figure 7.1.   Sample completed data sheet for using a system-of-least-prompts procedure in Sample Instructional Program 1.

Maintenance

Once Andrea reaches the criterion of 100% correct independent responses for 1 day, the instructor will fade praise for responses to an average of every five (i.e., variable ratio of 5, or VR5) for 1 day and to the end of the chained task (i.e., fixed ratio of 22, or FR22) for 1 day. Once criterion is reached and praise is faded, the instructor will continue to monitor maintenance during weekly CBI session at the self-service laundry.

Generalization

Generalization of laundry skills is facilitated by presenting multiple exemplars of laundry products and clothing during instruction. Generalization of reading is facilitated by presenting multiple exemplars of words presented on flashcards, laundry products, and appliances. Generalization also is facilitated during instruction by using multiple instructors. Generalization across settings, materials, and instructors is assessed during probes conducted by the job coach during CBI.

Behavior Management

Appropriate behavior will be facilitated by providing intermittent praise for attending during instruction.

Lesson Variations and Extension

Doing laundry is only one of many functional skills that learners with moderate and severe disabilities need for successful transition to an adulthood that is as independent as possible. The same procedure could be followed in teaching other domestic skills, such as cooking (teach in the consumer science room with multiple exemplars and then test in the home or an apartment for generalization). The following lesson is a variation that focuses on housekeeping skills.

Sample Instructional Program 2

As with many domestic skills, instruction on housekeeping skills has a dual outcome. First, housekeeping skills enable a person to live as independently as possible without having to pay someone else to perform the skills. Second, housekeeping skills can become a vocation through jobs in the hospitality industry, in the restaurant business, in janitorial services, or as private household help. In this instructional program, the instructor will facilitate generalization during school instruction and then assess generalization in a potential vocational setting. The procedures are based on a research study conducted by Smith et al. (1999).

Core Content Standards

Practical Living/ Vocational
- Students demonstrate skills that promote individual well-being and healthy family relationships.
- Students demonstrate skills and work habits that lead to success in future schooling and work.

Behavioral Objective

When presented with the housekeeping task of cleaning tables, Jeff will independently clean an array of tables by independently and correctly completing 100% of the steps of the task analysis for 5 days across the following settings: 1) the school teachers' lounge, 2) the school cafeteria, or 3) a community setting.

Instructional Context

Jeff is 16 years of age, and the transition plan that he has developed with his family and support team contains goals to make the transition to a supported living apartment and work in a local business in his community. Housekeeping skills will be needed for Jeff to live as independently as possible without having to hire housekeeping services. In addition, housekeeping skills may translate to a job for Jeff because he lives in a community in which a number of jobs that use these skills are available and he likes to work independently. The job coach has identified a number of school settings in which Jeff can learn housekeeping skills before trying them in the community as one of several work experiences that he will sample during the coming year. In addition, Jeff and his parents have identified housekeeping skills as being important in his present home as well as being important for Jeff to make independent or supported living a future option. The job coach has identified cleaning tables as the first housekeeping task that Jeff will learn. To facilitate generalization, the job coach will teach this skill in the consumer science classroom, the teachers' lounge, and the school cafeteria. The job coach will conduct generalization probes in a nearby church that is within walking distance of the school.

Instructional Materials

Teaching across settings will ensure that Jeff will experience cleaning a variety of tables during instruction that vary in color (i.e., brown, black, gray), shape (i.e., rectangular, square, octagonal), and size (i.e., small, large). In addition, cleaning materials also will be varied (see Smith et al., 1999, p. 345) to include different colors of cleaning cloths (i.e., red, white, tan) and buckets (i.e., brown, black, blue).

Instructional Procedure

Each instructional session will proceed as follows.

Attentional Cue
- When the materials are assembled and the job coach is standing beside Jeff, the job coach will secure his attention by asking, "Are you ready to clean the tables?" and waiting for an affirmative response (e.g., head nod or verbal reply).

System-of-Least-Prompts Procedure
- The task direction will be, "Jeff, clean the table." The instructor will wait 5 seconds for Jeff to initiate the first step of the task analysis. If Jeff fails to perform the correct response, the instructor first will provide a verbal prompt, then a model prompt, and then a physical prompt, waiting 5 seconds between each prompt in the hierarchy for Jeff to perform a correct response. Instruction will continue in this manner for each step of the task analysis.

Consequence
- Verbal praise will follow each prompted or unprompted correct response.

Nontargeted Information

Before instruction, the job coach will take Jeff to the sink and cleaning supply area of the consumer science classroom, the cafeteria, or the janitor's room. As Jeff watches, the job coach will describe each step as the materials for cleaning tables are assembled (i.e., opening the cabinet, taking out the bucket, taking out the soap, putting soap in the bucket, turning on the water, turning off the water when the bucket is full, taking out the cleaning cloth, and putting the cloth in the bucket). The job coach will praise Jeff for observing and listening after every five steps (i.e., fixed ratio of 5, or FR5). After instruction, the job coach and Jeff will return to the same area, and the job coach will describe putting away the cleaning materials (i.e., putting the bucket in the sink, taking out the cleaning cloth, turning on the water, rinsing out the cloth, pouring out the cleaning water, rinsing the bucket, turning off the water, putting the bucket in the cabinet, putting the soap in the cabinet). Again, the job coach will praise Jeff for watching and listening on a FR5 schedule.

Data Collection

For each step of the task analysis, the job coach will record *I* for each independent response, *V* for each correct response after a verbal prompt, *M* for each correct response after a model

SYSTEM-OF-LEAST-PROMPTS DATA SHEET

Student: _Jeff_   Skill: _Cleaning tables_
Instructor: _Ms. Nolan_   Setting: _Cafeteria_

Task analysis	June 1	June 2	June 3	June 4	June 5
1. Place bucket of water on table	P	V	M	M	V
2. Pick up cleaning cloth	P	P	V	M	V
3. Place cloth in soap and water	V	I	V	I	I
4. Wring out cloth	P	I	P	I	I
5. Wash first quarter of table	I	M	M	I	I
6. Place cloth in soap and water	I	V	M	I	I
7. Wring out cloth	M	V	P	M	V
8. Wash second quarter of table	V	P	P	V	I
9. Place cloth in soap and water	V	M	I	I	I
10. Wring out cloth	P	M	M	I	I
11. Wash third quarter of table	M	P	V	I	I
12. Place cloth in soap and water	M	P	V	I	I
13. Wring out cloth	P	V	P	V	I
14. Wash final quarter of table	P	P	M	M	V
15. Place cloth in bucket	I	I	M	I	I
Number/% independent	3/20%	3/20%	1/7%	9/60%	11/73%

Key: I, independent; M, model; P, physical; V, verbal.

Figure 7.2.   Sample completed data sheet for using a system-of-least-prompts procedure in Sample Instructional Program 2.

prompt, and *P* for each correct response after a physical prompt. A sample completed data sheet is shown in Figure 7.2.

Maintenance

Once Jeff reaches the criterion of 100% correct independent responses for 1 day, the job coach will fade praise for responses to an average of every five (i.e., variable ratio of 5, or VR5) for 1 day and to the end of the chained task (i.e., fixed ratio of 15, or FR15) for 1 day. Once criterion is reached and praise is faded, the job coach will continue to monitor maintenance during weekly CBI sessions at a local church.

Generalization

Generalization of housekeeping skills is facilitated by using multiple exemplars during instruction and teaching across settings. Generalization across settings and materials is assessed during probes conducted by the job coach in the social hall and kitchen of a nearby church. In addition to performing the task of cleaning tables at the church, Jeff will be asked to demonstrate observational learning by assembling the materials needed to clean tables and, later, putting away the materials after cleaning the tables in the church.

Behavior Management

Appropriate behavior will be facilitated by providing intermittent praise for attending during instruction as well as during pretask and posttask sessions used to facilitate observational learning of nontargeted portions of the task.

Lesson Variations and Extension

Cleaning tables is only one of many housekeeping tasks needed for successful transition to independent or supported living as well as for vocations in which housekeeping skills are needed. Other housekeeping skills that can be taught in this manner include dusting furniture, cleaning appliances or fixtures, vacuuming or mopping floors, cleaning glass (e.g., mirrors, windows), making beds, washing dishes, and disposing of trash. Some transition programs may have access to domestic environments (e.g., apartments, homes) in which to teach these skills. Although everyone needs housekeeping skills for daily living, the decision to teach them as vocational skills should be based on student and family preferences. It should be noted that the instruction of housekeeping skills provides an appropriate venue for embedding core content, such as measuring cleaning products before use and reading labels on cleaning products for directions and safety issues. The skills also provide the opportunity to teach self-sufficiency and self-evaluation when learners are provided with checklists to complete as they perform housekeeping tasks. It is never too early to begin teaching learners to perform independent chores. Even in elementary classrooms, students are asked to keep their work areas tidy and to assist with classroom chores, such as picking up trash from the floor or cleaning desk and table tops.

SUMMARY

This chapter provided strategies for facilitating maintenance and generalization, two crucial phases of learning that are not always addressed in instructional programs. Yet, if learners fail to maintain or generalize, the content they have learned is meaningless.

QUESTIONS FOR REFLECTION

1. What is the difference between using multiple exemplars and general case programming?

2. How do fixed and variable ratios of thinning reinforcement differ? Which is more likely to maintain?

3. How can classroom simulations be structured to reflect the environments in which skills will be needed?

4. Provide examples of natural cues and natural reinforcers.

REFERENCES

Alberto, P.A., & Troutman, A.C. (2009). *Applied behavior analysis for teachers* (8th ed.). Upper Saddle River, NJ: Prentice-Hall.

Billingsley, F.F., Burgess, D., Lynch, V.W., & Matlock, G.L. (1991). Toward generalized outcomes: Considerations and guidelines for writing instructional objectives. *Education and Training in Mental Retardation, 26*, 351–360.

Branham, R., Collins, B.C., Schuster, J.W., & Kleinert, H. (1999). Teaching community skills to students with moderate disabilities: Comparing combined techniques of classroom simulation, videotape modeling, and community-based instruction. *Education and Training in Mental Retardation and Developmental Disabilities, 33*, 170–181.

Collins, B.C. (2007). *Moderate and severe disabilities: A foundational approach.* Upper Saddle River, NJ: Pearson, Merrill, Prentice-Hall.

Collins, B.C., & Griffen, A. (1996). Teaching students with moderate disabilities to have safe responses to product warning labels. *Education and Treatment of Children, 19*, 30–45.

Collins, B.C., Stinson, D.M., & Land, L. (1993). A comparison of in vivo and simulation prior to in vivo instruction in teaching generalized safety skills. *Education and Training in Mental Retardation, 28*, 128–142.

Colyer, S.P., & Collins, B.C. (1996). Using natural cues within prompt levels to teach the next dollar strategy to students with disabilities. *Journal of Special Education, 30*, 305–318.

Day, M.D., & Horner, R.H. (1986). Response variation and the generalization of a dressing skill: Comparison of single instance and general case instruction. *Applied Research in Mental Retardation, 7*(2), 189–202.

Dogoe, M.S., Banda, D.R., Lock, R.H., & Feinstein, R. (2011). Teaching generalized reading of product warning labels to young adults with autism using the constant time delay procedure. *Education and Training in Autism and Developmental Disabilities, 46*(2), 204–213.

Horner, R.H., Jones, D., & Williams, J.A. (1985). A functional approach to teaching generalized street crossing. *Journal of The Association for Persons with Severe Handicaps, 10*(2), 71–78.

Lerman, L.R. (1996). The differential effectiveness of general case programming and rule learning for learners with mental retardation. *Focus on Autism and Other Developmental Disabilities, 11*(1), 45–52.

Mechling, L.C., & Gast, D.L. (2003). Multi-media instruction to teach grocery word associations and store location. *Education and Training in Developmental Disabilities, 38*(1), 62–76.

Nietupski, J., Hamre-Nietupski, S., Clancy, P., & Veerhusen, K. (1986). Guidelines for making simulation an effective adjunct to in vivo community instruction. *Journal of The Association for Persons with Severe Handicaps, 8*, 71–77.

Singleton, D.K., Schuster, J.W., Morse, T.E., & Collins, B.C. (1999). A comparison of antecedent prompt and test and simultaneous prompting procedures in teaching grocery sight words to adolescents with mental retardation. *Education and Training in Mental Retardation and Developmental Disabilities, 34*, 182–199.

Smith, R.L., Collins, B.C., Schuster, J.W., & Kleinert, H. (1999). Teaching table cleaning skills to secondary students with moderate/severe disabilities: Measuring observational learning during downtime. *Education and Training in Mental Retardation and Developmental Disabilities, 34*, 342–353.

Snell, M.E., & Brown, F. (2011). Selecting teaching strategies and arranging educational environments. In M.E. Snell & F. Brown (Eds.), *Instruction of students with severe disabilities* (7th ed., pp. 122–185). Upper Saddle River, NJ: Pearson.

Spooner, F., Browder, D.M., & Richter, S. (2011). Community and job skills. In D.M. Browder & F. Spooner (Eds.), *Teaching students with moderate and severe disabilities* (pp. 342–363). New York, NY: Guilford.

Taylor, P., Collins, B.C., Schuster, J.W., & Kleinert, H. (2002). Teaching laundry skills to high school students with disabilities: Generalization of targeted skills and nontargeted information. *Education and Training in Mental Retardation and Developmental Disabilities, 37*, 172–183.

Walker, A.R., Uphold, N.M., Richter, S., & Test, D.W. (2010). Review of the literature on community-based instruction across grade levels. *Education and Training in Autism and Developmental Disabilities, 45,* 242–267.

Westling, D.L., & Fox, L. (2009). *Teaching students with severe disabilities* (4th ed.). Upper Saddle River, NJ: Pearson.

CHAPTER 8

Teaching Functional Core Content

CHAPTER OBJECTIVES

On completion of this chapter, the reader will be able to

- Provide a rationale for teaching both functional skills and academic core content to learners with moderate and severe disabilities
- Discuss two approaches to combining functional skills and academic core content in the same instructional program

So far, this text has focused on the presentation of effective and efficient instructional strategies for teaching learners with moderate and severe disabilities. The sample instructional programs in each chapter have illustrated each response-prompting procedure while demonstrating that the methods for facilitating the efficiency of instruction are not limited by the setting in which they are used or by the content that they deliver.

Since the 1990s, the focus of special education services for learners with moderate and severe disabilities has gone through a transformation. When possible, instruction has moved from segregated to inclusive settings (e.g., Collins, Branson, Hall, & Rankin, 2001; McDonnell et al., 2006). In addition, a new focus on academic skills has been added to a focus on functional skills (Bouck, 2008; Bouck, 2009; Browder et al., 2004; Browder, Spooner, Wakeman, Trela, & Baker, 2006; Browder, Wakeman, et al., 2007; Copeland & Cosbey, 2008–2009; Dymond, Renzaglia, Gilson, & Slagor, 2007; Flowers, Browder, & Ahlgrim-Delzill, 2006; Lynch & Adams, 2008; Parrish & Stodden, 2009). Research is beginning to investigate ways to ensure that learners with moderate and severe disabilities have the opportunity to learn alongside their same-age peers without disabilities while still acquiring the skills they will need to function as independently as possible in the least restrictive environments possible when they make the transition to adulthood (e.g., Collins et al., 2001; Collins, Evans, Creech-Galloway, Karl, & Miller, 2007; McDonnell et al., 2006). Instructors are faced with the challenge of how to deliver effective instruction in inclusive settings and how to provide access to academic core content so that the curriculum for learners with moderate and severe disabilities results in the acquisition of skills that are meaningful and relevant in their personal lives.

A functional approach to designing a curriculum for learners with moderate and severe disabilities is based on the foundational arguments provided by Brown et al. (1979). It is a top-down approach in which instructional content consists of the skills that learners need to function as independently as possible across current environments in their lives (e.g., home, school, community) as well as the skills they will need to function as independently as possible in future environments (e.g., supported living apartment, workplace, community) when they make the transition to adulthood at the age of 21. To determine these skills, the instructional team conducts an ecological inventory across four domains: 1) domestic, 2) community, 3) recreation/leisure, and 4) educational and/or vocational. For example, the instructional team would conduct an ecological inventory of an elementary learner's current school environment, dividing the school into relevant subenvironments (e.g., general education homeroom, cafeteria, hallways, restroom, playground, gymnasium, music class, art class). In each of these subenvironments, the instructional team would identify the routine activities in which the learner will participate (e.g., working at centers, placing personal articles in a desk or cubbyhole, making transitions to special classes, using a water fountain or restroom, using playground equipment, participating in group games). These are the activities in which the instruction of specific useful skills (e.g., communication, social skills, functional reading, functional math, fine and gross motor skills, self-care skills) can be embedded, using systematic instruction and adaptations (e.g., assistive technology, picture symbols) as needed. The instructional team also will want to consider the skills needed for a successful transition to a future environment (e.g., secondary school) and begin to teach the skills that will be needed in that environment when the learner makes transitions (e.g., making choices in the cafeteria line, making transitions independently to classes, following a schedule of classes).

With the 1997 reauthorization of the Individuals with Disabilities Education Act (PL 105-17), which mandated access to core content in the general education curriculum, and the No Child Left Behind Act of 2001 (PL 107-110), which mandated that all students be assessed on grade-level standards in math, reading, and science, the general education curriculum has become an important focus for learners with moderate and severe disabilities. Many will qualify to take part in an alternate assessment in which specific skills are selected for instruction and assessment that are aligned with national and state standards (Browder et al., 2004; Browder et al., 2006; Flowers et al., 2006). Because the assessment of students' progress on core content holds high stakes for schools, districts, and states, the instruction of core content to learners with disabilities has become a priority. Because much instructional time must be spent on teaching skills to criterion and even more on teaching a sufficient number of examples and nonexamples so that learners will begin to form abstract concepts, it is necessary for instructors to carefully plan the way in which core content will be presented and taught.

One of the barriers to acquiring core content for learners with disabilities who are in inclusive settings is that general education teachers most often use large-group lessons to present concepts and cover these in a time-limited unit format before moving to the next concept (e.g., McDonnell, Thorson, & McQuivey, 2000). For example, a secondary math teacher may spend 2 days covering the Pythagorean theorem in a general education geometry class and perhaps another day later in the semester reviewing the concept. Students are expected to master this in a brief period of time, yet this may be a difficult concept for learners with moderate and severe disabilities to acquire. Even if systematic instruction results in learning to perform a task-analyzed sequence to calculate the answer to a given problem, the acquisition of this skill may not result in a generalized response in which learners can apply the Pythagorean theorem to solve a meaningful problem in the real world. Teaching a concept takes time and the careful structuring and presentation of a lesson plan that may need to be repeated numerous times before learners reach criterion.

The practice of embedded instruction in which learners are taught content beyond the scope of a specific lesson is one way to teach needed skills in a meaningful way. As suggested by Collins, Karl, Riggs, Galloway, and Hager (2010) and by Kleinert, Collins, Wickham, Riggs, and Hager (2010), there are two ways to mesh functional content and core content to result in the acquisition of meaningful skills. The first is to add functional applications when teaching core content. The second is to embed core content when teaching functional skills. With the large amount of content that teachers are to cover and the large number of skills that learners need to acquire, embedded instruction is a strategy that is well suited to inclusive environments as well as an efficient way to ensure that a learner's curriculum results in the acquisition of meaningful and relevant skills that will be needed when the learner makes the transition to adulthood.

ADDING FUNCTIONAL APPLICATIONS TO CORE CONTENT INSTRUCTION

When designing the instruction of core content, all instructors need to identify ways in which the targeted content is relevant to all learners. When teaching learners with moderate and severe disabilities in particular, a number of questions should be answered: How can the content be applied in the real world both now and in the future? How does the content form a foundation for the instruction of future content? What skills are necessary to master the content? If the content is to result in a concept, what examples and nonexamples can be used during instruction to facilitate the formation of concepts? How will learners be expected to generalize the acquired content? How can maintenance be ensured? Is mastery at a set criterion necessary for content to be useful to learners or to allow progression in a determined sequence? Will learners have the opportunity to revisit content at future points in the curriculum? Can targeted skills be taught in isolation, or is it necessary for learners to master a broader scope of skills for content to be useful? Perhaps the key question, given the amount of time that may be necessary to teach core content to learners with moderate and severe disabilities, is to ask which content is most useful to learners to promote meaningful interactions in their lives, to facilitate independence, and to provide access to less restrictive environments across domains both now and in the future.

Sometimes the relevance of core content is easy to determine. Learners need to learn to read to the extent possible to gain information as well as for personal enjoyment. Learners need to communicate through the written word to provide information. Learners need to apply math concepts to increase personal independence (e.g., manage personal finances, ensure nutritional sustenance, schedule and participate in daily activities) and to increase vocational options (e.g., food industry, carpentry, sewing, plant and animal maintenance, retail industry). Learners need to be able to apply a foundation in science to activities in their personal lives (e.g., cooking, dressing appropriately, maintaining optimal health). Sometimes, it is more difficult to make core content relevant when its applications are more remote to the lives of learners (e.g., weather patterns or geographic events found in a different part of the world) and are difficult to convey in a way that is concrete to learners (e.g., atomic core of elements, gravitational pull of planets). Instructors must analyze why core content is important and how it has an effect on the lives of learners to formulate a context for instruction. Collins et al. (2010) and Kleinert et al. (2010) presented examples of how instruction on cellular division can be taught in lessons on heredity and made relevant by including examples on the inheritance of health-related traits (e.g., diabetes, high blood pressure, cancer) that may require adjustments in lifestyle (e.g., exercise routine, medical screening and check-ups, dietary precautions). Although systematic instruction may be required to facilitate the acquisition of core content, a simple strategy to ensure that the content is personally relevant to students is to include examples during instruction of how the content can be applied in real life. A simple way to do this to embed real-life examples as nontargeted information during instruction (see Chapter 5).

ADDING CORE CONTENT TO FUNCTIONAL SKILL INSTRUCTION

Because learners with moderate and severe disabilities may need an increased amount of exposure to core content to master it, embedding instructional trials on core content during natural routines throughout the day is advantageous. In addition to giving learners the opportunities to apply core content in their daily lives, this increases the opportunities to receive feedback on performance and to make relevant links between instruction and practice. A number of functional skills can be taught in instructional trials that are distributed throughout the day, and core content can be embedded in each of these. For example, a learner who is being taught to wash hands during restroom breaks can also be taught body parts (e.g., hands, wrists, fingers, knuckles, nails), hygiene (e.g., disease prevention), reading (e.g., boys/girls), antonyms (e.g., hot/cold, left/right, in/out), math (e.g., counting), and science (e.g., water conservation, bacteria, liquid and solid states of matter). In some cases, inclusive non–core-content general education classes (e.g., consumer science, health, computer science), recreational classes (e.g., art, music, drama, physical education), or vocational classes (e.g., carpentry, sewing) may focus on the instruction of functional life skills while also providing the opportunity to embed core content (e.g., reading and defining vocabulary, measuring, performing math computations) that is necessary for successful acquisition of skills. Collins et al. (2010) described a functional lesson on cooking taught in a consumer science class that also embedded core content on reading (i.e., identifying, defining, and applying vocabulary words found on product labels), math (i.e., computing sales tax when planning a shopping budget for preparing a food item), and science (i.e., changing states of matter turning a liquid to a solid or a gas during a cooking activity). Although embedding core content in functional activities may not replace the need for direct instruction during classes dedicated to specific content, embedding content provides the opportunity to increase the number of instructional trials while making a clear link to the usefulness of the content in the daily lives of learners.

SAMPLE INSTRUCTIONAL PROGRAMS

The following examples of instructional programs have links to core content standards across the curriculum (e.g., math, language arts, science, social studies, humanities). Although the examples were derived from the core content identified in the state in which the author resided at the time this text was written, they should provide the impetus for readers to align instructional targets to standards within their own states because all states should address standards identified at the national level. (For examples, see the Common Core State Standards and the standards of the National Science Teachers Association, the National Council of Teachers of Mathematics, and the National Council of Teachers of English.) The examples of instructional programs also focus on teaching skills with response-prompting strategies. Response-prompting strategies are evidence-based practices, and there is a growing body of evidence that these strategies can be used effectively to teach core content, such as math (e.g., Browder, Spooner, Ahlgrim-Delzell, Harris, & Wakeman, 2008; Collins et al., 2011; Jimenez, Courtade, & Browder, 2008), reading (e.g., Bradford, Shippen, Alberto, Houchins, & Flores, 2006; Browder, Ahlgrim-Delzell, Spooner, Mims, & Baker, 2009; Browder, Trela, & Jimenez, 2007; Cohen, Heller, Alberto, & Fredrick, 2008; Collins et al., 2007; Collins et al., 2011; Wakeman, Spooner, & Knight, 2007), science (e.g., Collins et al., 2011), and social studies (e.g., Falkenstine, Collins, Schuster, & Kleinert, 2009). The following sample lessons are intended to demonstrate the use of response-prompting procedures in combination with the two strategies for combining functional and core content described in this chapter. For additional information on teaching core content and functional skills, see Browder and Spooner (2011), Kleinert and Kearns (2010), McDonnell and Copeland (2011), and Westling and Fox (2009).

Sample Instructional Program 1

The first sample instructional program employs a simultaneous-prompting (SP) procedure to embed instruction on both functional and core content vocabulary within an inclusive general education class. The procedure is based on a research study conducted by Collins et al. (2007). Whereas the original investigation also included instruction on math vocabulary to middle school students with moderate and severe disabilities and instruction on social studies vocabulary to secondary students with moderate and severe disabilities, the following lesson will be based on the component of the investigation that focused on instruction of science vocabulary to an elementary student with a moderate disability.

In the research on which the following lesson plan was based, the authors found that there were differences across learners, with some first reaching criterion during embedded instruction only and others first reaching criterion through direct instruction presented either through direct massed trial or distributed trial format. Thus, it should be noted that the instructor of this lesson has several options, based on the learning profile and placement of the learner. First, instruction may consist solely of systematic trials that are embedded within the general education science lesson for fully included learners whose past instructional data have demonstrated the ability to master content in a relatively short amount of time. Second, instruction can consist of embedded instruction supplemented by massed trial instruction for learners whose past instructional data have demonstrated that the rate of learning increased when additional opportunities for learning were added. For learners who are fully included, supplemental instruction can take place in a one-to-one or small-group format within the inclusive science class when there is downtime or when peers are involved in independent seatwork. For learners who go to a resource room for a period each day as a supplement to an inclusive placement with their same-age peers without disabilities, additional direct instruction can be provided in that setting in a one-to-one or small-group format. Supplemental instruction has the benefit of being focused on instruction on content before its presentation within the general education curriculum, thus preparing learners to more fully interact with peers and participate in the subsequent lessons or unit of study.

Core Content Standards

Science   • Students will explain that sound is a result of vibrations, a type of motion.

   • Students will describe pitch (high, low) as a difference in sounds that are produced and related to the rate of vibration.

Reading   • Students will apply word recognition strategies (e.g., phonetic principles, context clues, structural analysis) to determine pronunciations or meanings of words in passages.

   • Students will interpret the meaning of specialized vocabulary (words and terms specific to understanding the content).

Behavioral Objective

When presented with science vocabulary words from the unit on motion and forces, Pat will identify the words with 100% accuracy during one-to-one or group instruction for 5 days.

Instructional Context

Pat is a 9-year-old girl with a moderate disability who is included in general education classes but also receives supplemental one-to-one instruction on key vocabulary and concepts as a precursor to group instruction to enable her to more fully participate in lessons with her same-age peers without disabilities. Because prior instructional data have shown that Pat may take from 2 weeks to 1 month of daily instruction to learn to identify 2 to 3 vocabulary words, Pat attends a resource room for one period each day to receive supplemental instruction on content targeted for instruction on her individualized education program and on core content targeted for instruction on the state's alternate assessment. Pat's special education resource room teacher also collaborates with the science teacher during science class each day. This allows the special education teacher to conduct one-to-one instructional trials with Pat in the resource room and also conduct embedded trials with Pat as he circulates in the science class.

Instructional Materials

In addition to the instructional materials provided in the general education class (e.g., textbook, worksheets, vocabulary posted on "word wall"), the instructor will prepare vocabulary flashcards containing words that are specific to the unit of force and motion. The flashcards will consist of white index cards on which each of the identified words is hand printed in black letters. The targeted vocabulary words will consist of 1) vibration, 2) sound, and 3) pitch.

Instructional Procedure

Each instructional session will proceed as follows.

Attentional Cue	• The instructor will tell the Pat to look as he presents a flashcard and will wait until Pat focuses on the flashcard.
Simultaneous-Prompting Procedure	• The task direction will be, "What word?" During daily probe trials, the instructor will wait 5 seconds for Pat to respond before recording a response. There will be two trials per word, for a total of six trials per session. During daily training trials, the instructor again will state the task direction; however, the instructor immediately will model the correct response for Pat (0-second delay interval) and then wait 5 seconds for her to repeat the response before providing feedback and moving to the next trial. Again, there will be two trials per word.
	• During massed trials in the resource room, the instructor will sit opposite Pat and proceed immediately from one trial to the next. During distributed trials in the general education science class, the instructor will provide trials whenever there is downtime (e.g., students getting out materials or putting away materials, students doing independent seatwork) or whenever there is a natural opportunity (e.g., students reading from text that contains the targeted words, students working on worksheets that contain the targeted words). During science class, the instructor will pause by Pat's desk as he circulates around the room and deliver a brief trial (i.e., probe trial requiring an independent response followed by a training trial requiring a prompted response). Again, there will be two trials per word for a total of six trials per session.
Consequence	• Verbal praise will follow each prompted or unprompted correct response during both probe and training trials.

Nontargeted Information

After each training trial, the instructor will state the definition of the vocabulary word being presented as well as an example of the application of the word (e.g., "Vibration is a type of motion that can be observed, described, measured, and compared. When you place your hand on your throat as you speak, can feel the vibration of your vocal chords, and you can hear the sounds that are made").

Data Collection

The instructor will record data on responses during probe trials only. A plus sign will be recorded for correct responses, a minus sign will be recorded for incorrect responses, and a zero will be recorded for failures to respond. A sample completed data sheet is shown in Figure 8.1.

SIMULTANEOUS-PROMPTING DATA SHEET

Name: _Pat_   Instructor: _Mr. Barger_
Targeted skill: _Science vocabulary_

Trials	Date				
	March 17	March 18	March 19	March 20	March 21
1. Vibration	+	+	0	+	+
2. Sound	–	–	+	+	+
3. Pitch	–	+	+	+	+
4. Sound	+	+	+	+	+
5. Pitch	–	+	+	+	+
6. Vibration	0	+	+	+	+
7. Pitch	+	+	+	–	+
8. Vibration	+	+	+	+	+
9. Sound	–	–	–	+	+
Number/% correct	4/44%	7/78%	7/78%	8/89%	9/100%

Key: Plus sign indicates correct response; minus sign indicates incorrect response; zero indicates no response.

Figure 8.1.   Sample completed data sheet for using a simultaneous-prompting procedure in Sample Instructional Program 1.

Maintenance

Once Pat reaches the criterion of 100% correct responses for 2 days across settings, the instructor will fade praise for responses to an average of every three responses (i.e., fixed ratio of 3, or FR3) for 2 days and to the end of the session (i.e., fixed ratio of 9, or FR9) for 1 day. Once criterion is reached and praise is faded, the instructor will continue to monitor maintenance during lessons and assessments on motion and force in science class as well as on performance during the state's alternate assessment.

Generalization

Generalization will be facilitated by conducting trials with materials used during science class in addition to teaching with flashcards. Science class materials may include, but are not limited to, passages in the science textbook, sentences and activities on worksheets, words written on the classroom word wall, words that appear in online resources on the Internet or science-related computer programs, and PowerPoint presentations used during class lessons.

Behavior Management

Appropriate behavior will be facilitated by providing intermittent praise for attending during instruction.

Lesson Variations and Extension

The scientific principles of force and motion can be found across the curriculum. For example, Pat may participate in a music class in which vibration, sound, and pitch are part of the discussion related to singing or playing a musical instrument. She can be directed to touch an instrument to feel its vibration or to listen for changes in pitch while singing. Peers without disabilities can be taught to provide examples found in the natural environment when interacting with Pat during activities, such as chorus, or when listening to music during leisure time. Increasing opportunities for learning that are embedded throughout the day is likely to increase the rate of acquisition as well as generalization and maintenance.

Sample Instructional Program 2

The second sample instructional programs focuses on teaching an applied science concept with a constant time-delay procedure to middle school students with moderate and severe disabilities. In this lesson, instruction is designed from the beginning to make clear functional links to academic core content. The procedures are based on one of several core content skills from math, reading, and science required on the state's alternate assessment that were taught during a research study conducted by Collins et al. (2011).

Core Content Standards

Science
- Students will classify substances according to their chemical/reactive properties.
- Students will classify elements and compounds according to their properties
- Students will describe the effect of the sun's energy on the earth system.
- Students will describe the connections/relationship between the sun's energy and seasons.

Behavioral Objectives

When presented with three pictures related to the weather, the students will indicate by pointing the pictures containing a solid, a liquid, or neither with 100% accuracy for 3 days.

When presented with three pictures related to appropriate dress for the weather, the students will indicate by pointing the pictures of clothing appropriate for ice, rain, and sunshine with 100% accuracy for 3 days.

Instructional Context

Chris is a 14-year-old boy with autism, and Barbara is a 15-year-old girl with Down syndrome. Both have a moderate intellectual disability and limitations in intelligible verbal expressive communication skills. In addition, both of their parents have stated that appropriate dressing will increase their independence as they prepare to make the transition to secondary school. The state's alternate assessment requires that they be assessed on science concepts related to 1) the structure and transformation of matter and 2) energy transformations in the universe. The special education teacher and the instructional assistant will rotate conducting instruction in a small-group setting (i.e., 1:2 format).

Instructional Materials

Instructional materials will consist of two sets of white 5″ × 7″ cards. One set contains the words *solid, liquid,* and *neither* handwritten in black lowercase letters. The other set contains computer-generated pictures that represent ice cycles, rain falling from a cloud, and a sun with the words *ice, rainy,* and *sunny* handwritten in black lowercase letters under each, respectively. A third set of white 3″ × 5″ cards contains computer-generated pictures of clothing that might be worn or used for each of these types of weather conditions (i.e., coat and mitten, rain coat and umbrella, bathing suits).

Three corresponding sets of cards will be used to assess generalization. These will include white 5″ × 7″ cards containing the words *solid, liquid, gas,* and *neither* handwritten in black lowercase letters and paired with picture symbols (e.g., ice cubes, raindrops); photographs of weather conditions (i.e., ice cycles, rain puddles, sunshine); and photographs of clothing for various types of weather.

Instructional Procedure

Each instructional session will proceed as follows.

Attentional Cue	• The instructor will lay the card choices for student responses in random order on the table in front of the two learners and will say, "Look," while pointing to each card and stating the word (i.e., ice, rain, sun).
Constant Time-Delay Procedure	• The task direction will be for the learner to point to the correct picture. During the first instructional session, the instructor will immediately model the desired response by pointing to the correct card while stating the response (i.e., 0-second delay interval). For example, the instructor will lay the cards with pictures of the weather in front of the learners. When she has their attention, she will give the task direction, "Chris, point to the picture of a solid," while holding up the card with the word *solid* written on it. The instructor will then model the desired response by pointing to the picture of ice while saying, "Ice is water in solid form." Immediately after this trial, the instructor will lay the pictures of clothing in front of the learners and say, "Point to the picture of what you might wear when if it is icy outdoors," and then immediately point to a picture of a coat and mittens. The session will proceed until each learner receives a trial on solid, liquid, and neither. After one day with the 0-second delay interval, the instructor will wait 3 seconds for the learners to make responses before providing the prompt. There will be six trials per learner (two per stimulus of solid, liquid, and neither) per session for a total of 12 instructional trials per session.
Consequence	• Verbal praise will follow each prompted or unprompted correct response, making sure that both learners are attending to the consequence (e.g., "Good job! Look, Barbara; Chris pointed to the solid ice").

Nontargeted Information

When delivering the consequence for states of matter, the instructor will provide additional information on the science concept (e.g., "Rocks are also a solid"; "Milk is also a liquid"). When delivering the consequences for appropriate dress related to the weather, the instructor will provide additional information (e.g., "In the winter season, we wear warm clothing because it

CONSTANT TIME-DELAY DATA SHEET

Instructor: __Ms. McClannahan__ Setting: __Science class__ Date: __September 25__

Student	Stimulus	States of matter		Clothing for weather	
		Before	After	Before	After
1. Chris	Liquid	–			0
2. Barbara	Neither	+		+	
3. Chris	Solid	+		+	
4. Barbara	Liquid	+		+	
5. Chris	Neither		–		+
6. Barbara	Liquid		+		+
7. Chris	Solid	+		+	
8. Barbara	Neither		0		+
9. Chris	Liquid		+	+	
10. Barbara	Solid	+		–	
11. Chris	Neither		+		+
12. Barbara	Solid	+		+	
Number/% correct: Chris		2/33%	2/33%	3/50%	2/33%
Number/% correct: Barbara		4/67%	1/17%	3/50%	2/33%

Key: Plus sign indicates correct; minus sign indicates incorrect; zero indicates no response.

Figure 8.2. Sample completed data sheet for using a constant time-delay procedure in a small-group format in Sample Instructional Program 2.

is colder due to less of the sun's energy hitting the earth's surface," or "In the summer season, we wear lighter clothing because it is warmer due to more of the sun's energy hitting the earth's surface").

Data Collection

The instructor will record a plus sign for correct responses before or after the prompt, a minus sign for incorrect responses before or after the prompt, and a zero sign for no responses after the prompt.

A sample completed data sheet is shown in Figure 8.2.

Maintenance

Once a learner reaches the criterion of 100% correct independent responses for 1 day, the instructor will fade praise to follow every other response (i.e., fixed ratio of 2, or FR2) for a minimum of 2 days. Instruction will continue until both learners have met criterion. In addition, the instructor will monitor maintenance of science information during the general education science class units on states of matter and energy transformation in the universe.

Generalization

After both learners meet criterion, the instructor will assess generalization by using different materials (i.e., novel photographs of states of matter, weather, and clothing). The data collected from these trials to assess generalization will be used to document performance for the state's alternate assessment in science.

Behavior Management

Appropriate behavior will be facilitated by providing intermittent praise for attending during instruction and assessment.

Lesson Variations and Extension

It should be noted that direct instruction on core content may or may not take place in inclusive settings. Regardless of the setting, direct instruction on core content may be needed as a supplement to instruction during science units in general education classes. Although this lesson was designed to be conducted as supplemental small-group instruction to ensure that the learners mastered the concepts, it is possible for the lesson to be embedded during the general education unit by providing discrete trials with picture choices within the context of general education lessons. There are multiple opportunities to reinforce learning of these concepts throughout the day. For example, the instructor can provide brief trials on solid and liquid during lunch (e.g., "Chris, point to the item on your lunch tray that is a liquid") or during art class (e.g., "Barbara, point to the art material you are using that is a solid").

SUMMARY

This chapter discussed the need for teaching both core content and functional skills to learners with moderate and severe disabilities and showed how the two can be meshed within a single lesson using systematic instruction. Regardless of the core content that is being taught, instructors should make an effort to present the content in a way that shows a real-life application that is meaningful to the learner. In addition, the combination of meshing functional skill instruction with core content is a more efficient use of instructional time, with the outcome of the acquisition of skills that will be needed for successful transitions to more independent living in less restrictive environments during adulthood.

QUESTIONS FOR REFLECTION

1. Why is the acquisition of functional skills important? Why is the acquisition of core content important? How can the two be meshed?

2. Why might it be necessary to provide supplemental instruction on core content for students with moderate and severe disabilities in addition to the academic units that are taught in general education settings?

3. Does a move to higher expectations for the acquisition of core content mean that functional skill instruction should be abandoned? Delayed? Taught outside of the school setting? Provide a rationale for your response.

4. What are some strategies that can be used to ensure that core content is meaningful to learners with moderate and severe disabilities?

REFERENCES

Bouck, E.C. (2008). Factors impacting the enactment of a functional curriculum in self-contained cross-categorical programs. *Education and Training in Developmental Disabilities, 43*, 294–310.

Bouck, E.C. (2009). No Child Left Behind, the Individuals with Disabilities Education Act, and functional curricula: A conflict of interest. *Education and Training in Developmental Disabilities, 44*, 3–13.

Bradford, S., Shippen, M.E., Alberto, P., Houchins, D.E., & Flores, M. (2006). Using systematic instruction to teach decoding skills to middle school students with moderate intellectual disabilities. *Education and Training in Developmental Disabilities, 41*, 333–343.

Browder, C., Flowers, C., Ahlgrim-Delzell, L., Karvonen, M., Spooner, F., & Algozzine, R. (2004). The alignment of alternate assessment content with academic and functional curricula. *Journal of Special Education, 37*, 211–224.

Browder, D., Ahlgrim-Delzell, L., Spooner, F., Mims, P.J., & Baker, J.N. (2009). Using time delay to teach literacy to students with severe developmental disabilities. *Exceptional Children, 75*, 343–363.

Browder, D.M., & Spooner, F. (Eds.). (2011). *Teaching students with moderate and severe disabilities.* New York, NY: Guilford.

Browder, D.M., Spooner, R., Ahlgrim-Delzell, L., Harris, A.A., & Wakeman, S. (2008). A meta-analysis on teaching mathematics to students with significant cognitive disabilities. *Exceptional Children, 74*, 407–432.

Browder, D.M., Spooner, F., Wakeman, S., Trela, K., & Baker, J.N. (2006). Aligning instruction with academic content standards: Finding the link. *Research & Practice for Persons with Severe Disabilities, 31*, 309–321.

Browder, D.M., Trela, K., & Jimenez, G. (2007). Training teachers to follow a task analysis to engage middle school students with moderate and severe developmental disabilities in grade-appropriate literature. *Focus on Autism and Other Developmental Disabilities, 22*, 206–219.

Browder, D.M., Wakeman, S.Y., Flowers, C., Rickelman, R.J., Pugalee, D., & Karvonen, M. (2007). Creating access to the general curriculum with links to grade-level content for students with significant cognitive disabilities: An explication of the concept. *Journal of Special Education, 41*, 2–16.

Brown, L., Branston, M.B., Hamre-Nietupski, S., Pumpian, I., Certo, N., & Gruenewald, L. (1979). A strategy for developing chronological-age-appropriate and functional curricular content for severely handicapped adolescents and young adults. *Journal of Special Education, 13*, 81–90.

Cohen, E.T., Heller, K.W., Alberto, P., & Fredrick, L.D. (2008). Using a three-step decoding strategy with constant time delay to teach word reading to students with mild and moderate mental retardation. *Focus on Autism and Other Developmental Disabilities, 23*, 67–78.

Collins, B.C., Branson, T.A., Hall, M., & Rankin, S.W. (2001). Teaching secondary students with moderate disabilities in an inclusive academic classroom setting. *Journal of Developmental and Physical Disabilities, 13*, 41.

Collins, B.C., Evans, A., Creech-Galloway, C., Karl, J., & Miller, A. (2007). Comparison of the acquisition and maintenance of teaching functional and core content sight words in special and general education settings. *Focus on Autism and Other Developmental Disabilities, 22*, 220–223.

Collins, B.C., Hager, K.D., & Galloway, C.C. (2011). The addition of functional content during core content instruction with students with moderate disabilities. *Education and Training in Developmental Disabilities, 46*, 22–39.

Collins, B.C., Karl, J., Riggs, L., Galloway, C.C., & Hager, K.D. (2010). Teaching core content with real-life applications to secondary students with moderate and severe disabilities. *Teaching Exceptional Children, 43*(1), 52–59.

Copeland, S.R., & Cosbey, J. (2008–2009). Making progress in the general curriculum: Rethinking effective instructional practices. *Research & Practice for Persons with Severe Disabilities, 33–34*, 214–227.

Dymond, S.K., Renzaglia, A., Gilson, C.L., & Slagor, M.T. (2007). Defining access to the general curriculum for high school students with significant cognitive disabilities. *Research & Practice for Persons with Severe Disabilities, 32*, 1–15.

Falkenstine, K.J., Collins, B.C., Schuster, J.W., & Kleinert, K. (2009). Presenting chained and discrete tasks as nontargeted information when teaching discrete academic skills through small group instruction. *Education and Training in Developmental Disabilities, 44*, 127–142.

Flowers, C., Browder, D., & Ahlgrim-Delzill, L. (2006). An analysis of three states' alignment between language arts and mathematics standards and alternate assessment. *Exceptional Children*, 201–215.

Individuals with Disabilities Education Act Amendments (IDEA) of 1997, PL 105-17, 20 U.S.C. §§ 1400 *et seq.*

Jimenez, B.A., Courtade, G.R., & Browder, D.M. (2008). Teaching an algebraic equation to high school students with moderate developmental disabilities. *Education and Training in Developmental Disabilities, 43*, 266–274.

Kleinert, H.L., Collins, B.C., Wickham, D., Riggs, L., & Hager, K.D. (2010). Embedding life skills, self-determination, social relationships, and other evidence-based practices. In H.L. Kleinert & J.F. Kearns, *Alternate assessment for students with significant cognitive disabilities: An educator's guide*. Baltimore, MD: Paul H. Brookes Publishing Co.

Kleinert, H.L., & Kearns, J.F. (2010). *Alternate assessment for students with significant cognitive disabilities: An educator's guide*. Baltimore, MD: Paul H. Brookes Publishing Co.

Lynch, S., & Adams, P. (2008). Developing standards-based individualized education program objectives for students with significant needs. *Teaching Exceptional Children, 40*, 36–39.

McDonnell, J., & Copeland, S.R. (2011). Teaching academic skills. In M.E. Snell & F. Brown (Eds.), *Instruction of students with severe disabilities* (7th ed., pp. 492–528). Upper Saddle River, NJ: Pearson.

McDonnell, J., Johnson, J.W., Polychronis, S., Riesen, T., Jameson, J., & Kercher, K. (2006). Comparison of one-to-one embedded instruction in general education classes with small group instruction in special education classes. *Education and Training in Developmental Disabilities, 41*, 125–138.

McDonnell, J., Thorson, N., & McQuivey, C. (2000). Comparison of the instructional contexts of students with severe disabilities and their peers in general education classes. *Journal of the Association for Persons with Severe Handicaps, 24*, 54–58.

No Child Left Behind Act of 2001, PL 107-110, 115 Stat. 1425, 20 U.S.C. §§ 6301 *et seq.*

Parrish, P.R., & Stodden, R.A. (2009). Aligning assessment and instruction with state standards for children with significant disabilities. *Teaching Exceptional Children, 41*(4), 46–56.

Wakeman, S.Y., Spooner, F., & Knight, V. (2007). Evidence-based practices for teaching literacy to students with significant cognitive disabilities. *TASH Connections, 33*(3/4), 16–19

Westling, D.L., & Fox, L. (2009). *Teaching students with severe disabilities* (4th ed.). Upper Saddle River, NJ: Pearson.

CHAPTER 9

Working with Peers, Paraprofessionals, and Staff

On completion of this chapter, the reader will be able to

- Identify individuals who can be prepared to provide systematic instruction to learners with moderate and severe disabilities, and explain why multiple instructors can be a beneficial practice
- Discuss considerations in involving peers as instructors or natural support
- Discuss considerations in assigning instructional responsibilities to paraprofessionals
- Explain how a transdisciplinary model can be used when working with related services delivery personnel

TERMS USED IN THIS CHAPTER

transdisciplinary team model
role release

As stated and demonstrated repeatedly throughout this text, the education of learners with moderate and severe disabilities is a team effort. Systematic instruction is not the sole responsibility of the special education teacher trained in its procedures but, rather, the responsibility of a number of individuals including, but not limited to, general education teachers (e.g., academic content teachers, music or art teachers, physical educators), support staff (e.g., paraprofessionals, job coaches), related services personnel (e.g., speech-language pathologists, occupational therapists, physical therapists), family members and caregivers (e.g., parents, siblings, guardians), and peers (e.g., tutors, coaches, or friends). As discussed in Chapter 7, increasing and varying the number of instructors facilitates generalization across settings in which learners will be required to respond to and interact with novel individuals (e.g., neighbors, community workers, employers). Rather than limiting instructional settings to ones in which staff have been prepared with the expertise to deliver systematic instruction, special education teachers should be collaborators who view their role as preparing others to implement systematic instruction throughout the day (e.g., Carothers & Taylor, 2004; Carter, Cushing, Clark, & Kennedy, 2005; Cavkaytar, 2007; Collins, 2002; Collins, Branson, & Hall, 1995; Collins, Branson, Hall, & Rankin, 2001; Collins, Hager, & Galloway, 2011; Collins, Hall, & Branson, 1997; Godsey, Schuster, Lingo, Collins, & Kleinert, 2008; Lafasakis & Sturmey, 2007; McDuffie, Mastropieri, & Scruggs, 2009; Miracle, Collins, Schuster, & Grisham-Brown, 2001; Mobayed, Collins, Strangis, Schuster, & Hemmeter, 2000; Mueller et al., 2003; Ozcan & Cavkaytar, 2009).

This chapter highlights the sharing of expertise with three groups most likely to serve as support for learners across educational settings: 1) peers, 2) paraprofessionals, and 3) staff. It should be noted, however, that the methods described can be implemented with others in addition to these groups of individuals. Chapter 10 focuses on the difficult issue of scheduling instruction across settings.

WORKING WITH PEERS

The importance of peers without disabilities in the education of learners with moderate and severe disabilities cannot be overstated. Peers are natural partners and role models in teaching communication and social skills. Peer interactions can result in relationships that extend beyond the walls of the school, providing support in current environments in which learners live and engage in recreation and in future environments in which learners will secure employment and live as independently as possible. There is a large body of evidence that peers can be trained as effective and reliable instructors to teach an array of skills across age levels, although most of the research has been with secondary learners (e.g., Collins et al., 1995; Collins et al., 2001; Collins et al., 1997; Godsey et al., 2008; Miracle et al., 2001). By providing peer tutoring for learners with disabilities, peers can strengthen their own skill level and fluency while becoming more empathetic to learning differences and becoming more aware of the abilities of all learners to acquire knowledge and skills. An advantage to using peers as instructors is that they are available across inclusive settings to serve as a system of natural support and not just through peer tutoring programs in which they work in the resource room either as volunteers or for academic credit.

Some researchers have cautioned that the drawback to using a peer tutoring model is that the tutor–tutee model can be unbalanced, setting one group of students up to feel superior to another (Carter et al., 2005; Carter et al., 2010). Alternative models that have been proposed are to use same-age peers without disabilities as peer coaches or peer buddies who engage in support roles rather than instructional roles or to involve peers with and without disabilities in cooperative projects, such as service learning, in which there are learning goals set for all students (Hughes & Carter, 2008).

Although the focus most often has been on older learners, the professional research literature has shown that peers without disabilities can be used to effectively deliver response-prompting procedures, such as the system-of-least-prompts (SLP) procedure (e.g., Collins et al, 2001; Collins et al., 1997) and constant time-delay (CTD) procedure (e.g., Collins et al., 1995; Godsey et al., 2008; Miracle et al., 2001) to teach both discrete skills and chained tasks. Although most of the research to support this has occurred in resource rooms, some has occurred in natural settings, such as academic classes (e.g., Collins et al., 2001) and school hallways (e.g., Collins, Hall, Rankin, & Branson, 1999). One option that special educators should consider is preparing peers with the skills to deliver trials of systematic instruction and then to have them embed these throughout the school day. For example, a peer can deliver instructional trials on reading, writing, and math skills or on communication and social skills across academic classes, in music and art classes, during physical education, during hallway or playground interactions, or during community outings (e.g., community-based instruction [CBI], field trips, service learning projects, recreational activities). The more learning opportunities a learner has, the faster the learner will acquire the skill being taught. Also, the more instructional trials that are embedded across settings and instructors (in this case, peer tutors), the more likely a learner will be to generalize skills that are acquired. Finally, the use of peers to deliver instruction increases the efficiency of instruction because it is impossible for the special education teacher to be with all learners all day long, each of whom are following individualized schedules across instructional settings.

When a peers assume the role of instructors, it is imperative that they are trained to a high degree of reliability (typically above 80%, ideally above 90%) on instructional strategies and data collection. This can be accomplished through a combination of written materials, role modeling, practice, and feedback on performance (e.g., Collins et al., 1995; Collins et al., 1997; Godsey et al., 2008; Miracle et al., 2001).

PARAPROFESSIONALS

Regardless of whether special education teachers rely on peers to supplement instruction, almost all rely on the support of paraprofessionals, and it is not uncommon for there to be several assigned to providing special education support within a single school. Because it is rare for paraprofessionals to have degrees or advanced training in special education, it is up to the instructional team to determine the amount of support that a learner with a moderate or severe disability will receive from a paraprofessional, and it is most often up to the special education teacher to determine the schedule and responsibilities of each paraprofessional. Although a collaborative relationship is important for shared ownership of instruction, the ultimate responsibility for managing and training paraprofessionals typically will fall on the special education teacher (Westling & Fox, 2009).

Paraprofessionals often are given an array of responsibilities in working with students with moderate and severe disabilities. These may include providing instruction and support, assisting with physical and personal management, helping to adapt materials and make accommodations across settings, collecting instructional data, implementing behavior management programs and providing positive behavioral support, administering medical procedures and monitoring physical states, assisting with the use of augmentative and assistive communication devices, and performing clerical tasks for the teacher. These responsibilities may occur in inclusive general education settings, in special education resource rooms, and within the context of CBI.

Although it is evident that paraprofessionals can be a huge source of help to teachers and a great source of support for learners, there are legitimate arguments for using their assistance with caution (Giangreco & Broer, 2007). Researchers have pointed out that, as adults, the constant presence of paraprofessionals across settings can be stigmatizing to learners with special needs and can diminish natural interactions between students with and without disabilities. There is also the risk that learners may become overly dependent on the support of paraprofessionals, thus decreasing the amount of independence that learners achieve. Likewise, teachers also may become overly dependent on the support of paraprofessionals, thus shirking responsibilities for instruction, especially in large-group activities in which all learners should be included.

To avoid these problems, the instructional team should clearly delineate the responsibilities of paraprofessionals, rotating them across learners and settings and teaching them strategies that will transfer full dependence on the paraprofessional to natural supports, such as peers and general education teachers across settings (Causton-Theoharis & Malmgren, 2005). In most cases, it will be up to the special education teacher to collaborate with each paraprofessional, teaching how and when to provide direct support and instruction as well as how and when to back away and facilitate support and instruction by others. The best way to do this is to make expectations clear in writing and to conduct frequent meetings for discussing the needs and progress of learners. As with peer tutors, paraprofessionals who are to provide direct instruction should receive training in which they demonstrate a high degree of reliability on the implementation of instructional strategies and data collection before being assigned to deliver instruction.

SUPPORT STAFF

In addition to general and special educators, paraprofessionals, and peers, the instructional team also can contain a number of other individuals with different types of expertise, such as speech-language pathologists, occupational therapists, physical therapists, vision and mobility specialists, and medical personnel. Although the primary responsibility of these individuals may not be instruction, using a **transdisciplinary team model** (Downing & Bailey, 1990) makes it possible for members of the instructional team to collaborate on instructional programs with the teacher, to share their respective areas of expertise with each other, and to use systematic instruction to embed instructional trials across activities, regardless of who may be working with a learner at a particular time (e.g., Roark, Collins, Hemmeter, & Kleinert, 2002). For example, a speech-language pathologist who is working on oral motor skills during lunch can embed trials on right and left, open and shut, colors, and counting, among other skills. A physical therapist who is working on mobility can embed trials of reading, counting, and identifying colors while facilitating independent mobility in the school halls. An occupational therapist who is working on fine motor skills during vocational training can embed trials of reading or counting while working with a learner on transition skills in the community or domestic settings. Through **role release,** a special educator can share strategies for gaining attention, providing clear task directions, providing and fading prompts, and providing feedback on responses (Bricker, 1976). Likewise, a special education teacher can learn to embed techniques used by related services delivery personnel when providing systematic instruction on academic and functional skills, such as placing a material out of reach so that a learner will have to request it or extend across midline to grasp it. This type of transdiciplinary approach for collaborating on instruction in which professionals are generous in relinquishing their roles to others is superior to other team approaches because the number of opportunities to respond are increased across the day, the skills that learners acquire are more integrated into natural activities, and generalization is more likely to occur due to multiple instructors across activities and settings.

OTHERS

It should be stressed that parents and other family members or caregivers also should remain integral parts of the instructional team (e.g., Carothers & Taylor, 2004; Cavkaytar, 2007; Lafasakis & Sturmey, 2007; Mobayed et al., 2000; Mueller et al., 2003; Ozcan & Cavkaytar, 2009). When instructional strategies are shared, these are the individuals who can ensure that learning continues in natural settings (e.g., the home, neighborhood, and community) when school is not in session (e.g., nights, weekends, holiday, summer breaks). In addition to facilitating the rate of learning and generalization, sharing instructional strategies empowers those who are close to a learner to share in the responsibility for providing an education and decreases feelings of helplessness and dependency on others. The term *generalist* can be used to describe parents who can take strategies to teach specific skills and apply them with success to the instruction of novel skills, a practice that can increase the number of skills that a learner will acquire over time.

SAMPLE INSTRUCTIONAL PROGRAMS

Chapter 4 contains a sample instructional program conducted by a speech-language pathologist and another sample instructional program conducted by a paraprofessional. The following instructional programs demonstrate how peer tutors can provide reliable systematic instruction to learners with moderate and severe disabilities. In the following lesson plans, the peer tutors are enrolled in a peer tutoring class for which they receive academic credit, a process that can be an effective tool for recruiting students into college personnel preparation programs in special education. Although peer tutors are the instructors in these programs, paraprofessionals or other personnel also could be used in the same manner.

Sample Instructional Program 1

In the first sample program, secondary peer tutors are used to teach a functional chained task using a CTD procedure—in this case, how to prepare a food during a lunch group that meets in the consumer science room. Before implementing instruction, the special education teacher will train the peer tutors in instructional strategies during after-school training sessions. This training will consist of teaching how to implement the CTD procedure and how to collect data until the peer tutors demonstrate 90% accuracy on a written quiz and through performance in simulations. During instruction, two peer tutors will be paired with each learner with a disability—one to deliver direct instruction and one to collect data. Peer tutors will alternate between these two roles across learners to facilitate generalization. The procedure is based on a research study conducted by Godsey et al. (2008).

Core Content Standards

Practical Living/ Vocational
- Students demonstrate the knowledge and skills they need to remain physically healthy and to accept responsibility for their own physical well-being.

Reading
- Students will interpret the meaning of jargon, dialect, or specialized vocabulary found in a passage.
- Students will identify essential information from a passage needed to accomplish a task.
- Students will apply the information contained in a passage to accomplish a task/procedure or to answer questions about a passage.
- Students will follow the sequence of information from a passage.

Behavioral Objective

When told to prepare an item for a meal, the learner will prepare the item with 100% accuracy for 3 days.

Instructional Context

Linda, Karen, Patty, and Paula are the 4 students with moderate and severe disabilities who will participate in the lesson. They are 15 to 20 years old and have food preparation listed on their individualized education programs (IEPs) as a skill to help them successfully make the transition to adulthood in the least restrictive environment. There will be 11 peer tutors between the ages of 16 and 18 years who are enrolled in a peer tutoring class for credit, after having been recommended by other faculty members in the high school. Some of the peer tutors are enrolled in advanced course work in a precollege curriculum, and some are enrolled in a vocational education track. Each day, the peer tutors meet in the consumer science classroom with the learners with moderate and severe disabilities to prepare a meal together. The peer tutors rotate in participating in this activity. Each day, one peer tutor per learner will conduct instruction in a 1:1 format using a CTD procedure while another peer tutor observes and records data on performance. The number of trials for making foods will depend on the number of peer tutors and learners present each day to eat lunch.

Instructional Materials

The food targeted for instruction are those preferred by the learners, as indicated through interviews with the learners and their parents. The food preparation skills include 1) making a milkshake in a blender, 2) making juice from concentrate, 3) making a grilled cheese sandwich, and 4) making a waffle in a toaster (Godsey et al., 2008, p. 114). The students will rotate making a milkshake and grilled cheese with making juice and a waffle across days with two learners preparing drinks and two learners preparing sandwiches or waffles. The special education teacher has made a picture recipe book for each of these tasks, with one step shown per page. The peer tutors will have data collection sheets for collecting formative data on the progress of the learners.

Instructional Procedure

Each instructional session will proceed as follows.

Attentional Cue	• The peer tutor will state the learner's name and then place the picture recipe book in front of the learner.
Constant Time-Delay Procedure	• The instructional session will begin with the task direction (e.g., "Let's make orange juice today"). On the first day of instruction, each peer tutor will use a 0-second delay interval by immediately providing a verbal/model prompt for the learner (e.g., point to picture recipe and say, "The first step is to get out the pitcher. Watch me….Now, you do it"). After delivering the prompt, the peer tutor will wait 5 seconds for the learner to initiate each step and then 20 seconds for the learner to complete each step. On all subsequent days, the peer tutor will wait 5 seconds before delivering each prompt.
Consequence	• When each step is completed, the peer tutor will praise the learner if the response was correct or will perform a correct response for the learner if there was an incorrect response or no response. Once all learners have completed the food tasks, they will share the meal with the peer tutors (a natural reinforcer).

Nontargeted Information

Preparing food provides the opportunity to provide nontargeted information related to core content. When providing prompts or praise, the peer tutors will be taught to add statements on good nutrition (e.g., "Cheese is a dairy product and provides calcium to build strong bones"), on caloric intake (e.g., "Low-fat milk is a good choice because it has fewer calories than whole milk"), on measurement (e.g., "Two cups equal one pint"), on fractions (e.g., "If you cut one sandwich in four equal parts, each part is equal to one fourth"), and on social studies (e.g., "Oranges grow in states like Florida and California where the climate is warmer").

Data Collection

The peer tutor who is designated as the data collector will record data on responses throughout instruction. A plus sign will be recorded for correct responses before or after the prompt, a minus sign will be recorded for incorrect responses before or after the prompt, and a zero will be recorded for no response after the prompt. If there are multiple trials on preparing a

CONSTANT TIME-DELAY DATA SHEET

Skill: ___Making juice___

Steps	April 15 Before	April 15 After	April 16 Before	April 16 After	April 17 Before	April 17 After	April 18 Before	April 18 After
Date	April 15		April 16		April 17		April 18	
Peer tutor	Bob		Randy		Ron		Tom	
Student	Linda		Karen		Patty		Paula	
1. Get out pitcher	+		+		+		–	
2. Get out juice can	+		+		+		+	
3. Get out spoon		–		+	+		+	
4. Open juice can		0		–	+			+
5. Empty in pitcher	+			–	+		–	
6. Add water		+	+		–		+	
7. Stir	+		+		+		+	
8. Pour in cups		–	+		–		+	
Number/% correct	4/50%	1/13%	5/63%	1/13%	6/75%	0/0%	5/63%	1/13%

Key: Plus sign indicates correct; minus sign indicates incorrect; zero indicates no response.

Figure 9.1. Sample completed data sheet for using a constant time-delay procedure with peers in Sample Instructional Program 1. Multiple students are listed on this data sheet, but just one activity (making juice) is included, which allows peers to keep track of their rotation and ensure that each student has taken his or her turn on the activity.

food (e.g., making more than one sandwich), data will be recorded for the first trial only. A sample completed data sheet is shown in Figure 9.1.

Maintenance

Once the learner reaches the criterion of 100% correct responses on a task analysis for 2 days, the peer tutor will fade praise for responses to an average of every three (i.e., fixed ratio of 3, or FR3) responses for 1 day. When all learners have reach criterion on the target foods, new foods (e.g., soup, salads) will be selected for instruction, and maintenance will be monitored on the mastered foods by continuing to prepare each once per month for the remainder of the school year.

Generalization

Generalization is facilitated by teaching learners to prepare foods across peer tutors, who will rotate daily, and by preparing a variety of foods. Parents will be asked to encourage the learners to prepare the target foods at home once they have met criterion.

Behavior Management

Appropriate behavior will be facilitated by providing intermittent praise for attending during instruction.

Lesson Variations and Extension

There are a variety of foods that are simple to prepare that will facilitate independence in adulthood, including foods prepared on the stove, in an oven, or in a microwave. Cooking with others also is a recreational activity enjoyed by children, adolescents, and adults that provides the opportunity for social interactions. In addition, those who become skilled at preparing certain foods (e.g., preparing vegetables for a salad) may be employed in that capacity as adolescents or as adults. For younger learners, preparing healthy snacks, such as popcorn or cheese and crackers, can be a fun activity that prepares them for more complex cooking tasks in the future. In addition to using picture recipe books, many products (e.g., cake mixes) come with pictures paired with simple written directions, and it is a simple task to prepare PowerPoint slides on a computer to provide directions for recipes or to download verbal direction, still pictures, or video on iPods to take advantage of the using technology as a natural support for preparing foods.

Sample Instructional Program 2

The second sample instructional program also uses peer tutors to deliver instruction. This program, however, focuses on a core content skill (e.g., reading) rather than on a functional skill. This program will take place in a resource room to which peer tutors come each day to work on reading vocabulary words with learners with moderate and severe disabilities. The peer tutors participating in this lesson will participate in a series of after-school classes to learn the instructional procedures. The special education teacher will train them by discussing the importance of response-prompting procedures, providing written materials on the procedures, and teaching the peer tutors how to deliver instruction (e.g., prompt, reinforce) and collect data through modeling, practice, and feedback until the peer tutors can perform the instructional procedure with no more than one incorrect response. The procedures are based on a research study conducted by Miracle et al. (2001).

Core Content Standard

Reading • Students will interpret the meaning of jargon, dialect, or specialized vocabulary found in a passage.

Behavioral Objective

When presented with five vocabulary words, the learner will read the word with 100% accuracy for 3 days.

Instructional Context

Four learners with moderate and severe disabilities (i.e., Lucy, Letha, Shirley, and Kay) and four peer tutors will participate in the lesson. The learners with disabilities range in age from 14 to

20 years and have objectives for basic sight words listed on their IEPs. The peer tutors will range in age from 17 to 18 years; three are in a college preparatory track, and one is in a vocational track. The special education teacher has selected functional vocabulary words for instruction that represent the basic food groups being taught in health class. These words also will enable the learners to be more independent in selecting foods from restaurant menus or shopping for foods in the grocery store when they make the transition to adulthood. The peer tutors will rotate the learner with whom they work in the resource room across days.

Instructional Materials

Instructional materials will consist of white, unlined, 4″ × 6″ index cards on which the target words have been written in black letters with a marker.

Instructional Procedure

Each instructional session will proceed as follows.

Attentional Cue	• The peer tutor will approach the learner assigned by the special education teacher and tell the learner it is time to work on reading vocabulary words. Once seated, the peer tutor will ask the learner if she is ready to begin working before beginning instruction.
Constant Time-Delay Procedure	• The task direction will be, "What word is this?" During the first instructional session, the peer tutor will immediately state the correct response (i.e., verbal model prompt at a 0-second delay interval). There will be three trials per word for a total of 15 trials per session. On all subsequent days, the peer tutor will wait a 3-second delay interval before delivering the prompt.
Consequence	• Specific verbal praise (e.g., "Yes, the word is yogurt") will follow each prompted or unprompted correct response. Incorrect responses after the prompt will be followed by error correction (e.g., "No, the word is yogurt"). If the learner makes an incorrect response before the prompt, the peer tutor will give a reminder to wait to respond (e.g., "No. Please wait if you do not know the word, and I will tell you. The word is yogurt").

Nontargeted Information

Peer tutors will be told to make statements that provide core content about words whenever possible (e.g., "Yes, the word is yogurt. Yogurt is a dairy product, and it is a good source of calcium. Calcium builds strong bones").

Data Collection

The instructor will record a plus sign for correct responses before or after the prompt, a minus sign for incorrect responses before or after the prompt, and a zero for no responses after the prompt.

A sample completed data sheet is shown in Figure 9.2.

Maintenance

Once the learner reaches the criterion of 100% correct independent responses for one day, the instructor will fade praise for responses to an average of every third response (i.e., variable ratio of 3, or VR3) for 2 days. The special education teacher will check maintenance once per month until the end of the school year.

CONSTANT TIME-DELAY DATA SHEET

Skill: ___Health/foods vocabulary___   Date: ___September 15___

Peer tutor	Roy		Stanley		John		Ebb	
Student	Lucy		Letha		Shirley		Kay	
Steps	Before	After	Before	After	Before	After	Before	After
1. Apple	–		+		+		–	
2. Yogurt	+		+		+		+	
3. Chicken		–		+	+		+	
4. Peas		0		–	+			+
5. Bread	+		–		+		–	
6. Apple	–		+		+		–	
7. Yogurt	+		+		+		+	
8. Chicken		–		+	+		+	
9. Peas		0		–	+			+
10. Bread	+		–		+		–	
11. Apple	–		+		+		–	
12. Yogurt	+		+		+		+	
13. Chicken		–		+	+		+	
14. Peas		0		–	+			+
15. Bread	+		–		+		–	
Number/% correct	6/40%	0/0%	6/40%	3/20%	15/100%	0/0%	6/40%	3/20%

Key: Plus sign indicates correct; minus sign indicates incorrect; zero indicates no response.

Figure 9.2.   Sample completed data sheet for using a constant time-delay procedure with peers in Sample Instructional Program 2.

Generalization

Generalization is facilitated by varying the peer tutors who work with each learner daily. In addition, all learners participate in CBI once per week with the peer tutors. During this time, peer tutors will monitor the reading of the vocabulary words across settings (e.g., grocery stores, restaurants) and across materials (e.g., product labels, menus).

Behavior Management

Appropriate behavior will be facilitated by providing intermittent praise for attending during instruction and assessment.

Lesson Variations and Extension

Whereas this lesson focuses on teaching academic words related to health class (i.e., foods from the basic food groups) that the learners all attend, they are pretaught in a resource room to facilitate successful inclusion in the health lesson when food groups are taught. In addition, the target words also are important for successful transition to make learners more independent in grocery shopping and ordering from menus. In this case, the learners all attend other classes focusing on core content during the day; thus, instruction on additional vocabulary words related to math, science, or social studies also would be appropriate. Although definitions are not targeted in this lesson, it is simple to have peer tutors provide them as nontargeted information.

SUMMARY

This chapter discussed the importance of involving peer tutors, paraprofessionals, related services delivery personnel, and others in systematic instruction for learners with moderate and severe disabilities. As noted, this is a strategy to facilitate generalization while also decreasing instructional downtime. The sample instructional programs took place with peer tutors in a resource room and in a consumer science class during lunch. It should be noted that peer tutors, as well as other staff, also can deliver effective and reliable instruction in inclusive academic settings. Ways of scheduling personnel across environments are discussed in Chapter 10.

QUESTIONS FOR REFLECTION

1. How can staff and peer tutors be trained to provide systematic instruction?

2. What are the benefits of using multiple instructors to teach skills to learners with moderate and severe disabilities?

3. What is a precaution in regard to using paraprofessionals to conduct instruction in inclusive settings?

4. How can a teacher ensure that instruction is reliably implemented across instructors?

REFERENCES

Bricker, D. (1976). Educational synthesizer. In T.M. Angele (Ed.), *Hey, don't forget about me: Education's investment in the severely, profoundly, and multiply handicapped* (pp. 84–97), Reston, VA: Council for Exceptional Children.

Carothers, D.E., & Taylor, R.L. (2004). How teachers and parents can work together to teach daily living skills to children with autism. *Focus on Autism and Other Developmental Disabilities, 19,* 102–104.

Carter, E.W., Cushing, L.S., Clark, N.M., & Kennedy, C.H. (2005). Effects of peer support interventions on students' access to the general curriculum and social interactions. *Research and Practice for Persons with Severe Disabilities, 30,* 15–25.

Carter, E.W., Sisco, L.G., Chung, Y., & Stanton-Chapman, T.L. (2010). Peer interactions of students with intellectual disabilities and/or autism: A map of the intervention literature. *Research and Practice for Persons with Severe Disabilities, 353*(3–4), 63–79.

Causton-Theoharis, J.M., & Malmgren, K.W. (2005). Increasing peer interactions for students with severe disabilities via paraprofessional training. *Exceptional Children, 4,* 431–444.

Cavkaytar, A. (2007). Turkish parents as teachers: Teaching parents how to teach self-care and domestic skills to their children with mental retardation. *Education and Training in Developmental Disabilities, 42,* 85–93.

Collins, B.C. (2002). Using peers to facilitate learning by students with moderate disabilities. *Behavior Analyst Today, 3,* 329–341.

Collins, B.C., Branson, T.A., & Hall, M. (1995). Teaching generalized reading of cooking product labels to adolescents with mental disabilities through the use of key words taught by peer tutors. *Education and Training in Mental Retardation and Developmental Disabilities, 30,* 65–75.

Collins, B.C., Branson, T.A., Hall, M., & Rankin, S.W. (2001). Teaching secondary students with moderate disabilities in an inclusive academic classroom setting. *Journal of Developmental and Physical Disabilities, 13,* 41–59.

Collins, B.C., Hager, K.D., & Galloway, C.C. (2011). The addition of functional content during core content instruction with students with moderate disabilities. *Education and Training in Developmental Disabilities, 46,* 22–39.

Collins, B.C., Hall, M., & Branson, T.A. (1997). Teaching leisure skills to adolescents with moderate disabilities. *Exceptional Children, 63,* 499–512.

Collins, B.C., Hall, M., Rankin, S.W., & Branson, T.A. (1999). Just say "No!" and walk away: Teaching students with mental disabilities to resist peer pressure. *Teaching Exceptional Children, 31,* 48–52.

Downing, J. & Bailey, B.R. (1990). Sharing the responsibility: Using a transdisciplinary team approach to enhance the learning of students with severe disabilities. *Journal of Educational and Psychological Consultation, 1,* 259–278.

Giangreco, M.F., & Broer, S.M. (2007). School-based screening to determine overreliance on paraprofessionals. *Focus on Autism and Other Developmental Disabilities, 22,* 149–158.

Godsey, J.R., Schuster, J.W., Lingo, A.S., Collins, B.C., & Kleinert, H.L. (2008). Peer-implemented time delay procedures on the acquisition of chained tasks by students with moderate and severe disabilities. *Education and Training in Developmental Disabilities, 43,* 111–122.

Hughes, C., & Carter, E.W. (2008). *Peer buddy programs for successful secondary school inclusion.* Baltimore, MD: Paul H. Brookes Publishing Co.

Lafasakis, M., & Sturmey, P. (2007). Training parent implementation of discrete-trial teaching: Effects on generalization of parent teaching and child correct responding. *Journal of Applied Behavior Analysis, 40,* 685–689.

McDuffie, K.A., Mastropieri, M.A., & Scruggs, T.E. (2009). Differential effects of peer tutoring in co-taught classes: Results for content learning and student-teacher interactions. *Exceptional Children, 75,* 493–510.

Miracle, S.A., Collins, B.C., Schuster, J.W., & Grisham-Brown, J. (2001). Peer versus teacher delivered instruction: Effects on acquisition and maintenance. *Education and Training in Mental Retardation and Developmental Disabilities, 36,* 375–385.

Mobayed, K.L., Collins, B.C., Strangis, D., Schuster, J.W., & Hemmeter, M.L. (2000). Teaching parents to employ mand-model procedures to teach their children requesting. *Journal of Early Intervention, 23,* 165–179.

Mueller, M.M., Piazza, C.C., Moore, J.W., Kelley, M.E., Bethke, S.A., Pruett, A.E., et al. (2003). Training parents to implement pediatric feeding protocols. *Journal of Applied Behavior Analysis, 36,* 545–562.

Ozcan, N., & Cavkaytar, A. (2009). Parents as teachers: Teaching parents how to teach toilet skills to their children with autism and mental retardation. *Education and Training in Developmental Disabilities, 44,* 237–243.

Roark, T.J., Collins, B.C., Hemmeter, M.L., & Kleinert, H. (2002). Including manual signing as nontargeted information when teaching receptive identification of packaged food items. *Journal of Behavioral Education. 11,* 19–38.

Westling, D.L., & Fox, L. (2009). *Teaching students with severe disabilities* (4th ed.). Upper Saddle River, NJ: Pearson.

Setting up Instructional Schedules and Classroom Environments

CHAPTER OBJECTIVES

On completion of this chapter, the reader will be able to

- Explain why inclusion in general education settings is a beneficial practice for learners with moderate and severe disabilities
- Discuss options for providing instructional support in inclusive settings
- Design a matrix that demonstrates how systematic instruction on individualized education program (IEP) objectives can be embedded across the day
- Design a schedule for learners with moderate and severe disabilities that shows inclusion and support across settings

One of the misconceptions about direct systematic instruction is that it takes places only in a massed trial format at a set time for instruction each day. Instead, trials of direct instruction should be viewed in a much broader context. Although there are planned times for instruction on specific content, direct instruction should be an ongoing process that takes place throughout the day whenever the opportunity arises under a variety of instructors (e.g., special or general education teachers, paraprofessionals, peers, parents, related services personnel). As noted in Chapter 7, teaching across natural activities and environments, as well as involving an array of individuals in the role of instructor, facilitates generalization. Thus, the outcome should be that learners with moderate and severe disabilities acquire skills that they can perform correctly when needed under a variety of conditions. Also, as described in Chapter 1, instruction can and should occur in massed, spaced, or embedded formats to increase opportunities for learning.

Setting up a daily schedule for learners with moderate and severe disabilities to ensure that instruction takes places across settings and individuals can be a challenge. This chapter discusses ways to ensure that ample instructional trials occur across the school day by using teachers, peers, paraprofessionals, and staff as instructors. A sample daily schedule is provided, as well as sample instructional programs in which instructional trials are scheduled to maximize opportunities for learning.

LEAST RESTRICTIVE ENVIRONMENTS

Typically, the least restrictive environment for learners with disabilities is in the setting in which their same-age peers without disabilities are learning content. There are a number of reasons for the argument that learners with moderate and severe disabilities should receive educational services alongside their peers without disabilities (e.g., Carter, Cushing, Clark, & Kennedy, 2005; Jackson, Ryndak, & Wehmeyer, 2008–2009; Owen-DeSchryver, Carr, Cale, & Blakely-Smith, 2008; Ryndak, Ward, Alper, Storch, & Montgomery, 2010). First, peers without disabilities can be models for appropriate social behavior. Peers can model age-appropriate dress, language, and behaviors that can result in learners with moderate and severe disabilities being more accepted by their peers. Second, the general education environment provides direct access to core content that is being taught to peers without disabilities. If the instructor applies principles of universal design for all learners to participate in instruction, learners with moderate and severe disabilities may acquire some of the core content that is presented. Even if they do not master this content when exposed to it, functional skills, such as communication, turn taking, fine motor skills, or basic functional academics (e.g., reading and writing letters of alphabet, counting, discriminating between colors) can be embedded within lessons that focus on core content. Third, placing learners with and without disabilities in the same environment increases the likelihood that friendships will form and allows peers without disabilities the opportunity to act as natural supports, as described in Chapter 9. Relationships that form in the school environment may extend to activities outside of school and may continue once the students make the transition to adult life. Finally, inclusion of learners with moderate and severe disabilities can be beneficial to their peers without disabilities, facilitating empathy while possibly planting the seeds for future careers (e.g., special education teacher, related services provider) or creating more understanding if these peers someday become parents to children with disabilities.

Inclusion should not be confused with instruction on general education core content, nor should it be limited to general education classroom settings. Inclusion occurs when learners with moderate and severe disabilities becomes part of the school environment across settings and activities. To be fully included, learners with moderate and severe disabilities should be included on the general education class roll and as a part of the activities of that class (Janney & Snell, 2011). This means that learners with moderate and severe disabilities will eat lunch, attend special classes (e.g., physical education, music), and go on field trips with same-age peers without disabilities from their homeroom. In short, general education classrooms should be considered the least restrictive environment, and time in resource rooms should be limited to the time necessary to master skills that data show learners with moderate and severe disabilities are not acquiring in general education settings. For example, time that learners with moderate and severe disabilities spend in resource rooms may be dedicated to working on life skills not taught in general education settings, to participate in drill and practice on academic skills that have not been acquired in general education settings, or to provide preteaching that focuses on the instruction of prerequisite skills (e.g., vocabulary for a unit of study) to enable learners with moderate and severe disabilities to more fully participate in and benefit from instruction in general education settings.

STAFFING AND SUPPORT

As described in Chapter 9, there are a number of options for supporting learners with moderate and severe disabilities during instruction, no matter where it occurs. These options include assistance from special and general education teachers, paraprofessionals, peers without disabilities, and related services personnel. Each learner's day should be individually scheduled to ensure that objectives from the IEP are covered within the daily schedule in the setting in which the learner with moderate and severe disabilities is most likely to acquire them (Downing & Bailey, 1990; Westling & Fox, 2009). Thus, the special education teacher has a number of responsibilities as a member of the instructional team (Bricker, 1976). Instead of setting up a classroom schedule in which each learner with moderate and severe disabilities progresses through the same activities at the same time, the special education teacher should collaborate with the general education teacher to determine where the learner will be included in general education settings and the amount of support that will be needed for each activity in those settings. The special education teacher will then need to identify what, if any, content cannot be covered in general education settings and determine settings in which instruction on those skills can take place, as well as the person who will be responsible for that instruction. The special education teacher may find that some learners with moderate and severe disabilities can be fully included for the entire day and only need support for certain activities, such as transitions or lunch. Others may need time in the resource room to work on either academic or functional instructional goals, to take part in therapy that cannot be embedded in general education settings, or to have health care procedures monitored or administered that might be stigmatizing in general education settings. Also, the special education teacher will need to consider whether learners with moderate and severe disabilities can benefit from participation in community-based instruction (CBI; Beck, Broers, Hogue, Shipstead, & Knowlton, 1994; Collins, 2003; Walker, Uphold, Richter, & Test, 2010). This decision will be based on whether a learner with a moderate or severe disability has difficulty generalizing skills outside of the classroom environment or if he or she is nearing the age to make the transition from school to adulthood and needs to acquire a number of critical skills (e.g., vocational) to make that transition successful (Brown et al., 1986).

It is clear that special education teachers who work with a group of learners with moderate and severe disabilities will have to meet a diverse group of needs in planning schedules. Although small-group instruction can address diverse needs, an instructor still may

Name: Jill

Activity	Time and person responsible	IEP objectives and procedures			
		Objective 1: Communicate using augmentative device	Objective 2: Increase fine motor skills	Objective 3: Read age-appropriate vocabulary	Objective 4: Make choice from selection of three
Arrival in home-room; journal and calendar activity	9:00 Peer buddy	Greet peer (MM)	Do fasteners on jacket and book bag; write name and paste picture in journal; put sticker on calendar date (SLP)	Read and select words for journal and calendar (e.g., date, weather, holiday) (SP)	Select color of pencil for writing; select sticker to put on calendar (SLP)
Resource room	10:00 Special education teacher	Greet teacher and staff (MM)	Cut and paste pictures on worksheet (GG); put coins and dollars in and out of wallet (SLP)	Work on scripted literacy curriculum; count out coins and dollars (CTD)	Select seat; select reinforcer at end of each lesson (SLP)
Language arts class	11:00 Paraprofessional	Greet classmates; respond to questions (MM)	Write name on paper; participate in hands-on activity; turn pages of book (GG)	Name letters in books; read unit sight words (SP)	Choose book for independent reading time (SLP)
Lunch	12:00 Peer buddy	Greet peers; make needs known; respond to questions (NTD)	Wash hands; use utensils; open milk carton; use napkin (SLP)	Read signage in hallways and on doors (SP)	Make choices in food line; select seat by peers (SLP)
Math class	1:00 Paraprofessional	Greet peers (MM)	Manipulate counters	Read number words; read measurement terms; read computation words (SP)	Select manipulatives for counting (SLP)
Science class	2:00 Peer tutor	Greet peers (MM)	Manipulate hands-on materials during experiments (GG)	Read vocabulary words; indicate comprehension of vocabulary (CTD)	Select peer to be partner during experiment (SLP)
Departure	3:00 Peer tutor	Say goodbye to peers (MM)	Do fasteners on jacket and book bag (SLP)	Read signage in hallways and on doors (SP)	Select peer to walk to bus (SLP)

Figure 10.1. Sample matrix demonstrating the embedding of individualized education program (IEP) objectives throughout the day for an elementary learner with moderate and severe disabilities. (*Key:* CTD, constant time-delay procedure; GG, graduated-guidance procedure; MM, mand-model procedure; NTD, naturalistic time-delay procedure; SLP, system-of-least-prompts procedure; SP, simultaneous-prompting procedure.)

Activity	Time	Students and person responsible for support			
		Special education teacher	Paraprofessional	Related services provider	Peer
First period	8:00	Resource room instruction: Ken, Marie	Make materials	Resource room services Dexter	Resource room instruction Grace
Second period	9:00	CBI: Dexter	CBI: Ken	CBI: Marie	CBI: Grace
Third period	10:00	Resource room instruction: Dexter, Grace	Job coaching: Ken	Physical education support: Marie	
Fourth period	11:00	Resource room instruction: Ken, Grace	Lunch break		Language arts support: Dexter, Marie
Lunch	12:00	Lunch and planning	Cafeteria support: Dexter	Cafeteria support: Ken	Cafeteria support: Marie, Grace
Fifth period	1:00	Social studies support: Marie, Grace	Math support: Dexter		Music support: Ken
Sixth period	2:00	Science collaboration: Dexter, Grace	Art support: Marie		Art support: Ken
Departure	3:00	Data analysis	Home room: Marie, Grace		Home room: Dexter, Ken

Figure 10.2. Sample staff schedule to provide support for secondary learners with moderate and severe disabilities throughout the day. (*Key:* CBI, community-based instruction.)

need support while conducting a lesson. Most resource rooms will have a concurrent combination of ongoing small-group and individual instruction, requiring more than one instructor across learners. Learners who are included across settings (e.g., extracurricular activities, service learning project) or engaging in CBI also will need support in those settings. Although most support will come from skilled instructors and trained peers, it is important to note that support also can come from technology (e.g., Ayres & Langone, 2005; Parette & McMahan, 2002), such as computer programs (e.g., commercial instructional software, PowerPoint slides, teacher-made video) or devices (e.g., iPads, iPods). Whether high- or low tech, technology can be used to provide new instruction, to provide drill and practice, or to guide performance of skills. More information on how to increase the use of technology during systematic instruction is presented in Chapter 11.

Figure 10.1 provides an example of how a special education teacher might create a schedule for an elementary learner with a moderate or severe disability by creating a matrix that demonstrates where each IEP objective will be embedded throughout the day. Note that the instructor may need to embed more objectives than those shown on the chart. Figure 10.2 provides an example of how a special education teacher might create a schedule for staff to provide support for learners with moderate and severe disabilities throughout the day.

SAMPLE INSTRUCTIONAL PROGRAMS

In the following instructional programs, special education teachers have designed schedules to teach skills to students with moderate and severe disabilities across settings. Both of the instructional programs are designed to be implemented with secondary students because this is the age when learners are the most likely to be engaging in instruction across a variety of settings as they prepare for transition. In the first instructional program, the schedule is set up to provide time in the resource room to assess learning that is taking place in an inclusive setting. In the second instructional program, the schedule is set up to provide opportunities for instruction and assessment in the community. In the instructional programs, different types of support are provided to keep learners engaged in instruction as they acquire skills needed for successful transition.

Sample Instructional Program 1

In the first sample instructional program, the learner is included in a secondary English class each day, during which time peers without disabilities are working on writing portfolios required in their state's assessment. The learner with a disability also works on a writing assignment. The special education teacher and the English teacher have collaborated and agreed that the special education teacher will ensure that the learner has all writing materials before going to English class and will collect and monitor progress toward meeting objectives each day after class. During the English class, the English teacher will provide support and feedback for the learner as he does for all students in the class. The learner's daily schedule is constructed for the learner to stop by the resource room on the way to English class each day to get his writing assignment and to return to the resource room after English class each day so that his writing progress can be assessed. The procedure is based on a research study conducted by Collins, Hall, Branson, and Holder (1999).

Core Content Standards

Writing
- Students will exemplify effective language choices by applying correct grammar and usage.
- Students will communicate clearly by applying correct punctuation: Students will correctly punctuate declarative, exclamatory, interrogative, and imperative sentences; students will use commas in a series, a date, a compound sentence, and the greeting and closing of a letter; and students will correctly apply the rules of punctuation for periods in abbreviations.
- Students will communicate clearly by applying correct capitalization: Students will capitalize proper nouns (e.g., names, days, months), students will capitalize the beginning of sentences, and students will capitalize the pronoun *I*.

Behavioral Objective

When told to write a paragraph on a topic, Rob will write a paragraph using correct indentation and complete sentences with correct grammar, capitalization, and punctuation with 100% accuracy for 3 days.

Instructional Context

Rob is a 21-year-old with Down syndrome who is preparing to make the transition to adulthood and who plans to hold a job in a retail farm equipment store. His mother has indicated that he enjoys writing to people and that writing is an appropriate objective to allow him to continue social interactions with others after he leaves school. Thus, he is included in an English class with peers without disabilities who also are preparing to make the transition from school to college or work. The peers are working on writing essays for their state-required writing portfolios. Rob also will work on writing, although his assignments will consist of writing complete paragraphs on topics that he selects with the help of his resource room teacher, Ms. Johnson. Each day, Ms. Johnson will brief him on his writing assignment for the day and make sure he has his materials ready for English class. When Rob arrives in English class, he will work independently on his assignment alongside the other students in the class. His English teacher, Mr. Criscillis, will circulate during the class, providing assistance to all students in the class, as needed. Because Mr. Criscillis is not doing direct instruction, he will not use a systematic response-prompting strategy. Instead, he will provide support by systematically delivering nontargeted information to Rob each time he passes by as he circulates around the room. When the class ends, Ms. Johnson will assess Rob's progress in the class.

Instructional Materials

Rob will take the following materials with him to the English class each day: 1) a notebook with his assignment (e.g., topic for writing) written inside, 2) writing paper, and 3) a pencil.

Procedure

English Class—
Nontargeted
Information

- At least twice during each class as he circulates, Mr. Criscillis will walk by Rob's desk, stop, look at his written work, and make a comment, such as, "I like how you are working to quietly on your writing assignment," or "You are doing a great job on this assignment today." He will then present nontargeted information that includes one of the following statements: 1) "Remember that every sentence should begin with a capital letter," 2) "Remember that every sentence should end with a period," or 3) "Remember to indent a new paragraph by counting over a few spaces before you begin writing." Because Ms. Johnson has told Mr. Criscillis that Rob can benefit from learning information about his community before he makes the transition to adulthood, Mr. Criscillis also will make statements about current events, such as the names of candidates running for local elections, the offices for which they are seeking election, and their primary campaign platform, as he chats with Rob before leaving his desk.

Resource Room—
Data Collection

- After each English class, Rob will go to the special education resource room, where Ms. Johnson will conduct a brief assessment of his progress. She will first look at and comment on his written work. Then, she will collect formative data as follows.

- *Attentional cue.* Ms. Johnson will ask, "Are you ready to listen?"

- *Task directions.* When Rob is attending, Ms. Johnson will first ask questions about writing. These will include 1) "How do you begin a sentence?" 2) "How do you end a sentence?" and 3) "How do you begin a

TIME-DELAY DATA SHEET

Name: _Rob_   Instructor: _Ms. Johnson_   Skill: _Writing_

	Date									
	January 3		January 4		January 5		January 6		January 7	
Trials	Before prompt	After prompt	Before prompt	After prompt	Before prompt	After prompt	Before prompt	After prompt	Before prompt	After prompt
1. Indent	–			–		+	+		+	
2. Capital letter		+	+		+		+		+	
3. Period		0	+		+		+		+	
4. Capital letter		+	+		+		+		+	
5. Period		+	+		+		+		+	
6. Indent		–		+		+	+		+	
Number correct	0	3	4	1	4	2	5	1	6	0
Number incorrect	1	1	0	1	0	0	0	0	0	0
Number no response	0	1	0	0	0	0	0	0	0	0

Key: Plus sign indicates correct response; minus sign indicates incorrect response; zero indicates no response.

Figure 10.3. Sample completed data sheet for assessing non-targeted information presented in an inclusive English class in Sample Instructional Program 1.

paragraph?" She will wait 3 seconds after each question for Rob to respond.

- *Consequence.* If Rob answers a question correctly, Ms. Johnson will praise his response. If he answers a question incorrectly, she will ignore the response.

- *Date recording.* Ms. Johnson will record a plus sign for all each correct response, a minus sign for each incorrect response, and a zero for failure to respond. A sample completed data sheet can be found in Figure 10.3. In addition, Ms. Johnson will collect permanent products of Rob's writing assignments to be placed in his writing portfolio as evidence of his progress over time.

Maintenance

Because there is no formal instructional trial with a task direction, a response, and a consequence, there is no need to fade reinforcement. Both the English and special education teachers, however, will continue to monitor maintenance of Rob's writing skills throughout the remainder of the school year.

Generalization

Generalization is facilitated by having Rob receive feedback on his writing across two teachers.

Behavior Management

Because Rob is social and talkative, the English teacher will give him reminders to remain quiet while everyone is working on their writing assignments in class. Appropriate behavior also is facilitated by allowing Rob to choose his writing topic to match his interests each day.

Lesson Variations and Extension

Once Rob has mastered the skills of indenting paragraph, capitalizing the first words of sentences, and ending sentences with periods, his teachers will move on to new skills that include, but are not limited to, writing sentences that require other types of punctuation, using commas to separate items in seriation, putting periods after abbreviations, and capitalizing proper nouns. After assessing Rob's writing progress each day, Ms. Johnson also will ask Rob what else he learned from Mr. Criscillis during English class (e.g., the current election). This can provide the impetus for future writing assignments (e.g., writing a letter to a candidate or a paragraph about a party's political platform).

Sample Instructional Program 2

The second sample instructional program shows how a teacher can teach community skills even without going into the community every day (e.g., Nietupski, Hamre-Nietupski, Clancy, & Veerhusen, 1986). In this case, the teacher plans a learner's weekly schedule to take advantage of peer tutors as instructors and to take advantage of technology as an instructional tool. In this way, she can alternate instruction in the community with simulations conducted by peers without disabilities and with instruction via video loaded on a computer. The procedures are based on a research study conducted by Branham, Collins, Schuster, and Kleinert (1999).

Core Content Standard

Practical Living   •   Students will apply financial management practices, including budgeting, banking (e.g., check writing, balancing a checking account), savings and investments (e.g., advantages and disadvantages of savings accounts, stocks, bonds, mutual funds, certificates of deposit, individual retirement accounts, 401[k]s, and credit (e.g., responsible use of debit and credit cards, establishing and maintaining good credit, cause and effect of bankruptcy) and explain their importance in achieving short- and long-term financial goals.

Behavioral Objective

When presented with a bank check, Emily will perform the steps of the task analysis to cash the check with 100% accuracy for 3 out of 3 opportunities across settings.

Instructional Context

Emily is a 20-year-old with a severe disability who will soon be making the transition to adult-hood. She and her family expect her to hold a job in their community. Because she will be earning money, she will be more independent if she can perform banking skills. Thus, the first banking skill she is learning is how to cash a check. Because Emily attends a rural school, she cannot go out into the community every day, but her teacher schedules CBI for her each week on Friday. On the days she does not go on CBI, she uses the same block of time to work on community skills in the resource room. Because Emily's school is on a block schedule, the class schedules are different for *A* days and *B* days. On *A* days, peer tutors come into the re-source room and conduct a banking simulation for Emily to practice banking skills. On *B* days, she works independently at the computer on a video that allows her to go through task anal-yses for banking skills. Regardless of the setting or the format, a CTD procedure is used as the instructional strategy.

Instructional Materials

Community-Based Instruction	• When Emily is in the community, she goes to a local bank with a check that has been written to her by her teacher. The teacher has prearranged for Emily to do an on-site instructional simulation at a time when the bank is not busy. The bank teller cashes the check for Emily and gives her real money. The teacher returns the money to the teller after the instructional session.
Simulation	• During the simulation, a peer tutor assumes the role of the bank teller and stands behind a desk. Another peer tutor writes a check to Emily that Emily then cashes during the simulation. She receives photocopies of real money that are slightly larger that the actual size to prevent con-fusion with real money.
Video Modeling	• During video modeling, Emily sits at the computer and watches a pre-loaded video that shows a peer cashing a check at a real bank. The teacher has prepared the video to pause for 10 seconds after each step of the task analysis to provide time for Emily to state what comes next before being prompted by the video. An instructor (e.g., teacher, para-professional, peer tutor) sits by Emily during the session.

Instructional Procedure

The instructor for this instructional program varies from day to day and may be the special education teacher, the job coach, a paraprofessional, or a peer tutor. Each instructional ses-sion will proceed as follows.

Attentional Cue	• The instructor will state Emily's name to get her attention before in-struction begins.
Constant Time-Delay Procedure	• The task direction will be, "Cash the check." The controlling prompt will be verbal directions, and the first day of instruction will consist of a 0-second delay interval before the prompt is delivered. On all subse-quent days, the delay interval will be 3 seconds. During CBI and simula-tions, Emily will perform the steps of the task analysis to cash a check. During video modeling, the instructor will ask Emily, "What do you do

next?" and wait for Emily to give a verbal response before watching the next step performed on the video.

Consequence
- Specific verbal praise will follow each prompted or unprompted correct response. If Emily makes an incorrect response, the instructor will say, "Wait," and correct it before allowing her to continue.

Nontargeted Information

Instructive feedback when praising Emily for completing the task will consist of stating information related to banking, such as, "If you save your money in a bank, you can earn extra interest or extra money," or "If you cash a check when you do not have enough money in the bank, your account will be overdrawn and you will have to pay a fee."

Data Collection

The instructor will record a plus sign for correct responses before or after the prompt, a minus sign for incorrect responses before or after the prompt, and a zero for no responses after the prompt.

A sample completed data sheet is shown in Figure 10.4.

Maintenance

Once Emily reaches the criterion of 100% correct independent responses for 1 day, the instructor will fade praise for responses to the end of the task analysis (i.e., fixed ratio of 5, or

CONSTANT TIME-DELAY DATA SHEET

Name: Emily   Skill: Cashing a check   Date: February 14
Instructor: Alex   Setting: Class simulation   Time: 2:00

Steps	Before prompt	After prompt
1. Approach bank teller		+
2. Sign back of check		+
3. Hand check to teller		+
4. Say, "Cash please"	+	
5. Wait for money	+	
6. Place money in wallet		+
Number/% correct	2/33%	4/67%
Number/% incorrect	0/0%	0/0%
Number/% no response	0/0%	0/0%

Key: Plus sign indicates correct response; minus sign indicates incorrect response; zero indicates no response.

Figure 10.4. Sample completed data sheet for using a constant time-delay procedure in Sample Instructional Program 2.

FR5) for 2 days. The instructor will monitor maintenance once per month until the end of the school year.

Generalization

Generalization is facilitated by teaching across settings, instructors, and materials. Instruction will not end until Emily has demonstrated 100% correct performance of the skill for at least 1 day in the community setting.

Behavior Management

Appropriate behavior will be facilitated by providing intermittent praise for attending during instruction and assessment.

Lesson Variations and Extension

When Emily reaches criterion, she will continue the same sequence of instruction on a new community skill. This may be related to banking (e.g., making a deposit, using an automated teller machine) or to other community skills (e.g., making a transaction at the post office, crossing different examples of community streets). The goal is that Emily become as independent as possible in the community before making the transition from school to adulthood.

SUMMARY

This chapter focused on planning instructional schedules for students across settings and instructors. The chapter also showed how instructional trials can be increased by embedding instruction on IEP objectives throughout the day. Although it may take a large initial investment of time to construct matrices to show where IEP objectives can be embedded and to set up schedules that take advantage of various individuals to provide instructional support, doing this will be an efficient use of the teacher's time in the long run.

QUESTIONS FOR REFLECTION

1. Why is inclusion a beneficial practice for learners with moderate and severe disabilities? Why is CBI a beneficial practice?

2. How can instructional opportunities be increased in a learner's daily or weekly schedule?

3. Who are some of the people who can serve as instructors throughout the day? Where are some of the places that instruction can take place?

REFERENCES

Ayres, K.M., & Langone, J. (2005). Intervention and instruction with video for students with autism: A review of the literature. *Education and Training in Developmental Disabilities, 40*, 183–196.

Beck, J., Broers, J., Hogue, E., Shipstead, J., & Knowlton, E. (1994). Strategies for functional community-based instruction and inclusion for children with mental retardation. *Teaching Exceptional Children, 26*, 44–48.

Branham, R., Collins, B.C., Schuster, J.W., & Kleinert, H. (1999). Teaching community skills to students with moderate disabilities: Comparing combined techniques of classroom simulation, videotape modeling, and community-based instruction. *Education and Training in Mental Retardation and Developmental Disabilities, 33,* 170–181.

Bricker, D. (1976). Educational synthesizer. In T.M. Angele (Ed.), *Hey, don't forget about me: Education's investment in the severely, profoundly, and multiply handicapped* (pp. 84–97), Reston, VA: Council for Exceptional Children.

Brown, L., Nisbet, J., Ford, A., Sweet, M., Shiraga, B., York, J., & Loomis, R. (1986). The critical need for nonschool instruction in educational programs for severely handicapped students. *Journal of The Association for Persons with Severe Handicaps, 11,* 12–18.

Carter, E.W., Cushing, L.S., Clark, N.M., & Kennedy, C.H. (2005). Effects of peer support interventions on students' access to the general curriculum and social interactions. *Research and Practice for Persons with Severe Disabilities, 30,* 15–25.

Collins, B.C. (2003). Meeting the challenge of conducting community-based instruction in rural settings. *Rural Special Education Quarterly, 22*(2), 31–35.

Collins, B.C., Hall, M., Branson, T., & Holder, M. (1999). Acquisition of related and nonrelated nontargeted information presented by a teacher within an inclusive setting. *Journal of Behavioral Education, 9,* 223–237.

Downing, J., & Bailey, B.R. (1990). Sharing the responsibility: Using a transdisciplinary team approach to enhance the learning of students with severe disabilities. *Journal of Educational and Psychological Consultation, 1,* 259–178.

Jackson, L.B., Ryndak, D.L., & Wehmeyer, M.L. (2008–2009). The dynamic relationship between context, curriculum, and student learning: A case for inclusive education as a research-based practice. *Research & Practice for Persons with Severe Disabilities, 33–34,* 175–195.

Janney, R.E., & Snell, M.E. (2011). Designing and implementing instruction for inclusive classrooms. In M.E. Snell & F. Brown (Eds.), *Instruction of students with severe disabilities* (7th ed., pp. 224–256). Upper Saddle River, NJ: Pearson.

Nietupski, J., Hamre-Nietupski, S., Clancy, P., & Veerhusen, K. (1986). Guidelines for making simulation an effective adjunct to in vivo community instruction. *Journal of The Association for Persons with Severe Handicaps, 8,* 71–77.

Owen-DeSchryver, J.S., Carr, E.G., Cale, S.I., & Blakely-Smith, A. (2008). Promoting social interactions between students with autism spectrum disorders and their peers in inclusive school settings. *Focus on Autism and Other Developmental Disabilities, 23,* 15–28.

Parette, P., McMahan, G.A. (2002). What should we expect of assistive technology? *Teaching Exceptional Children, 35*(1), 56–61.

Ryndak, D., Ward, T., Alper, S., Storch, J.F., & Montgomery, J.W. (2010). Long-term outcomes of services in inclusive and self-contained settings for siblings with comparable significant disabilities. *Education and Training in Autism and Developmental Disabilities, 45,* 38–53.

Walker, A.R., Uphold, N.M., Richter, S., & Test, D.W. (2010). Review of the literature on community-based instruction across grade levels. *Education and Training in Autism and Developmental Disabilities, 45,* 242–267.

Westling, D.L., & Fox, L. (2009). *Teaching students with severe disabilities* (4th ed.). Upper Saddle River, NJ: Pearson.

CHAPTER 11

Teaching with Technology

CHAPTER OBJECTIVES

On completion of this chapter, the reader will be able to

- Identify ways in which the addition of technology can be beneficial to learners to with moderate and severe disabilities
- List considerations in selecting appropriate technology for individual learners with moderate and severe disabilities
- Explain the difference between assistive and instructional technology, as well as the way the two may overlap
- Explain the difference between video modeling and video prompting, providing examples of each
- Design systematic instructional programs that incorporate the use of technology

TERMS USED IN THIS CHAPTER

assistive technology	video modeling
instructional technology	video prompting

The use of technology in special education has been embraced for its capacity to increase learning, to facilitate communication, and to enable learners to more fully participate in their environments, including the classroom setting (Ayres & Langone, 2005; Mechling, 2008; Westling & Fox, 2009). Technology, however, is a tool to be used by instructors and learners and is not, in itself, a means to an end. Both instructors and learners must be taught to evaluate the appropriateness of types of technology for the purposes for which they are to be used and then how to use the technology in an appropriate way (Parette & McMahan, 2002). For example, an instructor never should provide a learner with a specific type of technology without first assessing the learner's needs and the role that the technology can play in instruction and adaptive behavior. Likewise, the instructor never should introduce technology to a learner without also teaching the learner how to access and use the technology. Finally, an instructor never should make the assumption that a learner is acquiring knowledge or accessing the environment without monitoring to ensure that such an assumption is true. Although the role of technology in special education is far too vast to be covered in a single chapter in this text, this chapter addresses the use of technology as a tool to be used in conjunction with systematic instruction to increase the acquisition of skills.

The specific purpose of technology use with learners with moderate and severe disabilities is to enable them to acquire skills that might be difficult or impossible to perform otherwise. Technology can allow those with physical or sensory impairments to access the world available to those who do not have these impairments (Campbell, 2011; Spooner, Browder, & Mims, 2011), it can be used to facilitate communication (Browder, Spooner, & Mims, 2011; Downing, 2011), and it can help learners monitor appropriate behavior (e.g., Cihak, Wright, & Ayres, 2010). Computer access can open up a realm of instructional possibilities. In addition to facilitating academic learning (e.g., Zisimopoulos, Sigafoos, & Koutromanos, 2011), technology can facilitate the performance of functional skills across domains, including community skills (e.g., Ayres, Langone, Boon, & Norman, 2006; Branham, Collins, Schuster, & Kleinert, 1999; Cihak, Alberto, Taber-Doughty, & Gama, 2006; Mechling & Gast, 2003; Mechling & O'Brien, 2010), domestic skills (e.g., Ayres & Cihak, 2010; Ayres, Maguire, & McClimon, 2009; Canella-Malone et al., 2006; Graves, Collins, Schuster, & Kleinert, 2005; Mechling, Gast, & Gustafson, 2009; Mechling & Stephens, 2009; Norman, Collins, & Schuster, 2001), leisure skills (e.g., Hammond, Whatley, Ayres, & Gast, 2010), and vocational skills (e.g., Cihak, 2008; Ellerd, Morgan, & Salzberg, 2006; Mitchell, Schuster, Collins, & Gassaway, 2000).

ASSISTIVE AND INSTRUCTIONAL TECHNOLGY

Assistive technology can be low tech or high tech and enables a learner to access his or her environment. Some devices, such as communication boards, are simple to create and use; others, such as complex augmentative communication devices, may require skill to program and instruction to use. The type of assistive technology that is selected for an individual learner is a decision that should be made by the learner's instructional team (e.g., teachers, parents, related service personnel) with input from the learner. The team's decision should be based on the personal characteristics of the learner (e.g., age, gender, strengths and abilities) and on the outcomes that the device can help the student achieve (e.g., communication, mobility, access, skill performance). Cost, mobility, durability, availability, ease of repair, ease of programming and maintenance, cultural values, and necessary training also may be factors in determining the type of device that is selected (Westling & Fox, 2009). Regardless of the device, systematic instruction may be required to teach the learner how to use it.

The focus of **instructional technology** is to facilitate the acquisition of knowledge and skills, whether or not a learner has a cognitive disability. Instructional technology may consist of computer software that introduces new content to facilitate acquisition, provides drill and practice to increase fluency, or presents multiple application examples to increase generalization. Learners may access graphic, audio, and video instructional content through instructional devices (e.g., computers, iPods, iPads, interactive whiteboards). Instructional technology should not be used for technology's sake but, rather, to enhance learning in a way that may be novel, provide greater clarity, and facilitate independence. Although the goal may be to meet criterion on a skill taught through instructional technology, it may be appropriate, in some cases, for users to continue to use the technology as support over time. For example, a learner may learn to prepare a meal by viewing a Power-Point display of a recipe on a computer. The technology may or may not be faded over time, just as a person who uses a cookbook may or may not continue to use it to prepare a favorite recipe over time. In this way, instructional technology may overlap with assistive technology, depending whether or not the technology results in independent performance of a skill or continues to be used to assist the learner over time.

TECHNOLOGY AND SYSTEMATIC INSTRUCTION

As technology has emerged as a major component in the field of special education, the research on systematic instruction has broadened to include technology use as the focus of instruction (e.g., Zisimopoulos et al., 2011) and technology use as a means to provide instruction (e.g., Ayres & Langone, 2005; Mechling, 2008). As technological advances continue and technology becomes more accessible and affordable to all, the coming years should be filled with new and different practices that merge technology and systematic instruction. The following examples are just a sampling of how this can occur.

First, systematic instruction can be used to teach a learner how to use technology. For example, the system-of-least-prompts procedure might be used to prompt a student to activate a simple switch in order to respond to a task direction (e.g., press a button switch to indicate *yes* or *no* when asked to select the correct answer to a math problem) by working through a prompt hierarchy of independence, verbal direction, modeling, and physical guidance. The simultaneous-prompting procedure might be used to teach a learner to use word processing on a computer (e.g., enter personal information) by first conducting a probe trial to see if the learner can correctly and independently respond to the task direction and then conducting training trials to prompt the learner through the task, if necessary. The graduated-guidance procedure can be used to assist a learner in using an adaptive device (e.g., a walker or a manual wheelchair) by shadowing the learner's movements and providing physical guidance as needed. The time-delay procedure can be used to teach a learner to perform a math calculation (e.g., compute sales tax) by providing a delay interval for an independent response before providing a model prompt with a second calculator. The mand-model procedure can be used to teach a learner to communicate using an augmentative communication device (e.g., iPad) by waiting for a response, then manding a response, and then modeling how to make the response, as needed.

Second, technology can provide instruction in a systematic way on how to perform a skill. **Video modeling** and **video prompting** are two examples of this (e.g., Norman et al., 2001). In video modeling, the learner observes a task being performed and then attempts to perform the task independently (e.g., Hammond et al., 2010). If the learner cannot perform the task, the instructor can use a systematic procedure, such as the system-of-least-prompts procedure, to assist the learner in performing the task. For example, the learner may view a video of someone (e.g., the learner or a peer) performing a daily routine or a vocational task before attempting to perform it independently. The instructor would then systematically use a hierarchy to prompt the learner to perform the task, if necessary. The purpose of the video model is to facilitate the rate of learning, and it would be faded when no longer needed. In video prompting, the learner does not view the video until it is needed, with the video providing the prompt (e.g., Graves et al., 2005). For example, the learner may listen to audio and watch video on an iPod when getting money from an automatic teller machine in the community. Under the supervision of the instructor using a time-delay procedure, the learner would first attempt to perform a step of the task during a set time delay before using the iPod to access the prompt. If the learner masters the task over time, the technology is naturally faded, but it can remain in place as an adaptive device if the learner needs it.

Instructors can easily program many types of technology to be used within the context of a systematic procedure. It is simple and inexpensive to make clear digital photos to show steps of task analyses or to shoot a short video to show how to perform both discrete and chained tasks. In teaching academic core content, an instructor can compile a series of pictures to teach a science concept, such as states of matter. The student can click on a PowerPoint slide that asks a question (e.g., "This is a rock. Is it a solid or a liquid or a gas?"). The student can either respond or wait a delay interval to be prompted with the correct response. Over time, multiple exemplars of the states of matter that sample the range can be added (e.g., balls, books, boards) to increase the likelihood that the learner will grasp the concept (e.g., solids can come in various shapes and colors as long as they are not fluid or do not evaporate into the air). In teaching functional skills, an instructor can compile a series of videos to demonstrate the steps of grocery shopping (e.g., "This is the entrance to the store; which aisle contains dairy products?" or "This is an aisle in the dairy department; which case contains milk?" or "This is the dairy case with milk; which milk is fat free?"). Again, the student can either respond or wait a delay interval to be prompted with the correct response. Examples can come from the store at which the learner's family shops or from multiple stores to facilitate generalization. One of the advantages is that technology used in this way can be a less expensive option than community-based instruction.

SAMPLE INSTRUCTIONAL PROGRAMS

The following instructional programs demonstrate how special education teachers designed instruction to teach two life skills to learners with moderate and severe disabilities. In the first, an elementary instructor uses video prompting with a constant-time-delay (CTD) procedure to teach a personal management skill to a small group of elementary learners. In the second, a secondary instructor uses video prompting to teach a personal management skill to a single learner.

Sample Instructional Program 1

In the first sample program, the special education teacher has prepared a video that will show learners how to use the zippers on their jackets before going out to recess. The video incorporates a CTD procedure using a visual and audio prompt. The procedure is based on a research study conducted by Norman et al. (2001).

Core Content Standards

Practical Living/ Vocational
- Students perform physical movement skills effectively in a variety of settings.
- Students will identify technology tools (e.g., electronic games, phones, computers) that are used in homes and schools.

Science
- Students will describe patterns in weather and weather data in order to make simple predictions based on those patterns discovered.
- Students will make generalizations and/or predictions about weather changes from day to day and over seasons based on weather data.

Behavioral Objective

When told to put on their jackets before going outdoors, the learners will zip their jackets with 100% accuracy for 3 days.

Instructional Context

The three students with moderate and severe disabilities engaging in the lesson are 8 to 12 years old. Morgan and Erin are girls who have Down syndrome, and Reed is a boy who has autism. All have personal management skills listed on their individualized education programs (IEPs) to facilitate independence. In addition, all participate in a morning calendar session during homeroom in which they identify the day's weather and the season and then discuss how they should dress appropriately for the weather (e.g., wear a jacket). In addition, all participate in an inclusive science class in which one of the units focuses on charting and predicting the weather. Before going outdoors for recess each day, the learners watch a video that uses video prompting to teach them to zip their jackets along with support from an instructor. The learners all find the video to be motivating, as assessed by their attention when viewing it.

Instructional Materials

The instructional materials will include a video, made by the special education teacher, that focuses on zipping jackets. The special education teacher made the video by having the school technology support person video her from a subjective viewpoint as she performed the task. To do this, the technology support person aimed the camera over her shoulder so that the resulting video would allow the learners to see the same view as when they perform the task. Once the video was shot, the teacher added graphic print for each step of the task analysis and paired this with corresponding audio stating each step (e.g., "Engage the zipper"). The video first showed the task being performed from beginning to end (i.e., video model). Then, the teacher edited the video to pause for a set delay interval between each step so that the learners would have an opportunity to perform a step before viewing the model prompt. In addition to the video, instructional materials will include the learners' personal jackets.

Instructional Procedure

Each instructional session will proceed as follows.

Attentional Cue • The instructor will say, "It's cool outside today. You need to put on your jackets." Once the learners are attending, the instructor will position the learners, one at a time, in front of the computer on which the video has been loaded. Thus, two learners will watch as the third zips the jacket. The learners will watch a preview of the entire task before instruction begins.

Task Direction • After the preview, the video will show the words *Zip your jacket* while stating the task direction.

Constant Time-Delay Procedure • On the first 2 days of instruction, the video immediately will show the video model prompt for each step of the task accompanied by the written text and the audio directions for each step. The instructor will pause the video to allow the learner to perform the step following each prompt. On subsequent days, the preview will be dropped, and the instructor will use a video that has been edited to provide a 20-second delay interval between each step before providing the video model prompt. If a learner makes an error, the instructor will pause the video and provide physical guidance to assist the learner in performing the step.

Consequence • When each step is completed, the instructor will praise the learner. Once all learners have zipped their jackets, they will get to go outdoors for recess (natural reinforcer).

Nontargeted Information

Before or after the video prompting, the instructor will tie the activity to the day's calendar lesson or the science unit on weather (e.g., "We need to wear jackets today because it is spring, and spring is cool with an average temperature of 45 degrees"). Learners also may acquire the ability to read some of the words printed on the video during prompting.

Data Collection

The instructor will record data on responses throughout instruction. A plus sign will be recorded for correct responses before or after the prompt, a minus sign will be recorded for incorrect responses before or after the response, and a zero will be recorded for no response after the prompt. A sample completed data sheet is shown in Figure 11.1.

Maintenance

Once the learner reaches the criterion of 100% correct responses on a task analysis for 1 day, the instructor will fade praise for responses to an average of every four (i.e., variable ratio of 4, or VR4) responses for 1 day and then to the end of the task (i.e., fixed ratio of 8, or FR8).

CONSTANT TIME-DELAY DATA SHEET

Instructor: _Ms. Riley_   Skill: _Zipping a jacket_   Date: _March 17_

Steps	Reed Before	Reed After	Morgan Before	Morgan After	Erin Before	Erin After
1. Hold zipper—right hand	+		+		+	
2. Hold zipper teeth—left hand	+			0	−	
3. Align zipper	−		+	+		+
4. Engage zipper		+	−		+	
5. Hold zipper at bottom—left hand	+		+			0
6. Pull zipper up—right hand	+		0	+		
7. Stop at top		−		+		−
8. Adjust waistband		0	+		+	
Number correct	4	1	4	2	4	1
Number incorrect	1	1	1	0	2	0
Number no response	0	1	0	2	0	1

Key: Plus sign indicates correct response; minus sign indicates incorrect response; zero indicates no response.

Figure 11.1.   Sample data sheet for using the constant time-delay procedure with video prompting in Sample Instructional Program 1.

Generalization

Generalization is facilitated by teaching learners to put on their own jackets. Parents will be asked to also do this at home.

Behavior Management

Appropriate behavior will be facilitated by using video because this has been shown to be motivating to the learners and by conducting the instructional session before recess. The instructor also will praise learners who are watching while the other performs the skill (e.g., "I like the way you are watching Reed while he zips his jacket").

Lesson Variations and Extension

In addition to teaching learners how to zip jackets, videos can be created to teach other personal management skills to facilitate independence (e.g., cleaning sunglasses before putting them on to go outdoors). Many of the videos that focus on personal management skills also can be tied to core content (e.g., stating the time after putting on a watch). These activities also are a good time to embed motor skills identified by physical or occupational therapists.

Sample Instructional Program 2

In the second sample instructional program, the special education teacher has prepared a video that will show a learner how to prepare a simple meal. The video also incorporates a CTD procedure with a video/audio prompt but does not contain the text that was included in the first program. The procedure is based on a research study conducted by Graves et al. (2005).

Core Content Standards

Practical Living/ Vocational
- Students will analyze the effect of individual behavior choices and habits relating to diet, exercise, rest, and other choices on various body systems (e.g., circulatory, respiratory, nervous, digestive).
- Students will explain risks associated with unhealthy habits and behaviors (e.g., dietary).

Behavioral Objective

When told to prepare lunch, Becky will prepare a simple meal with 100% accuracy for 3 days.

Instructional Context

Becky is a 16-year-old student with Down syndrome. She has personal management skills that include making a simple meal listed on her IEP as well as on her transition plan. In addition, she participates in an inclusive health class in which one of the units focuses on making healthy dietary choices. Her teacher has prepared a series of videos on how to prepare healthy foods that Becky likes. Each day, she will go to the consumer science room at lunch to prepare her meal. The meals will vary between a meal that can be prepared on the counter (i.e., sandwich), a meal that can be prepared in the microwave (i.e., frozen meal), and a meal that can be prepared on the stove top (i.e., soup). Each of these meals will use healthy products that are low in sugar, fat, sodium, and calories.

Instructional Materials

The instructional materials will include videos made by the special education teacher that focus on preparing simple meals. She made the inexpensive videos with the assistance of students in the school's video production class using a subjective viewpoint that will allow Becky to see the same view when she performs the task. To insert a delay interval, she covered the lens of the video camera with a blue sheet of paper for 20 seconds between each step. This kept her from having to edit the video once it was shot.

Instructional Procedure

Each instructional session will proceed as follows.

Attentional Cue
- The instructor will ask, "Are you ready to fix lunch today?" When Becky responds, the instructor will tell her to select the video of the meal she wants to prepare.

Task Direction
- Once the video is ready, the instructor will say, "Let's fix lunch," and begin the video, first showing a preview of the entire task.

Constant Time-Delay Procedure	• On the first day of instruction, the video immediately will show the video model prompt for each step of the task accompanied audio directions for each step. The video will pause with a blue screen for 20 seconds as Becky performs each step of the task analysis. On subsequent days, Becky will see the blue frame before completing the step. If she cannot do the step independently, she can wait for the video prompt. If Becky makes an error, the instructor will back up the video so that Becky can again watch the video model prompt.
Consequence	• As each step is completed, the instructor will praise Becky. Once she completes the task, Becky will get to eat the lunch she has prepared (natural reinforcer).

Nontargeted Information

When Becky has made her lunch selection, the instructor will deliver information about the wise decision she has made (e.g., "A sandwich of low-fat peanut butter on wheat bread is a good choice because peanut butter is a good source of protein and wheat bread is a good source of fiber").

Data Collection

The instructor will record data on responses throughout instruction. A plus sign will be recorded for correct responses before or after the prompt, a minus sign will be recorded for incorrect responses before or after the response, and a zero will be recorded for no response after the prompt. A sample completed data sheet is shown in Figure 11.2.

Maintenance

Once the learner reaches criterion of 100% correct responses on a task analysis for 2 days, the instructor will fade praise for responses to an average of every four (i.e., variable ratio of 4, or VR4) responses for 1 day. Once Becky has met criterion, she will continue to fix meals for the remainder of the school year.

Generalization

Generalization will be facilitated by having Becky prepare meals with her parents in her home. Becky has a computer at home so she can access the video there as well. Over the course of instruction, the brands of the products that are used will vary.

Behavior Management

Appropriate behavior will be facilitated by using video because this has been shown to be motivating to Becky and by conducting the activity at lunch when Becky is more likely to be hungry. Allowing Becky to make her own choices about what she will prepare for lunch also will facilitate appropriate behavior.

Lesson Variations and Extension

Using a video recipe to prepare a meal is an appropriate way to cook because it is similar to watching a cooking program on television or a commercial video on television or the computer. The goal will be for Becky to build a collection of videos that she can take with her

CONSTANT TIME-DELAY DATA SHEET

Name: _Becky_   Skill: _Making a sandwich_   Date: _April 8_
Instructor: _Ms. Pennington_   Setting: _Consumer science_   Time: _11:30_

Steps	Before	After
1. Wash hands		+
2. Get out plate		+
3. Get out two bread slices		+
4. Get out peanut butter	+	
5. Get out knife	+	
6. Open peanut butter		+
7. Put knife in jar		+
8. Spread peanut butter on bread		+
9. Put bread slices together		+
10. Clean up	+	
Number/% correct	3/30%	7/70%
Number/% incorrect	0/0%	0/0%
Number/% no response	0/0%	0/0%

Key: Plus sign indicates correct response; minus sign indicates incorrect response; zero indicates no response.

Figure 11.2.   Sample data sheet for using the constant time-delay with video prompting in Sample Instructional Program 2.

when she makes the transition to a supported living apartment. Thus, she will have the videos for reference if she fails to maintain the cooking skills. To increase social interactions during the instructional program, Becky can take her lunch with her as she joins peers in the cafeteria, or she can invite peers to come eat with her in the consumer science room. If the instructor also is preparing a personal lunch, they can compare the health factors across their meals (e.g., calorie count, fat content).

SUMMARY

This chapter discussed the emergence of assistive and instructional technology in the field of special education and described ways in which technology can be used in conjunction with systematic instruction. This can focus either on teaching learners how to use technology as a personal tool or on teaching learners other content with the support of technology. In particular, the sample instructional programs focused on video modeling and video prompting, two effective procedures for teaching skills with technology in a systematic fashion. As technology continues to improve and become more affordable, it should play an increasing role in facilitating independence and providing instruction.

QUESTIONS FOR REFLECTION

1. What is the difference between assistive and instructional technology?

2. What is the difference between video modeling and video prompting?

3. What are some factors that should be considered in purchasing technology for learners with moderate and severe disabilities?

REFERENCES

Ayres, K., & Cihak, D. (2010). Computer- and video-based instruction of food-preparation skills: Acquisition, generalization, and maintenance. *Intellectual and Developmental Disabilities, 48*(3), 195–208.

Ayres, K.M., & Langone, J. (2005). Intervention and instruction with video for students with autism: A review of the literature. *Education and Training in Developmental Disabilities, 40,* 183–196.

Ayres, K.M., Langone, J., Boon, R.T., & Norman, A. (2006). Computer-based instruction for purchasing skills. *Education and Training in Developmental Disabilities, 41,* 253–263.

Ayres, K.M., Maguire, A., & McClimon, D. (2009). Acquisition and generalization of chained tasks taught with computer based video instruction to children with autism. *Education and Training in Developmental Disabilities, 44,* 493–508.

Branham, R., Collins, B.C., Schuster, J.W., & Kleinert, H. (1999). Teaching community skills to students with moderate disabilities: Comparing combined techniques of classroom simulation, videotape modeling, and community-based instruction. *Education and Training in Mental Retardation and Developmental Disabilities, 33,* 170–181.

Browder, D.M., Spooner, F., & Mims, P.J. (2011). Communication skills. In D.M. Browder & F. Spooner (Eds.), *Teaching students with moderate and severe disabilities* (pp. 262–282). New York, NY: Guilford.

Campbell, P.H. (2011). Addressing motor disabilities. In M.E. Snell & F. Brown (Eds.), *Instruction of students with severe disabilities* (7th ed., pp. 340–376). Upper Saddle River, NJ: Pearson.

Canella-Malone, H., Sigafoos, J., O'Reilly, M., de la Cruz, B., Edrisnha, C., & Lancioni, G.E. (2006). Comparing video prompting to video modeling for teaching daily living skills to six adults with developmental disabilities. *Education and Training in Developmental Disabilities, 41,* 344–356.

Cihak, D.F. (2008). Use of a handheld prompting system to transition independently through vocational tasks for students with moderate and severe intellectual disabilities. *Education and Training in Developmental Disabilities, 43,* 102–110.

Cihak, D., Alberto, P.A., Taber-Doughty, T., & Gama, R.I. (2006). A comparison of static picture prompting and video prompting simulations using group instructional procedures. *Focus on Autism and Other Developmental Disabilities, 21,* 89–99.

Cihak, D.F., Wright, R., & Ayres, K.M. (2010). Use of self-modeling static-picture prompts via a handheld computer to facilitate self-monitoring in the general education classroom. *Education and Training in Autism and Developmental Disabilities, 45,* 136–149.

Downing, J.E. (2011). Teaching communication skills. In M.E. Snell & F. Brown (Eds.), *Instruction of students with severe disabilities* (7th ed., pp. 461–491). Upper Saddle River, NJ: Pearson.

Ellerd, D.A., Morgan, R.L., & Salzberg, C.L. (2006). Correspondence between video CD-ROM and community-based job preferences for individuals with developmental disabilities. *Education and Training in Developmental Disabilities, 41,* 81–90.

Graves, T.B., Collins, B.C., Schuster, J.W., & Kleinert, H.L. (2005). Using video prompting to teach cooking skills to secondary students with moderate disabilities. *Education and Training in Developmental Disabilities, 40,* 34–46.

Hammond, D., Whatley, A.D., Ayres, K.M., & Gast, D.L. (2010). Effectiveness of video modeling to teach iPod use to students with moderate intellectual disabilities. *Education and Training in Autism and Developmental Disabilities, 45*(4), 525–538.

Mechling, L.C. (2008). High tech cooking: A literature review of evolving technologies for teaching a functional skill. *Education and Training in Developmental Disabilities, 43,* 474–485.

Mechling, L.C., & Gast, D.L. (2003). Multi-media instruction to teach grocery word associations and store location: A study of generalization. *Education and Training in Developmental Disabilities, 38,* 62–76.

Mechling, L.C., Gast, D.L., & Gustafson, M.R. (2009). Use of video modeling to teach extinguishing of cooking related fires to individuals with moderate intellectual disabilities. *Education and Training in Developmental Disabilities, 44,* 67–79.

Mechling, L., & O'Brien, E. (2010). Computer-based video instruction to teach students with intellectual disabilities to use public bus transportation. *Education and Training in Autism and Developmental Disabilities, 45,* 230–241.

Mechling, L.C., & Stephens, E. (2009). Comparison of self-prompting of cooking skills via picture-based cookbooks and video recipes. *Education and Training in Developmental Disabilities, 44,* 218–236.

Mitchell, R.J., Schuster, J.W., Collins, B.C., & Gassaway, L.J. (2000). Teaching vocational skills through a faded auditory prompting system. *Education and Training in Mental Retardation and Developmental Disabilities, 35,* 415–427.

Norman, J.M., Collins, B.C., & Schuster, J.W. (2001). Using video prompting and modeling to teach self-help skills to elementary students with mental disabilities in a small group. *Journal of Special Education Technology, 16,* 5–18.

Parette, P., & McMahan, G.A. (2002). What should we expect of assistive technology? *Teaching Exceptional Children, 35*(1), 56–61.

Spooner, F., Browder, D.M., & Mims, P.J. (2011). Sensory, physical, and health care needs. In D.M. Browder & F. Spooner (Eds.), *Teaching students with moderate and severe disabilities* (pp. 241–261). New York, NY: Guilford.

Westling, D.L., & Fox, L. (2009). *Teaching students with severe disabilities* (4th ed.). Upper Saddle River, NJ: Pearson.

Zisimopoulos, D., Sigafoos, J., & Koutromanos, G. (2011). Using video prompting and constant time delay to teach an internet search basic skill to students with intellectual disabilities. *Education and Training in Autism and Developmental Disabilities, 46*(2), 238–250.

Procedural Flowcharts

FLOWCHART FOR CONDUCTING A BASELINE SESSION (CONDUCTED IN A ONE-TO-ONE FORMAT)

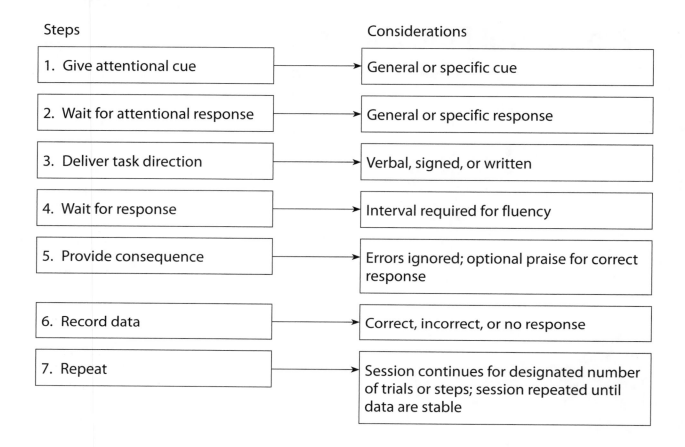

Steps | Considerations

1. Give attentional cue → General or specific cue

2. Wait for attentional response → General or specific response

3. Deliver task direction → Verbal, signed, or written

4. Wait for response → Interval required for fluency

5. Provide consequence → Errors ignored; optional praise for correct response

6. Record data → Correct, incorrect, or no response

7. Repeat → Session continues for designated number of trials or steps; session repeated until data are stable

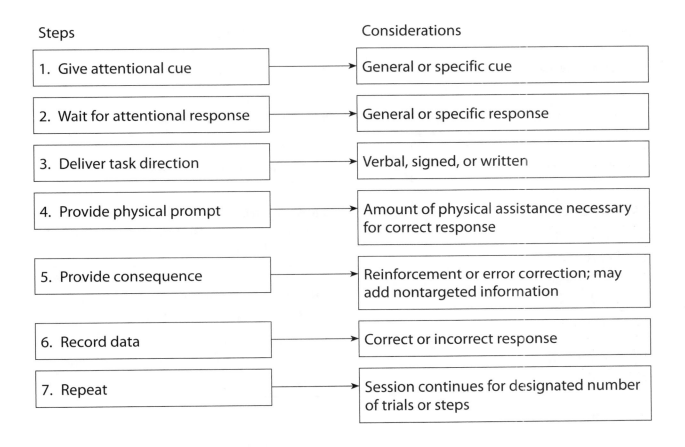

Steps   Considerations

1. Give attentional cue	General or specific cue
2. Wait for attentional response	General or specific response
3. Deliver task direction	Verbal, signed, or written
4. Provide physical prompt	Amount of physical assistance necessary for correct response
5. Provide consequence	Reinforcement or error correction; may add nontargeted information
6. Record data	Correct or incorrect response
7. Repeat	Session continues for designated number of trials or steps

FLOWCHART FOR IMPLEMENTING A MOST-TO-LEAST PROMPTING PROCEDURE (ONE-TO-ONE FORMAT)

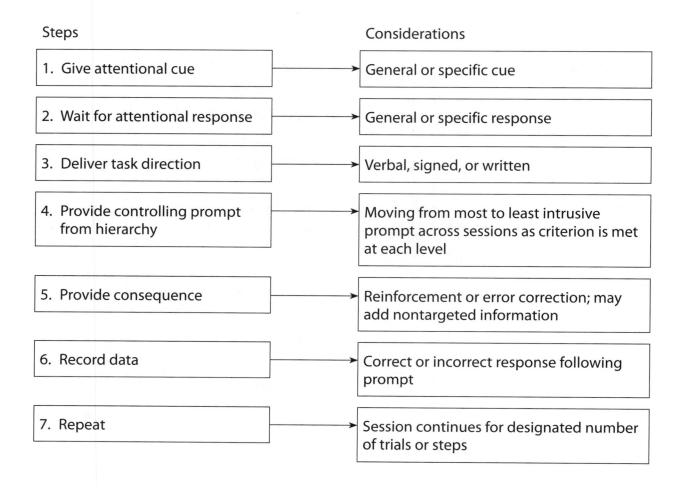

Steps

Considerations

1. Give attentional cue → General or specific cue

2. Wait for attentional response → General or specific response

3. Deliver task direction → Verbal, signed, or written

4. Provide controlling prompt from hierarchy → Moving from most to least intrusive prompt across sessions as criterion is met at each level

5. Provide consequence → Reinforcement or error correction; may add nontargeted information

6. Record data → Correct or incorrect response following prompt

7. Repeat → Session continues for designated number of trials or steps

FLOWCHART FOR IMPLEMENTING A SYSTEM-OF-LEAST-PROMPTS PROCEDURE (ONE-TO-ONE FORMAT)

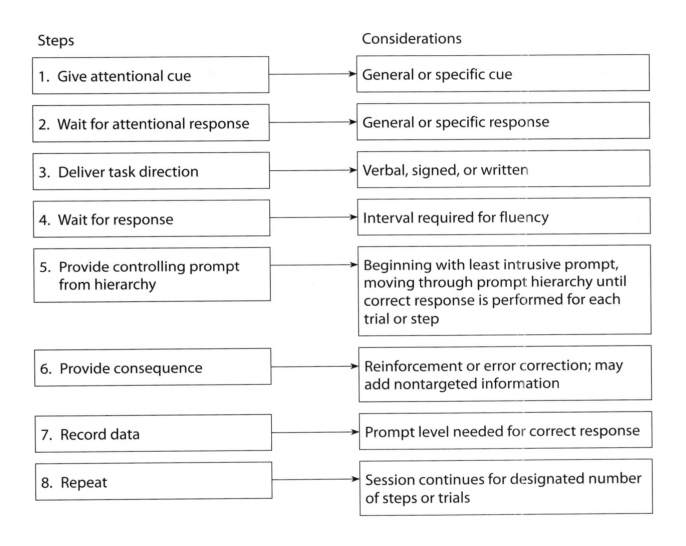

Steps	Considerations
1. Give attentional cue	General or specific cue
2. Wait for attentional response	General or specific response
3. Deliver task direction	Verbal, signed, or written
4. Wait for response	Interval required for fluency
5. Provide controlling prompt from hierarchy	Beginning with least intrusive prompt, moving through prompt hierarchy until correct response is performed for each trial or step
6. Provide consequence	Reinforcement or error correction; may add nontargeted information
7. Record data	Prompt level needed for correct response
8. Repeat	Session continues for designated number of steps or trials

FLOWCHART FOR IMPLEMENTING A PROGRESSIVE TIME-DELAY PROCEDURE (ONE-TO-ONE FORMAT)

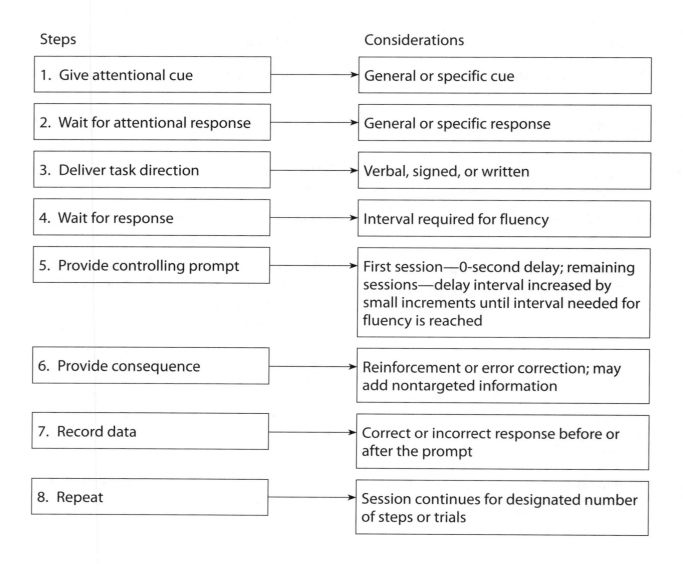

Steps

Considerations

1. Give attentional cue → General or specific cue

2. Wait for attentional response → General or specific response

3. Deliver task direction → Verbal, signed, or written

4. Wait for response → Interval required for fluency

5. Provide controlling prompt → First session—0-second delay; remaining sessions—delay interval increased by small increments until interval needed for fluency is reached

6. Provide consequence → Reinforcement or error correction; may add nontargeted information

7. Record data → Correct or incorrect response before or after the prompt

8. Repeat → Session continues for designated number of steps or trials

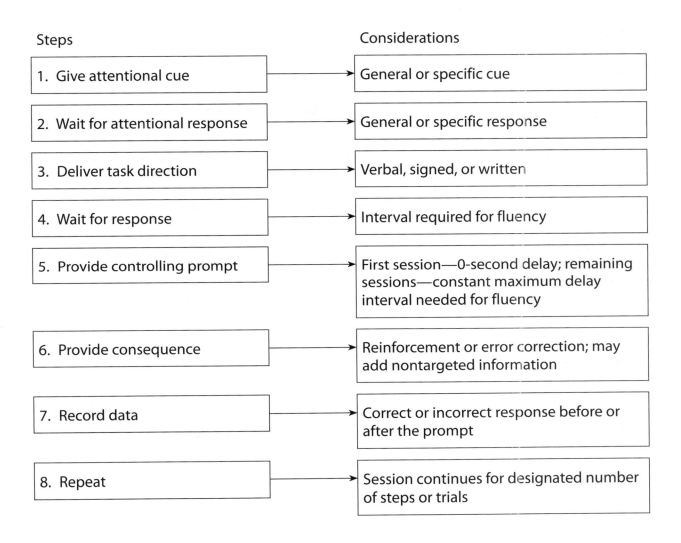

Steps | Considerations

1. Give attentional cue → General or specific cue

2. Wait for attentional response → General or specific response

3. Deliver task direction → Verbal, signed, or written

4. Wait for response → Interval required for fluency

5. Provide controlling prompt → First session—0-second delay; remaining sessions—constant maximum delay interval needed for fluency

6. Provide consequence → Reinforcement or error correction; may add nontargeted information

7. Record data → Correct or incorrect response before or after the prompt

8. Repeat → Session continues for designated number of steps or trials

I. Probe Trials

Steps   Considerations

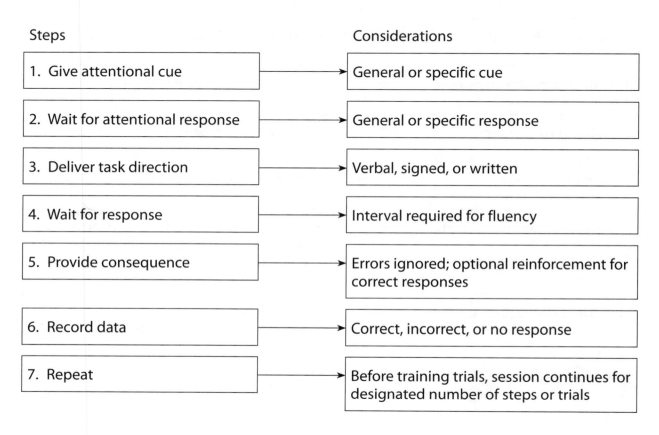

Steps	Considerations
1. Give attentional cue	General or specific cue
2. Wait for attentional response	General or specific response
3. Deliver task direction	Verbal, signed, or written
4. Wait for response	Interval required for fluency
5. Provide consequence	Errors ignored; optional reinforcement for correct responses
6. Record data	Correct, incorrect, or no response
7. Repeat	Before training trials, session continues for designated number of steps or trials

II. Training Trials

Steps   Considerations

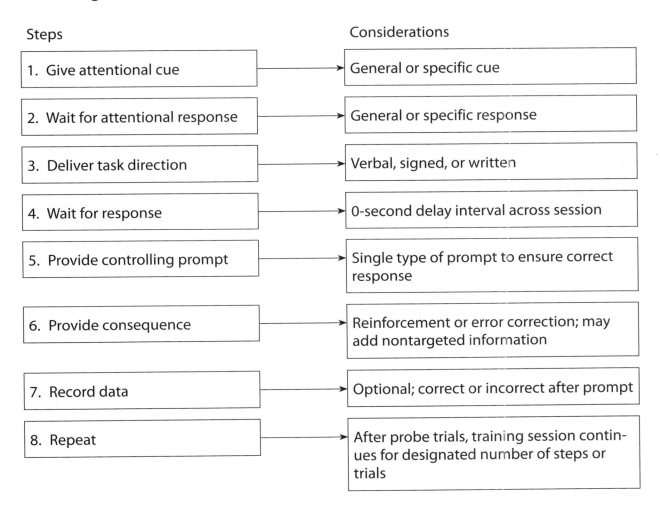

Steps	Considerations
1. Give attentional cue	General or specific cue
2. Wait for attentional response	General or specific response
3. Deliver task direction	Verbal, signed, or written
4. Wait for response	0-second delay interval across session
5. Provide controlling prompt	Single type of prompt to ensure correct response
6. Provide consequence	Reinforcement or error correction; may add nontargeted information
7. Record data	Optional; correct or incorrect after prompt
8. Repeat	After probe trials, training session continues for designated number of steps or trials

FLOWCHART FOR IMPLEMENTING RESPONSE PROMPTING IN A SMALL-GROUP FORMAT

Steps	Considerations
1. Give attentional cue	General or specific; individual or choral
2. Wait for attentional response	General or specific; individual or choral
3. Deliver task direction	Verbal, signed, or written; same or different skill for each group member
4. Implement response-prompting procedure for each group member	Graduate guidance, most-to-least prompting, system of least prompts, time delay, or simultaneous prompting (training trials only)
6. Provide consequence	Reinforcement or error correction; may add nontargeted information; praise for attending to facilitate observational learning
7. Record data	Correct or incorrect response before or after the prompt
8. Repeat	Session continues for designated number of steps or trials per student; massed or spaced trial format

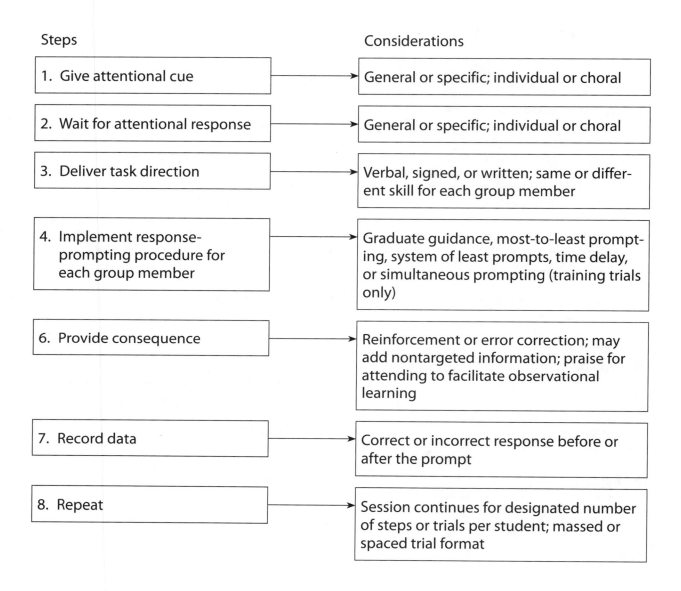

I. Modeling Procedure

Steps   Considerations

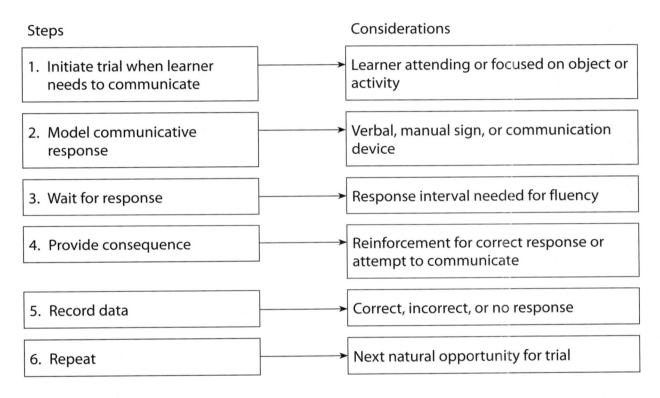

Steps	Considerations
1. Initiate trial when learner needs to communicate	Learner attending or focused on object or activity
2. Model communicative response	Verbal, manual sign, or communication device
3. Wait for response	Response interval needed for fluency
4. Provide consequence	Reinforcement for correct response or attempt to communicate
5. Record data	Correct, incorrect, or no response
6. Repeat	Next natural opportunity for trial

II. Mand-Model Procedure

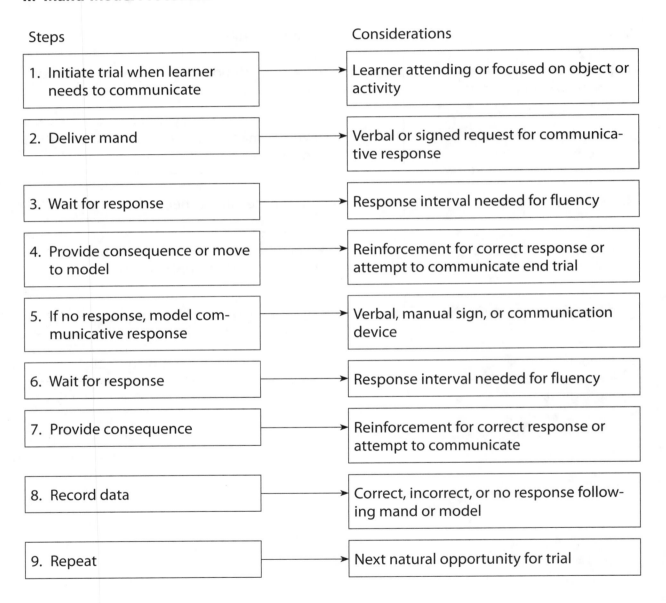

Steps

Considerations

Steps	Considerations
1. Initiate trial when learner needs to communicate	Learner attending or focused on object or activity
2. Deliver mand	Verbal or signed request for communicative response
3. Wait for response	Response interval needed for fluency
4. Provide consequence or move to model	Reinforcement for correct response or attempt to communicate end trial
5. If no response, model communicative response	Verbal, manual sign, or communication device
6. Wait for response	Response interval needed for fluency
7. Provide consequence	Reinforcement for correct response or attempt to communicate
8. Record data	Correct, incorrect, or no response following mand or model
9. Repeat	Next natural opportunity for trial

III. Incidental-Teaching Procedure

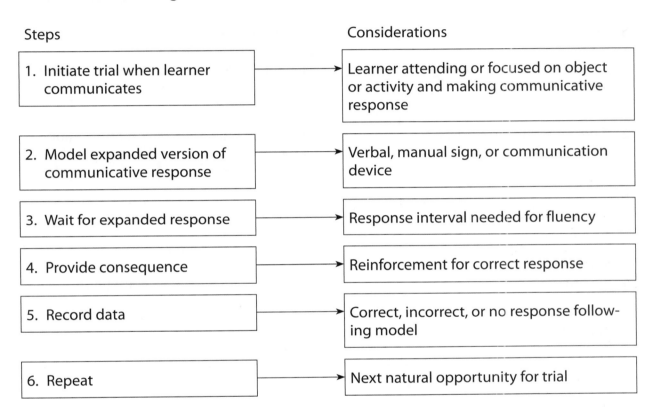

Steps | Considerations

1. Initiate trial when learner communicates → Learner attending or focused on object or activity and making communicative response

2. Model expanded version of communicative response → Verbal, manual sign, or communication device

3. Wait for expanded response → Response interval needed for fluency

4. Provide consequence → Reinforcement for correct response

5. Record data → Correct, incorrect, or no response following model

6. Repeat → Next natural opportunity for trial

IV. Naturalistic Time-Delay Procedure

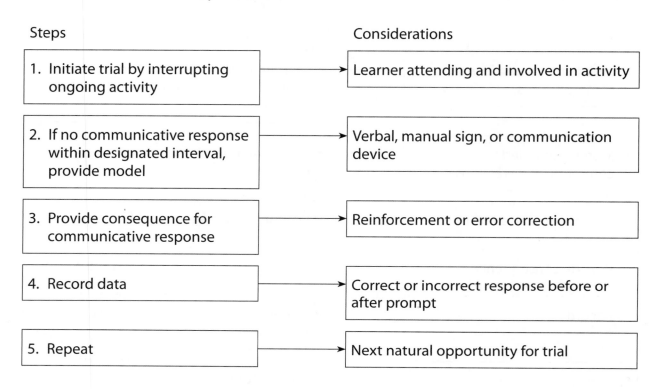

Steps | Considerations

1. Initiate trial by interrupting ongoing activity → Learner attending and involved in activity

2. If no communicative response within designated interval, provide model → Verbal, manual sign, or communication device

3. Provide consequence for communicative response → Reinforcement or error correction

4. Record data → Correct or incorrect response before or after prompt

5. Repeat → Next natural opportunity for trial

APPENDIX B

Blank Data Collection Sheets

BASELINE DATA SHEET

Name: _____   Instructor: _____

Skill: _____   Setting: _____

Trials or steps	Date		
1.			
2.			
3.			
4.			
5.			
6.			
7.			
8.			
9.			
10.			
11.			
12.			
13.			
14.			
15.			
16.			
17.			
18.			
19.			
20.			
Number correct			
% correct			

Key: Plus sign indicates correct; minus sign indicates incorrect; zero indicates no response.

GRADUATED-GUIDANCE DATA SHEET

Name: _____ Skill: _____ Date: _____

Instructor: _____ Setting: _____ Time: _____

Trials or steps	Response
1.	
2.	
3.	
4.	
5.	
6.	
7.	
8.	
9.	
10.	
11.	
12.	
13.	
14.	
15.	
16.	
17.	
18.	
19.	
20.	
Number correct	
% correct	

Key: I, independent response; P, physical prompt.

MOST-TO-LEAST PROMPTING DATA SHEET

Name: _____ Skill: _____ Date: _____

Instructor: _____ Setting: _____ Time: _____

Prompt level: _____

Trials or steps	Response
1.	
2.	
3.	
4.	
5.	
6.	
7.	
8.	
9.	
10.	
11.	
12.	
13.	
14.	
15.	
16.	
17.	
18.	
19.	
20.	
Number correct	
% correct	

Key: Plus sign indicates correct; minus sign indicates incorrect; zero indicates no response.

SYSTEM-OF-LEAST-PROMPTS DATA SHEET

Name:_____ Skill:_____ Date:_____

Instructor:_____ Setting:_____ Time:_____

Trials or steps	Response
1.	
2.	
3.	
4.	
5.	
6.	
7.	
8.	
9.	
10.	
11.	
12.	
13.	
14.	
15.	
16.	
17.	
18.	
19.	
20.	
Number/% independent	
Number/% verbal	
Number/% model	
Number/% physical	

Key: I, independent; M, model; P, physical; V, verbal.

TIME-DELAY DATA SHEET

Name: _____ Skill: _____ Date: _____

Instructor: _____ Setting: _____ Time: _____

Delay interval: _____

Trials or steps	Before prompt	After prompt
1.		
2.		
3.		
4.		
5.		
6.		
7.		
8.		
9.		
10.		
11.		
12.		
13.		
14.		
15.		
16.		
17.		
18.		
19.		
20.		
Number/% correct		
Number/% incorrect		
Number/% no response		

Key: Plus sign indicates correct; minus sign indicates incorrect; zero indicates no response.

Name: _____ Skill: _____ Date: _____

Instructor: _____ Setting: _____ Time: _____

Delay interval: _____

Trials or steps	Correct before prompt	Incorrect before prompt	Correct after prompt	Incorrect after prompt	No response
1.					
2.					
3.					
4.					
5.					
6.					
7.					
8.					
9.					
10.					
11.					
12.					
13.					
14.					
15.					
16.					
17.					
18.					
19.					
20.					
Number/%					

Key: Check appropriate column.

SIMULTANEOUS-PROMPTING DATA SHEET

Name: _____ Skill: _____ Date: _____

Instructor: _____ Setting: _____ Time: _____

Trials or steps	Probe trial	Training trial
1.		
2.		
3.		
4.		
5.		
6.		
7.		
8.		
9.		
10.		
11.		
12.		
13.		
14.		
15.		
16.		
17.		
18.		
19.		
20.		
Number/% correct		
Number/% incorrect		
Number/% no response		

Key: Plus sign indicates correct; minus sign indicates incorrect; zero indicates no response.

SMALL-GROUP DATA SHEET

Date: _____   Instructor: _____

Skill: _____   Procedure: _____

Trials or steps	Student names									
1.										
2.										
3.										
4.										
5.										
6.										
7.										
8.										
9.										
10.										
Number correct										
% correct										

Key: Plus sign indicates correct response; minus sign indicates incorrect response; zero indicates no response.

MODELING DATA SHEET

Name: _____   Date: _____

Instructor: _____   Target response: _____

Opportunity to respond (activity, time)	Response
1.	
2.	
3.	
4.	
5.	
6.	
7.	
8.	
9.	
10.	
11.	
12.	
13.	
14.	
15.	
16.	
17.	
18.	
19.	
20.	
Number correct	
% correct	

Key: Plus sign indicates correct; minus sign indicates incorrect; zero indicates no response.

MAND-MODEL DATA SHEET

Name: _____   Date: _____

Instructor: _____   Target response: _____

Opportunity to respond (activity, time)	Initiation	Mand	Model
1.			
2.			
3.			
4.			
5.			
6.			
7.			
8.			
9.			
10.			
11.			
12.			
13.			
14.			
15.			
16.			
17.			
18.			
19.			
20.			
Number correct			
% correct			

Key: Check appropriate column.

INCIDENTAL-TEACHING DATA SHEET

Name: _____ Date: _____

Instructor: _____ Target response: _____

Opportunity for expansion (activity, time)	Response
1.	
2.	
3.	
4.	
5.	
6.	
7.	
8.	
9.	
10.	
11.	
12.	
13.	
14.	
15.	
16.	
17.	
18.	
19.	
20.	
Number correct	
% correct	

Key: Plus sign indicates correct; minus sign indicates incorrect; zero indicates no response.

NATURALISTIC TIME-DELAY DATA SHEET

Name: _____   Date: _____

Instructor: _____   Target response: _____

Opportunity to respond (activity, time)	Before prompt	After prompt
1.		
2.		
3.		
4.		
5.		
6.		
7.		
8.		
9.		
10.		
11.		
12.		
13.		
14.		
15.		
16.		
17.		
18.		
19.		
20.		
Number correct		
% correct		

Key: Plus sign indicates correct; minus sign indicates incorrect; zero indicates no response.

Resources from the Professional Literature

Readers may be interested in the following articles that contain more detailed information on the procedures presented in this book.

INSTRUCTIONAL DESIGN

Sometimes it can be difficult to know where to begin in designing instruction for learners with moderate and severe disabilities. These articles provide guidelines that expand on the procedures described in this text and may assist instructors in designing instruction by providing additional clarification.

Billingsley, F.F., Burgess, D., Lynch, V.W., & Matlock, B.L. (1991). Toward generalized outcomes: Considerations and guidelines for writing instructional objectives. *Education and Training in Mental Retardation, 9*(3), 186–192.

Collins, B.C., Gast, D.L., Ault, M.J., & Wolery, M. (1991). Small group instruction: Guidelines for teachers of students with moderate to severe handicaps. *Education and Training in Mental Retardation, 26*, 18–32.

Collins, B.C., Karl, J., Riggs, L., Galloway, C.C., & Hager, K.D. (2010). Teaching core content with real-life applications to secondary students with moderate and severe disabilities. *Teaching Exceptional Children, 43*(1), 52–59.

Lignugaris/Kraft, B., Marchand-Martella, N., & Martella, R.C. (2001). Writing goals and better short-term objectives or benchmarks. *Teaching Exceptional Children, 34*(1), 52–58.

Wolery, M., & Schuster, J.W. (1997). Instructional methods with students who have significant disabilities. *Journal of Special Education, 31*(1), 61–79.

LITERATURE REVIEWS

All educators are now required to use research-based practices in providing instruction for learners with moderate and severe disabilities. These articles consist of reviews of research investigations in the professional literature that have established response-prompting procedures as research-based practices.

Browder, D., Ahlgrim-Delzell, L., Spooner, F., Mims, P.J., & Baker, J.N. (2009). Using time delay to teach literacy to students with severe developmental disabilities. *Exceptional Children, 75*(3), 343–364.

Doyle, P.M., Wolery, M., Ault, M.J., & Gast, D.L. (1988). System of least prompts: A literature review of procedural parameters. *Journal of The Association for Persons with Severe Handicaps, 13*(1), 28–40.

Morse, T.E., & Schuster, J.W. (2004). Simultaneous prompting: A review of the literature. *Education and Training in Developmental Disabilities, 39*(2), 153–168.

Schuster, J.W., Morse, T.E., Ault, M.J., Doyle, P.M., Crawford, M.R., & Wolery, M. (1998). Time delay with chained tasks: A review of the literature. *Education and Treatment of Children, 21*(1), 74–106.

Walker, G. (2008). Constant and progressive time delay procedures for teaching children with autism: A literature review. *Journal of Autism and Developmental Disorders, 38*(2), 261–175.

COMPARATIVE RESEARCH STUDIES

Instructors may be confused as to which procedure is the best. These articles describe research studies that have compared the instructional efficiency of various response-prompting procedures.

Ault, M.J., Gast, D.L., & Wolery, M. (1988). Comparison of progressive and constant time delay procedures in teaching community-sign word reading. *American Journal on Mental Retardation, 93*(1), 44–56.

Ault, M.J., Wolery, M., Gast, D.L., Doyle, P.M., & Martin, C.P. (1990). Comparison of predictable and unpredictable trial sequences during small group instruction. *Learning Disability Quarterly, 13*(1), 12–29.

Collins, B.C., Evans, A., Creech-Galloway, C., Karl, J., & Miller, A. (2007). Comparison of the acquisition and maintenance of teaching functional and core content sight words in special and general education settings. *Focus on Autism and Other Developmental Disabilities, 22*(4), 220–233.

Cromer, K., Schuster, J.W., Collins, B.C., & Grisham-Brown, J. (1998). Teaching information on medical prescriptions using two instructive feedback schedules. *Journal of Behavioral Education, 8*, 37–61.

Doyle, P.M., Wolery, M., Gast, D.L., & Ault, M.J. (1990). Comparison of constant time delay and the system of least prompts in teaching preschoolers with developmental delays. *Research in Developmental Disabilities, 11*(1), 1–22.

Gast, D.L., Ault, M.J., Wolery, M., Doyle, P.M., & Bellanger, S. (1988). Comparison of constant time delay and the system of least prompts in teaching sight word reading to students with moderate retardation. *Education and Training in Mental Retardation, 23*(2), 117–128.

Godby, S., Gast, D.L., & Wolery, M. (1987). A comparison of time delay and system of least prompts in teaching object identification. *Research in Developmental Disabilities, 8*(2), 283–305.

Kurt, O., & Tekin-Iftar, E. (2008). A comparison of constant time delay and simultaneous prompting within embedded instruction on teaching leisure skills to children with autism. *Topics in Early Childhood Special Education, 28,* 53–64.

Libby, M.E., Weiss, J.S., Bancroft, S., & Ahearn, W.H. (2008). A comparison of most-to-least and least-to-most prompting on the acquisition of solitary play skills. *Behavioral Analysis in Practice, 1*(1), 37–43.

Miracle, S.A., Collins, B.C., Schuster, J.W., & Grisham-Brown, J. (2001). Peer versus teacher delivered instruction: Effects on acquisition and maintenance. *Education and Training in Mental Retardation and Developmental Disabilities, 36,* 375–385.

Singleton, D.K., Schuster, J.W., Morse, T.E., & Collins, B.C. (1999). A comparison of antecedent prompt and test and simultaneous prompting procedures in teaching grocery sight words to adolescents with mental retardation. *Education and Training in Mental Retardation and Developmental Disabilities, 34,* 182–199.

West, E.A., & Billingsley, F. (2005). Improving the system of least prompts: A comparison of procedural variations. *Education and Training in Developmental Disabilities, 40*(2), 131–144.

Wolery, M., Ault, M.J., Doyle, P.M., & Mills, B.M. (1990). Use of choral and individual attentional responses with constant time delay when teaching sight word reading. *Remedial and Special Education, 11*(5), 47–58.

Wolery, M., Cybriwsky, C.A., Gast, D.L., & Boyle-Gast, K. (1991). Use of constant time delay and attentional responses with adolescents. *Exceptional Children, 57,* 462–474.

Glossary

abscissa   Labeled with the dimension of time (e.g., sessions, days) when instruction is conducted, the abscissa is the x-axis on the graph on which formative instructional data are plotted for visual analysis.

acquisition   Acquisition is the initial phase of learning during which learners acquire new skills.

aim star   A strategy for conducting a visual analysis of graphed instructional data to determine whether a learner is making progress, the aim star marks the spot at which a learner is expected to meet criterion on the acquisition of a skill.

antecedent   In an instructional trial, the antecedent is the stimulus that signals the performance of a targeted response or behavior by the learner.

applied behavior analysis (ABA)   ABA is the theoretical foundation for systematic instruction in which behaviors or responses are elicited by a specific antecedent or stimulus and are followed by consequences that either increase the likelihood of future correct responses or decrease the likelihood of future incorrect responses.

assistive technology   Assistive technology consists of an array of high- or low-tech devices that enable individuals with disabilities (e.g., cognitive, sensory, communicative, motor) to perform behaviors that would be difficult or impossible without the support of the devices.

attentional cue   A specific or general attentional cue signals learners to respond that they are attending and ready for the instructional session or trial to begin.

attentional response   A specific or general attentional response signals the instructor that learners are attending and ready for the instructional session or trial to begin.

backward chaining   Backward chaining is a slow format for teaching a task analysis in which the learner first masters the final step in a sequence and then learns the remaining steps, one at a time, from the final step to the first.

baseline condition   The baseline condition consists of assessment trials and sessions that document the ability of a learner to perform a skill or behavior before instruction and should continue until data are stable or show a contratherapeutic trend.

behavior   In an instructional trial, the behavior is the measurable and observable response that a learner performs after the presentation of an antecedent or stimulus.

behavioral objective   A behavioral objective is a statement that makes clear the behavior or skill that a learner is to perform to a specific criterion under a specific condition to verify that learning has occurred.

chained task   A chained task consists of a sequence of measurable and observable behaviors that are linked together to form a complex behavior.

choral response   In a choral response, all learners in a small-group format simultaneously perform a behavior after the presentation of a stimulus (e.g., task direction).

community-based instruction (CBI)   CBI is the practice of teaching skills in the setting in which they will be needed outside of the school, thus facilitating generalization.

community-referenced instruction   Community-referenced instruction is the classroom-based practice of teaching skills with realistic materials in realistic simulations that reflect the setting in which they will be needed outside of school, thus facilitating generalization.

concurrent model of instruction   A concurrent model of instruction consists of teaching simultaneously across a sufficient number of multiple exemplars (e.g., settings, materials, instructors) to increase the likelihood that the learner will generalize to a novel exemplar.

condition change lines   Solid vertical condition change lines on a graphic display of instructional data indicate when the learner changed from baseline assessment to instruction.

consecutive model of instruction   A consecutive model of instruction consists of teaching with one exemplar (e.g., setting, material, instructor) at a time until the learner demonstrates a generalized response to a novel exemplar.

consequence   In an instructional trial, the consequence is the feedback that follows the performance of a response or behavior by the learner and either increases or decreases the likelihood that the response will occur again in the future.

constant time-delay (CTD) procedure   The CTD procedure is a systematic and errorless instructional strategy in which a controlling prompt is provided after a set delay interval (0 seconds during initial instruction and a consistent number of seconds during subsequent instruction) and naturally fades as learners begin to perform the correct response before the delivery of the prompt.

contratherapeutic trend   A contratherapeutic trend in graphed instructional data is established by a minimum of three data points and provides evidence that progress is failing to occur in the desired direction.

controlling prompt   A controlling prompt is the least intrusive variable possible (e.g., verbal direction, physical guidance, picture) that is added to the instructional trial to ensure that the desired behavior or response will be performed.

data paths   Data paths connect consecutive data points that represent student performance during assessment or instruction on a graphic display and can be broken to show a change in conditions or phases or to indicate an unplanned absence from instruction.

data points   Data points are graphic symbols that represent student performance during assessment or instructional conditions and are connected by data paths to show the continuity of sessions.

delay interval   In the time-delay procedure, the delay interval is the set allotment of time (e.g., 3 seconds) after the presentation of a stimulus (e.g., task direction) in which a learner can respond independently before a prompt is provided to elicit the correct response.

differential reinforcement   In systematic instruction, differential reinforcement is a strategy for decreasing dependency on prompts by providing positive reinforcement (e.g., praise) for correct responses before delivery of a prompt and withholding positive reinforcement for correct responses that follow the delivery of a prompt.

discrete behavior   A discrete behavior consists of a single action that can be observed and measured.

distributed trial format   In a distributed trial format, instructional trials are naturally embedded in ongoing activities throughout the day, a practice that facilitates generalization.

efficiency   Efficiency is a measure that compares one instructional strategy with another to determine which strategy results in fewer trials or sessions to criterion, fewer errors made by the learner to criterion, or less instructional time to criterion.

embedded instruction   In embedded instruction, trials are naturally distributed across ongoing activities throughout the day, a practice that facilitates generalization.

errorless learning   Errorless learning is systematic instruction using response-prompting procedures that results in less than 20% incorrect responses by learners because the opportunity to make errors is minimized by providing the level of assistance needed to make correct responses.

fixed ratio (FR) schedule of reinforcement   An FR schedule of reinforcement during instruction facilitates maintenance once criterion is met and consists of providing positive reinforcement (e.g., praise) after a set number of correct responses (e.g., FR3 = reinforcement delivery following every third correct response).

fluency   Fluency is the phase of learning during which learners begin to use acquired skills more efficiently and with greater ease.

form   The form of a behavior is the specific way in which it is to be performed consistently (e.g., talking or using manual signs are both forms that result in the function of communication).

formative data   Formative data provide evidence of learning as instruction occurs and can be used to make instructional decisions if a learner is failing to make desired progress.

forward chaining   Forward chaining is a slow format for teaching a task analysis in which the learner masters the first step in a sequence before proceeding to instruction, one step at a time, on the remaining steps.

function   The function of a behavior is the specific outcome that occurs as a result of the performance of a behavior (e.g., talking or using manual signs are both forms that result in the function of communication).

general case programming   General case programming is the process of selecting and teaching with a sufficient number of multiple exemplars that sample the range of variables that the learner may encounter and is likely to result in a generalized response to an array of stimuli.

generalization   Generalization is the phase of learning during which learners demonstrate the ability to apply acquired skills in different ways or across a number of variables (e.g., settings, individuals, materials).

gestural prompt   A gestural prompt consists of an action by the instructor (e.g., pointing, miming) that increases the likelihood that the learner will make a correct response.

graduated-guidance procedure   The graduated-guidance procedure is a systematic and errorless instructional strategy in which the instructor provides the minimum amount of physical guidance necessary to ensure a correct response by the learner on a moment-to-moment basis; the guidance is naturally faded when the physical prompt no longer is needed.

heterogeneous group   During small-group instruction, a heterogeneous group may consist of learners who are at different skill levels or require different levels of support.

incidental-teaching procedure   Incidental teaching is a naturalistic or milieu response-prompting language strategy that focuses on increasing the length and complexity of utterances through modeling new forms during instructional trials that are based on the interest of the learner and are embedded in ongoing activities.

indiscriminable contingency   Using an indiscriminable contingency is an instructional practice in which the antecedent or stimulus to respond reflects the real world to the extent that the learner is likely to generalize the response across environmental variables (e.g., settings).

instructional program   An instructional program consists of sessions of instructional trials that are repeated until the learner masters a skill by reaching a set criterion of performance in contrast to a lesson plan that is short term and likely to be presented only once.

instructional session   An instructional session consists of a designated number of instructional trials on a discrete skill or the presentation of at least one trial on a chained task.

instructional technology   Instructional technology consists of software and devices that are used to facilitate and enhance learning.

instructional trial   An instructional trial is a single opportunity to facilitate learning that consists of 1) an antecedent or stimulus to elicit a response, 2) a targeted behavior or response from the learner, and 3) a consequence to provide feedback to the learner on the accuracy of the response.

instructive feedback   Instructive feedback consists of nontargeted information that is inserted in the consequence of an instructional trial; this feedback can increase the efficiency of instruction if the learner acquires the additional information.

intersequential model   In a small-group instructional format, an intersequential model occurs when learners all work together to master a single behavior or skill.

intrasequential model   In a small-group instructional format, an intrasequential model occurs when learners each work independently at their own pace on individual skills within the group.

in-vivo instruction   In-vivo instruction is a practice in which learners are taught to perform skills in the natural environment in which they will be needed, thus facilitating generalization.

maintenance   Maintenance is the phase of learning during which learners demonstrate the ability to continue performing acquired skills over time.

mand-model procedure   The mand-model procedure is a naturalistic or milieu response-prompting language strategy that focuses on teaching learners to initiate communication and consists of trials that are based on the interest of the learner and are embedded in ongoing activities for which a mand (a request or directive for performing a response) and then a model are provided if the learner fails to initiate the targeted form.

massed trial format   In a massed trial format, instructional trials occur one after the other with no time between each, a practice that facilitates acquisition or initial learning.

mean levels of performance   Computing and indicating mean levels of performance is a strategy for conducting a visual analysis of graphed instructional data to determine whether a learner's average correct responses increase across baseline and instructional conditions.

measurable behaviors   Measurable behaviors are those that can be seen, described, and measured to verify that learning has occurred.

milieu strategies   Milieu or naturalistic language response-prompting strategies consist of brief trials that are based on the interest of the learner and are embedded in ongoing activities to facilitate communication.

model prompt   A model prompt consists of a verbal or physical demonstration of a targeted behavior by the instructor that increases the likelihood that the learner will make a correct response.

modeling procedure   The modeling procedure is a naturalistic or milieu response-prompting language strategy that focuses on teaching initial communication skills to learners and consists of trials that are based on the interest of the learner and are embedded in ongoing activities for which a model of the targeted form is provided.

most-to-least prompting procedure   The most-to-least prompting procedure is a systematic and errorless instructional strategy that uses a prompting hierarchy in which the learner is first provided with the most intrusive level of assistance; the assistance is faded over time as the learner responds to less intrusive prompts until independence is reached.

multiple-exemplar approach   In a multiple-exemplar approach to instruction, the instructor simultaneously teaches across a sufficient number of variables (e.g., settings, individuals, materials) to facilitate generalization to a novel variable.

multiple-opportunity format   In a multiple-opportunity format, baseline assessment of a task analysis continues when the learner makes an error or fails to respond on a step, thus allowing assessment of the learner's ability to perform any of the steps of a chained task.

natural reinforcers   Natural reinforcers are consequences that occur naturally in the environment in response to a performed behavior and that increase the likelihood that learners will continue to perform the behavior.

naturalistic language strategies   Milieu or naturalistic language response-prompting strategies consist of brief trials that are based on the interest of the learner and are embedded in ongoing activities to facilitate communication.

naturalistic time-delay procedure   The naturalistic time-delay procedure is a naturalistic or milieu response-prompting language strategy that focuses on teaching generalized communication skills to learners and consists of trials in which brief delay intervals are inserted in ongoing activities to allow learners to independently use the targeted form of communication before the delivery of a prompt.

nontargeted information   Nontargeted information consists of content that is inserted in an instructional trial (i.e., the antecedent, the prompt, or the consequence) and that can increase the efficiency of instruction if the learner acquires the additional information.

observable behaviors   Observable behaviors are those that can be seen, described, and measured to verify that learning has occurred.

observational learning   Observational learning occurs when a learner acquires nontargeted information through watching others perform a behavior and is facilitated by teaching in a small-group format.

one-to-one supplemental instruction   One-to-one supplemental instruction occurs when an individual learner receives instructional trials in addition to those conducted in a small-group instructional format.

ordinate   Labeled with the measure of the targeted behavior (e.g., number or percent correct response), the ordinate is the y-axis on the graph on which formative instructional data are plotted for visual analysis.

overlap   Computing the percentage of data points in baseline condition that overlap with data points during instruction is a strategy for conducting a visual analysis of graphed instructional data across conditions to determine the magnitude of the effectiveness of instruction.

performance data   On a formative assessment data sheet, the recording of performance data indicates responses as a learner performs a behavior.

phase change lines   Broken vertical phase change lines on a graphic display of instructional data indicate when the learner experienced a change in instruction within the instructional condition.

physical prompt   A partial or full physical prompt consists of bodily assistance provided by the instructor that increases the likelihood that the learner will make a correct response.

prerequisite skills   Prerequisite skills are behaviors (e.g., academic, motor) that learners must have in their repertoire to increase the likelihood that they will be able to acquire a new skill or behavior.

probe trial   A probe trial is a single opportunity to assess learning that consists of 1) an antecedent or stimulus to elicit a response, 2) a targeted behavior or response from the learner, and 3) a consequence that may consist of either acknowledging or ignoring a response but not correcting an error.

progressive time-delay (PTD) procedure   The PTD procedure is a systematic and errorless instructional strategy in which a controlling prompt is provided following a delay interval that slowly increases in designated increments over time (0 seconds during initial instruction and increasingly larger increments in the number of seconds provided during subsequent instruction) and naturally fades as learners begin to perform the correct response before the delivery of the prompt.

prompt   A prompt consists of assistance (e.g., verbal, gestural, model, physical) provided by the instructor that increases the likelihood that the learner will make a correct response.

prompt hierarchy   In a prompt hierarchy, levels of assistance are sequenced by intrusiveness from most to least or from least to most.

reinforcer preference testing   Conducted prior to instruction, reinforcer preference testing is an assessment to identify consequences that will increase the likelihood that a learner will make a correct response during instruction.

response   In an instructional trial, the response is the measurable and observable behavior that a learner performs following the presentation of an antecedent or stimulus.

response cards   Response cards are materials that learners may chorally present following a task direction in a small-group instructional format to indicate whether they have acquired the targeted behavior.

response generalization   Response generalization occurs when a learner can perform a class of equivalent behaviors in response to a single stimulus.

response interval   In an instructional trial, the delay interval is the set allotment of time (e.g., 3 seconds) following the presentation of a stimulus in which a learner can perform a behavior.

response prompt   A response prompt consists of assistance (e.g., verbal, gestural, model, physical) from the instructor that is inserted in an instructional trial after presenting the antecedent or stimulus; this assistance increases the likelihood that the learner will make a correct response.

role release   Role release occurs when a trained professional shares his or her expertise with other members of the instructional team, allowing them to perform tasks typically performed by the professional.

screening   Screening is an informal assessment used to identify skills that learners do not have in their repertoire and, thus, need to acquire through instruction.

simulations   Simulations are a context for providing school-based instruction using stimuli (e.g., instructional materials, antecedents, consequences) that reflect the natural environment in which the skills will be needed, thus facilitating generalization.

simultaneous-prompting (SP) procedure   The SP procedure is a systematic and error-less instructional strategy in which probe trials to determine when acquisition of a behavior has occurred are conducted before training trials using a controlling prompt and 0-second delay interval.

single-opportunity format   In a single-opportunity format, baseline assessment of a task analysis ends when the learner makes an error or fails to respond on a step, thus eliminating the chance for the learner to perform any of the remaining steps of a chained task.

situational information   On a formative assessment data sheet, situational data (e.g., student and instructor names, date, target skill, setting, instructional procedure) provide information about the variables involved in instruction.

spaced trial format   In a spaced trial format, a learner's instructional trial is followed by an interval of time in which other learners respond before the learner again is asked to respond.

stimulus   In an instructional trial, the stimulus is the antecedent that signals the performance of a targeted response or behavior by the learner.

stimulus control   Stimulus control occurs when a learner can make a specific response to a specific stimulus.

stimulus generalization   Stimulus generalization occurs when a learner can perform a specific behavior in response to the presentation of multiple exemplars of stimuli that fall in the same class.

stimulus prompt   A stimulus prompt consists of assistance (e.g., picture, verbal statement, color cue) that is inserted in the antecedent of the instructional trial and increases the likelihood that the learner will make a correct response.

summary information   On a formative assessment data sheet, summary information (e.g., number or percentage of correct responses) provides information about the performance data recorded during instruction and can be transferred to a graph for visual analysis.

summative data   Summative data consist of evidence of learning that is collected after instruction and can be used to determine whether a learner has mastered a skill.

system-of-least-prompts (SLP) procedure   The SLP procedure is a systematic and errorless instructional strategy that uses a prompting hierarchy in which the learner is first given the opportunity to independently perform a behavior before being provided with the least intrusive level of assistance from a hierarchy until the target response is performed correctly; the assistance is naturally faded over time as the learner requires progressively less assistance.

tandem model   A tandem model of instruction occurs when an individual learner begins receiving instruction in a one-to-one format and then, over time, begins to receive instruction in a small-group format as learners are added, one at a time, to the group.

task analysis   A task analysis is the process of breaking down a chained task into smaller steps to receive individual instruction.

therapeutic trend   A therapeutic trend in graphed instructional data is established by a minimum of three data points and provides evidence that progress is occurring in the desired direction.

tic marks   On a graphic display of data, tic marks are small lines on the abscissa (x-axis) that indicate the passage of time and on the ordinate (y-axis) that indicate the measure of competence.

time-delay procedure   The constant and progressive time-delay procedures are systematic and errorless instructional strategies in which a controlling prompt is provided after a delay interval (0 seconds during initial instruction and a larger increment[s] in the number of seconds provided during subsequent instruction) and naturally fades as learners begin to perform the correct response before the delivery of the prompt.

total task presentation   In a total task presentation, instruction occurs on each step of a task analysis during each session.

training trial   A training trial is a single opportunity to provide instruction that consists of 1) an antecedent or stimulus to elicit a response, 2) a targeted behavior or response from the learner, and 3) a consequence that provides feedback on the accuracy of the response.

transdisciplinary team model   A transdisciplinary team model occurs when a trained professional shares his or her expertise through role release with other members of the instructional team, allowing them to perform tasks typically performed by the professional.

universal design   When employing a universal design of instruction, the instructor adapts instructional procedures and materials so that all learners can participate regardless of ability.

variable ratio (VR) schedule of reinforcement   A VR schedule of reinforcement during instruction facilitates maintenance once criterion is met and consists of providing positive reinforcement (e.g., praise) after an average number of correct responses (e.g., VR3 = reinforcement delivery after an average of every third correct response).

verbal prompt   A direct or indirect verbal prompt consists of auditory assistance (e.g., verbal model or directions) provided by the instructor; such assistance increases the likelihood that the learner will make a correct response.

video modeling   Video modeling is an instructional strategy in which the learner views the performance of a behavior via technology before attempting to perform it.

video prompting   Video prompting is an instructional strategy in which the learner views a prompt via technology, as needed, to facilitate the performance of a behavior.

wait training   Wait training consists of teaching a learner to wait for a prompt when unsure of how to perform a behavior and consists of reinforcing the learner for pausing instead of attempting to perform a novel behavior.

Index

Page numbers followed by *f* indicate figures.